STAYING ALIVE

real poems for unreal times

'This is a book to make you fall in love with poetry...Go out and buy it for everyone you love' – CHRISTINA PATTERSON, *Independent*

'A revelation...An anthology like this should make poetry reviewers feel not just enthusiastic but evangelical. Buy it. Leave it around the house. Give it to friends. It could keep them alive' – JOHN CAREY, *Sunday Times*

'Anyone who has the faintest glimmer of interest in modern poetry must buy it. If I were master of the universe or held the lottery's purse strings, there would be a copy of it in every school, public library and hotel bedroom in the land. On page after page I found myself laughing, crying, wondering, rejoicing, reliving, wishing, envying. It is a book full of hope and high art which restores your faith in poetry' – ALAN TAYLOR, *Sunday Herald*

'The book is without equal as a handbook for students and readers' – SIAN HUGHES, *Times Educational Supplement*

'*Staying Alive* is a book which leaves those who have read or heard a poem from it feeling less alone and more alive. Its effect is deeply political – in a way that nobody ten years ago could have foreseen. Why? The 500 poems in it are not political as such. But they have become subversive because they contest the way the world is being (and has been) manipulated and spoken about. They refuse the lies, the arrogant complacencies, the weak-kneed evasions. They offer 500 examples of resistance' – JOHN BERGER

'One should only read books which bite and sting one.
If the book we are reading does not wake us up with
a blow to the head, what's the point in reading?
A book must be the axe which smashes
the frozen sea within us.'

FRANZ KAFKA

'If I read a book and it makes my whole body so cold
no fire ever can warm me I know *that* is poetry.
If I feel physically as if the top of my head were
taken off, I know *that* is poetry.'

EMILY DICKINSON

NEIL ASTLEY founded Bloodaxe Books in 1978, and was given a D.Litt by
Newcastle University for his pioneering work. As well as *Staying Alive* and
Being Alive, he has edited over 800 poetry books, and has published several
other anthologies, including *Poetry with an Edge*, *New Blood*, *Pleased to See Me*,
and *Do Not Go Gentle: poems for funerals*, and two poetry collections,
Darwin Survivor and *Biting My Tongue*. His first novel, *The End of My Tether*,
was shortlisted for the Whitbread First Novel Award; his second,
The Sheep Who Changed the World, is due out in 2005.

STAYING ALIVE

real poems for unreal times

edited by
NEIL ASTLEY

BLOODAXE BOOKS

ISBN: 1 85224 588 3

First published 2002 by
Bloodaxe Books Ltd,
Highgreen,
Tarset,
Northumberland NE48 1RP.

Seventh impression 2005

www.bloodaxebooks.com
For further information about Bloodaxe titles
please visit our website or write to
the above address for a catalogue.

Bloodaxe Books Ltd acknowledges
the financial assistance of
Arts Council England, North East.

This book is published with the support of
the Lannan Foundation, with special thanks
to J. Patrick Lannan for making it possible.

For Simon

Printed in Great Britain by
Bell & Bain Limited, Glasgow, Scotland.

CONTENTS

3 Dead or alive

4 Bittersweet

5 Growing up

6 Man and beast

7 In and out of love

9 War and peace

10 Disappearing acts

11 Me, the Earth, the Universe

12 The art of poetry

POETS ON POETRY

Coleridge: 'Poetry; the *best* words in the best order.'

Dana Gioia: 'Poetry is the art of using words charged with their utmost meaning.'

Keats: 'It should strike the reader as a wording of his own highest thoughts, and appear almost a remembrance.'

Yeats: 'Poetry is truth seen with passion.'

Boswell: 'Sir, what is poetry?'
Johnson: 'Why Sir, it is much easier to say what it is not. We all *know* what light is; but it is not easy to *tell* what it is.'

Christopher Logue: 'Poetry cannot be defined, only experienced.'

Wordsworth: 'Poetry is the breath and finer spirit of all knowledge ...Poetry is the spontaneous overflow of powerful feelings: it takes its origin from emotion recollected in tranquillity...'

T.S. Eliot: '...it is neither emotion, nor recollection, nor, without distortion of meaning, tranquillity. It is a concentration, and a new thing resulting from the concentration, of a very great number of experiences...a concentration which does not happen consciously or deliberation...Poetry is not a turning loose from emotion, but an escape from emotion; it is not the expression of personality, but an escape from personality.'

David Constantine: 'It is a widening of consciousness, an extension of humanity. We sense an ideal version when we read, and with it arm ourselves, to quarrel with reality.'

Sylvia Plath: 'My poems do not turn out to be about Hiroshima, but about a child forming itself finger by finger in the dark. They are not about the terrors of mass extinction, but about the bleakness of the moon over a yew tree in a neighboring graveyard...In a sense, these poems are deflections. I do not think they are an escape.'

Archibald MacLeish:
A poem should not mean
But be.

R.S. Thomas:
Poetry is that
which arrives at the intellect
by way of the heart.

INTRODUCTION

The best contemporary poetry is life-affirming and directly relevant to all our lives. Yet most of us could only name one or two modern poems which have moved us profoundly and unforgettably. These are the kinds of poems which speak to us with the same unnerving power now as when we first came across them, like W.H. Auden's 'Funeral Blues' in *Four Weddings and a Funeral* ('Stop all the clocks...') and Dylan Thomas's 'Do Not Go Gentle into that Good Night'. And there are also those rare poems we encounter almost by accident. That short poem we stared at, read and re-read, on the underground or subway train. Or the one photocopied by a friend, now a personal talisman pinned to the kitchen noticeboard or kept in a wallet, the poem which says everything about Life, the Universe and little me. They're like word-of-mouth books, because a poem which makes important personal connections for a trusted friend is likely to affect you in similar ways.

Such poems are remarkable because there seem to be so few of them. Or so we believe. For most people think contemporary poetry is either boring and irrelevant or pretentious and superficial. And that these single, powerful poems are somehow the exceptions. But they aren't. One of the problems with modern poetry is that because there is so much of it – and so many poems hold little interest for the general reader – you don't know where to find those exceptional poems. I hope you'll discover many such gems in this book.

Staying Alive is quite unlike any other anthology. It doesn't just give you 500 exceptional poems by all kinds of poets from around the world, it is a book with a particular vision of what poetry should be about – drawn from the poems themselves, not the critical reputations of the poets. I've been editing and publishing poetry now for nearly 30 years, so *Staying Alive* is the culmination of one committed reader's lifetime trawl through thousands and thousands of poems; it also includes poems recommended over the years by friends and writers whose taste I trust. It is a book about what poetry means and how it can help us as people. A book about staying alive.

Many people turn to poetry only at unreal times, whether for consolation in grief or affirmation in love. This book includes many of the great modern love poems and elegies, such as those by Auden and Neruda which reached a wider audience through recent films, as well as many less familiar but equally powerful poems about love and death. But *Staying Alive* also shows the power of poetry in celebrating the ordinary miracle, taking you, the reader, on a journey around many of the different aspects of life explored in poems. David Constantine believes that poetry 'helps us understand common things better'. A poem is not just for crisis.

I've put Kafka's comment about books which 'bite and sting' at the front of *Staying Alive* because there are many poems here which 'wake us up with a blow to the head'. Kafka says a book 'must be the axe which smashes the frozen sea within us'. Yet poems with that kind of power are rarely simplistic and often formally complex. Their immediacy and directness are the result of skilful but unobtrusive artistry. The poem and the "message" are one and the same thing. The paraphrasable meaning is less than the poem itself. What affects you is the experience of reading or re-reading the poem. For if what the poem says could be expressed by some other means, in prose or through conversation, you wouldn't need the poem. Basil Bunting always stressed the importance of the sound of the poem. 'Poetry, like music, is to be heard,' he wrote, believing that without the sound, readers would look at the lines of a poem as they look at prose, 'seeking a meaning. Prose exists to convey meaning, and no meaning such as prose conveys can be expressed as well in poetry. That is not poetry's business.'

Staying Alive has many poems written in response to unreal times which have great personal force for readers faced with similar tribulations in their own lives, like Mary Oliver's 'Wild Geese' (see page 28) as well as her 'Journey' (78). Such poems can be so valuable to us that they become personal mantras, poems to be committed to memory and taken fully to heart. When Nehru lay dying, he had written out the last verse of Robert Frost's 'Stopping by Woods on a Snowy Evening' (73) on a piece of paper by his bed, and kept repeating the lines ('And miles to go before I sleep...'). Another Frost poem, 'The Road Not Taken' (55), became America's favourite modern poem because it encapsulates everyone's anxieties about the roads we take – or might have taken – in life. Stevie Smith's 'Not Waving but Drowning' (57) has a similar force, contrasting the proactive approach to life we'd all like to take with the passive one we too often end up taking. Many of the poems in the second *Roads* section of *Staying Alive* dramatise these kinds of life decisions: the journeys we take, the roads we choose or have chosen for us.

I have tried to create a selection which has its own internal drama, so that different kinds of poems seem to answer or echo one another, developing a theme in such a way that the reader engages with what they say as a whole as well as with the poems individually. Some of these links reflect actual connections between certain poets. I have also selected poems which contradict one another, and set them side by side. In the third *Dead or Alive* section, poems about depression are immediately followed by others which lift you out of sadness into assertion. I've used oppositions of this kind through *Staying Alive* because, as William Blake says, 'without contraries is no progression', and just as Blake gives you his Songs of Innocence *and* Experience, here you will find body and soul, war and peace, God and atheism. Such a structure mirrors that of the poem. Readers often say they are drawn *either* to the emotional power or to the intellectual complexity of a poem, but all good poetry enacts an interplay between thought and feeling, challenging the intellect at the same time as it draws on emotion. The American poet Theodore Roethke said a poet should think *by* feeling. The same is true of reading. Randall Jarrell said you need to read good poetry 'with an attitude that is a mixture of sharp intelligence and of willing emotional empathy, at once penetrating and generous'.

Like this book's selection, its subtitle *Real Poems for Unreal Times* is double-edged. These are poems which relate to times which feel unreal as we experience extremes or anxieties in our lives, whether in response to love or death, or to how we deal with change, disruption or simply with living from day to day. But these are also poems relating to the unreal times we live through as people, poems in which language is used with the primal force and feeling too often lost in a modern world which insists on instant comment and immediate communication, in which time is money and everything is costed. And yet sensitivity to language is what distinguishes us as civilised people, both as human beings and as individuals, registering our intelligence as well as our alertness and attention to the lives of others. A poem lives in its language, which is body to its soul. Joseph Brodsky believed that our purpose in life as human beings was 'to create civilisation', and that 'poetry is essentially the soul's search for its release in language'.

Seamus Heaney thinks that poetry has a special ability to *redress* spiritual balance and to function as a counterweight to hostile and oppressive forces in the world. He calls this 'the imagination pressing back against the pressure of reality'. Heaney's personal mantra is a phrase by an earlier Nobel prizewinner, the Greek poet George Seferis, who felt that poetry should be 'strong enough to help', by which he didn't mean 'the kind of strength that is supposed to come from reading books of an uplifting nature' but rather that he valued poetry's 'response to conditions in the world at a moment when the world was in crisis'. This is what Heaney calls 'redress', whereby 'the poetic imagination seems to redress whatever is wrong or exacerbating in the prevailing conditions', offering 'a response to reality which has a liberating and verifying effect upon the individual spirit...tilting the scales of reality towards some transcendent equilibrium...This redressing effect of poetry comes from its being a glimpsed alternative, a revelation of potential that is denied or constantly threatened by circumstances.'

David Constantine develops this theme in a fascinating essay on Bertolt Brecht's poetry, showing how Brecht's dogmatic requirement that lyric poetry should be 'useful' was subverted in his own work. The effect of Brecht's poems on the reader is not an engagement with his political ideas, says Constantine, but rather 'a shock, a quickening of consciousness, a becoming alert to better possibilities, an extension, a liberation', for such poetry is, 'to put it mildly, a useful thing if, when reading it, we sense a better way of being in the world'.

Heaney has said he is not a political writer and he doesn't see literature as a way of solving political problems, yet he also believes in the poet as spiritual witness, in the transforming power of poetry: the spirit at bay, making a stand, the poet trying writing 'to teach the free man how to praise' as Auden put it in his elegy for Yeats, which Heaney calls 'a rallying cry that celebrates poetry for being on the side of life, and continuity of effort, and enlargement of the spirit'. Sylvia Plath wanted poetry to be 'solid and miraculous' in the face of adversity: 'Surely the great use of poetry is its pleasure – not its influence as religious or political propaganda.' Constantine adds that 'poetry will effect its greatest redress if, especially in the dark times, it asserts its traditional lyric freedom, treats the subjects it always has treated, and keeps its formal options as open as possible'.

Heaney's vision of poetry is of 'a glimpsed alternative', poetry being 'instrumental in adjusting and correcting imbalances in the world, poetry as an intended intervention into the goings-on of society – even then, poetry is involved with supreme fictions as well as actual conditions...To redress poetry in this sense is to know it and celebrate it for its forcibleness as itself, as the affirming spiritual flame which W.H. Auden wanted to be shown forth.' Auden held out that flame in his poem 'September 1, 1939' (357) as the world prepared for war. We need it just as much now.

If we look to poets for anything at a time when abuse of power goes hand in hand with abuse of language, when the threat to language is an attack on our lifeblood, it should be for their vigilance in defending and continually revitalising the language, whether that be in the countries of the former Soviet bloc where such abuse was blatant, or in the West where it is more insidious.

Joseph Brodsky said the poet 'shouldn't be viewed through any other prism than that of his poems', meaning that biography and politics come second. The reader engages not with the poet, but with the poem, experiencing the poem in its own terms. *The Poem Itself* was Stanley Burnshaw's simple, resonant phrase for this (and the title of his celebrated anthology presenting word by word translations of 150 modern European poems).

W.B. Yeats wrote great poetry despite having a highly confused love life and muddled ideas drawn from a hotchpotch of philosophies, but you don't go to poets for philosophical guidance any more than for models of good behaviour. One of the greatest disservices to poetry has been the modern tendency to read poems in terms of their paraphrasable meaning, leading to the misguided attempt to urge poets to "speak out" on political issues. These kinds of misreadings of poetry are the inevitable result of botched teaching: first the killing of poems by careless dissection at school, then their intellectual "decoding" as so-called "texts" in universities by literary theoreticians.

When Elizabeth Bishop taught at Harvard in the 1970s, she spurned the academic approach of New Criticism, insisting that poems should never be interpreted. Dana Gioia has described how her students would have to memorise a poem before talking about its meaning: 'To her, the images and the music of the lines were primary. If we comprehended the sound, eventually we would understand the sense …She wanted us to see poems, not ideas. Poetry was the particular way the world could be talked about only in verse…the medium was the message. One did not interpret poetry, one experienced it. Showing us how to experience it clearly, intensely, and, above all, directly was the substance of her teaching. One did not need a sophisticated theory. One needed only intelligence, intuition, and a good dictionary.'

In these unreal times when so much feels hostile to everything we hold dear, poetry can seem irrelevant, as hard to defend as it is to define. What's the point of poetry? people ask, or we ask ourselves. How can we spend time reading or writing poetry when humanity and civilisation are being trashed all around us? Aren't we fiddling while Rome burns? And what *is* poetry anyway?

This book is an attempt to address all those difficult but necessary questions, though not necessarily to answer them. The comments by poets at the beginning of this introduction offer some possible responses, or at least clues. Seamus Heaney's notion of the 'redress of poetry' is another helpful yardstick, and I would hope that there is much common ground between Heaney's position and the poetry map of *Staying Alive*. You don't go to poetry for answers or absolutes, just as you shouldn't expect a psychotherapist to give you solutions to your problems, to make your decisions for you. But whether with a therapist or a trusted friend, dialogue helps you think and feel your way through difficulties or anxieties, leading to self-knowledge. A similar process is enacted, telescoped into three hours, in a Shakespeare play, when we witness how someone learns 'to thine own self be true', for then 'Thou canst not then be false to any man.'

While *Staying Alive* includes many classic and timeless poems from the past hundred years, it's primarily a book showing the wide range of contemporary poetry from the past three decades, much of which is closer to Shakespeare than to Modernism in its address to concerns shared by the reader and in the way the poet often celebrates human and spiritual values instead of mirroring cultural fragmentation. This is particularly true of major figures such as Seamus Heaney, Ted Hughes and the European writers they have championed, including Joseph Brodsky, Osip Mandelstam, Anna Akhmatova and Miroslav Holub.

Poets no longer live in ivory towers, although there are a few still cocooned in academic isolation, especially in America. Today's poets come from all kinds of backgrounds and cultures, women as well as men; they are much more tuned in to how people think about the world and feel about themselves than the poets of 50 years ago. What the best poets write is relevant to people's lives and to their experience of the world, on an everyday as well as on a more spiritual level. Poetry includes not just the personal but the social, political and analytical; self-regard has given way to self-awareness.

In these unreal times, poetry could be a great source of nourishment to many more people who are trying to make sense of a new age of information and double-speak, technology and terrorism, of war and world poverty. In politics, television, newspapers and advertising, language is often negative, reductive, stripped of full expression to put across a message – or it's spun or twisted out of recognition, by democrats as well as by extremists. Instead of being used to communicate, it is used to control thinking, as a tool of power. Our continual exposure to this manipulative, dulling force discourages openness, otherness, imagination, wonder, reaching out. Contemporary poetry can offer fresh slants, new views and broader perspectives. And poets like Jo Shapcott, Selima Hill and Paul Muldoon have been reclaiming language for the imagination with a new kind of protean poetry whose energy comes from the way in which it slips from your grasp the more you read it – and yet the more you read, the more you are drawn into its almost otherworldly take on the unreal "real" world we live in.

Poetry doesn't give answers as such, but it engages readers intellectually and emotionally. Readers identify with the inner debates explored by poets, with the personal conflicts explored through poetry. It also engages readers at a very basic level through its music, energy and concentrated interplay of ideas through imagery and metaphor, and through its exhilarating engagement with language.

Poets like Paul Durcan, Brendan Kennelly and Ken Smith have shown you can be serious and funny at the same time. Their black humour points up a telling social or political point. Many of them tell stories. Contemporary poetry is remarkable for its mixture of bizarre intelligence and anarchic humour, popular culture and learning, eroticism and sensuality of language.

European poets such as Miroslav Holub, Marin Sorescu and Zbigniew Herbert have encouraged a new, highly inventive approach to narrative in contemporary poetry by Americans such as Billy Collins, Stephen Dobyns, Thomas Lux and the Yugoslav-born Charles Simic, as well as by their British and Irish counterparts. Often bizarrely humorous, this fantastical mode has been ridiculed by serious-minded writers, including the American Robert Pinsky, who called it the 'jackanapes' strain of modern poetry, citing a poem about throwing old gramophone records at cows. Some poets writing in this vein are certainly overindulgent, but others achieve great emotive power and intellectual resonance, like Selima Hill, writing 'I want to be a cow / and not my mother's daughter' (237), or Jo Shapcott, telling her 'Life' (266) as a bat, a frog and an iguana.

One 'jackanapes' fabulist, Matthew Sweeney, differentiates what he calls 'alternate realism' from Surrealism, which was concerned with the irrational and the unconscious, often using dreams, free association or automatic writing. Sweeney makes a comparison with Kafka and Dante: 'You enter a world in which everything is operating in its own very realistic way, but it is an alternative to our world.' This blackly comic, alternative poetry might owe much to Monty Python satire as well as to comics and cartoons (from Mickey Mouse and *The Beano* to Steve Bell and *The Simpsons*), but there's also a darker emotional edge, as in Beckett's plays or in magic realist fiction. In Charles Simic's poems, 'the magic dance is being kept up to keep calamity at bay', according to Heaney – himself a very different kind of poet – while the American critic Helen Vendler finds in Simic 'the search for explanation, knowing there is none; and the finding of plots or images to match the burden of feeling'.

There has also been a still shifting redefinition of spiritual poetry at a time when many people have become disillusioned not only with the established church but with New Age beliefs and alternative religion. Dylan Thomas believed that 'the joy and function of poetry is, and was, the celebration of man, which is also the celebration of God'. More recently, while R.S. Thomas won a wide readership for his poetry of doubt-wracked engagement with God and belief, other poets have been writing a more tentative kind of visionary poetry, exploring humanity and nature in spiritual terms, often enacting their own hesitancy and disquiet within the poem.

Yet an art which could offer so much to so many people is generally ignored or ridiculed. For contemporary poetry, one of this country's greatest treasures, is one of its best kept secrets. One reason for this is historical: the reading public lost touch with poetry when modern poets lost touch with their audience early in the 20th century (for further comment on this, see pages 458-63).

Another problem is poetry's supposed difficulty. Appreciating the technical complexity of a poem is part of its appeal for me. I read a poem first for the experience of 'the poem itself', then re-read it to see how its effects are achieved, returning to it later when I'm less conscious of that previous reading. Just as I go back to the same pictures when I visit a gallery, I keep revisiting particular poems which have exerted a strong pull on my imagination. And yet you hear highly intelligent people complaining on arts programmes that a particular poetry book was too difficult because they didn't get 'its meaning' at one reading but had to keep going back to the poem. You sense their impatience at the poem's refusal to explain itself, as if this somehow contravened new rules that all thought must be instantly communicable and language immediately accessible, and therefore disposable: difficulty equals obscurity, and we don't have time for this. But this is the strength and beauty of the well-wrought, challenging poem: it makes you stop and think, it gives you back that private time and space which are so much under threat in our culture.

A great modern poem like Derek Mahon's 'A Disused Shed in Co. Wexford' (166) doesn't just make you pause for thought as you read and re-read it, it almost makes you feel more human. The poem's evolving interplay between thought and feeling – enacted through its engagement with language – produces a delicately balanced response in the reader. Those particular sensations of sound and symbol evoked by this poem trouble the meaning, but you shouldn't expect to understand any poem at one reading. Just as you listen to songs – or sing them – again and again, so poems need to be read, re-read, read out loud and read again.

In selecting many different kinds of poems for *Staying Alive*, I've tried to produce a selection specifically for interested readers who have little knowledge of contemporary poetry, but I've also tried to stay true to the spirit of poetry. Editors are too often pressured to publish what's called 'accessible poetry', but instead of directing people towards lively, challenging work, you are expected to give readers more of what they already know, or worse, to patronise intelligent and critical readers with second-rate or diluted forms of poetry.

Many poems ask the reader to settle into their own slower, more contemplative time-frame in order to enter into a gradual unfolding of thought and feeling, enacted through the language and formal structure. A good example of this would be Edward Thomas's 'As the team's head-brass' (349), a carefully achieved poem set during war-time in a once unchanging English landscape. Many of his poems use rhyme, but Thomas knows intuitively that this kind of a meditative poem needs to be written in unrhymed "blank verse" – as used by Shakespeare in his plays as well as in English landscape poetry from Thomson, Crabbe and Wordsworth to Robert Frost – set off by a gentle undertow of unobtrusive, irregularly placed half-rhymes suggesting the turn of the plough at the end of a line or furrow. You cannot rush this kind of poem.

The dedicated reader knows all this, but while *Staying Alive* is essentially an anthology for new readers of poetry, it should also appeal to readers already familiar with much contemporary poetry because it draws upon such a wide range of poetry from around the world, and I hope that such readers will make many astonishing discoveries in the course of these pages.

For the new reader, I've introduced each section with a short comment. Most of the poems speak for themselves and don't need any glossing, but some context is helpful in places as a means of giving the reader some bearings (most of the sections include one particularly challenging or densely written poem). I also mention forms used by certain poets, and any technical terms employed in this introduction or in the prefatory comments are defined in the glossary at the back of the book. This is preceded by 'The Sound of Poetry', a short discussion of rhyme, metre and free verse, beginning with the widely held but totally mistaken belief that 'if it doesn't rhyme, it's not poetry' (458-63).

My hope is that having discovered a much fuller understanding and appreciation of contemporary poetry through *Staying Alive*, you will then want to go on to explore the full riches held in so many other books. Until you discovered *Staying Alive*, the problem was that you didn't know where to look, but after you've read and re-read the poems in this anthology, I hope you'll seek out books by many of the poets whose work you've liked. In the *Further Reading* note at the end, I've listed other anthologies and guides which I think you'll also find helpful.

NEIL ASTLEY

Wild Geese

You do not have to be good.
You do not have to walk on your knees
for a hundred miles through the desert, repenting.
You only have to let the soft animal of your body
    love what it loves.
Tell me about despair, yours, and I will tell you mine.
Meanwhile the world goes on.
Meanwhile the sun and the clear pebbles of the rain
are moving across the landscapes,
over the prairies and the deep trees,
the mountains and the rivers.
Meanwhile the wild geese, high in the clean blue air,
are heading home again.
Whoever you are, no matter how lonely,
the world offers itself to your imagination,
calls to you like the wild geese, harsh and exciting –
over and over announcing your place
in the family of things.

MARY OLIVER

1

Body and soul

Poems come out of wonder, not out of knowing.

LUCILLE CLIFTON

Poetry says more about the psychic life of an age than
any other art. Poetry is a place where all the fundamental
questions are asked about the human condition.

CHARLES SIMIC

THIS SECTION begins with poems that celebrate the joy of living, the beauty
of the natural world and the pleasures of the body and the senses. Denise
Levertov's 'Living' (31) captures the vitality of nature and the preciousness of
every life and every minute of life. The oneness with the body which Lucille
Clifton expresses in 'Homage to My Hips' (36) contrasts with Elizabeth Bishop's
'Chemin de Fer' (39), a cry for love which speaks to her own struggle to accept
her homosexuality when she wrote this poem in 1946; it could also be read as
a "coded" account of female masturbation. The Canadian writer Alden Nowlan
had a miserable childhood, leaving school at 12 to work in a papermill. Written
at a time when it was normal to talk about 'retarded' children, Nowlan's poem
(40), like those by Tess Gallagher (38) and Les Murray (41), is about not being
afraid to show our emotions: giving physical expression to the way we feel,
here by hugging or crying in public.

There's also a sense of mystery in this: no one knows why the man is cry-
ing in 'An Absolutely Ordinary Rainbow', and Les Murray evokes the baffled,
communal response to a spectacle both ordinary and extraordinary by echoing
a famous poem by 'Waltzing Matilda' author 'Banjo' Paterson in his opening
lines. Every Australian of Murray's generation would know by heart 'The Man
from Snowy River' which begins: 'There was movement at the station, for
the word had passed around / That the colt from old Regret had got away',
but instead of bushmen from different cattle-stations, Murray homes in on
men reacting from familiar Sydney locations, drinking or eating in Repins
and Lorenzinis, or watching the horse sales at Tattersalls.

Poets often draw on well-known poems, stories or myths to nudge us in
unexpected directions. At one time they could rely upon most readers sharing
their own knowledge and love of literature and history, of the Bible and clas-
sical mythology, but people today are generally less familiar with that cultural

heritage, so that poetry drawing on this tradition has less resonance. Myths restate recurring archetypal patterns and psychological truths. When poets use myth they make potent connections with living stories just as relevant to us as they were to the ancient Greeks. Our growing separation from that heritage is even more telling in relation to the poetry itself, for the single most important stylistic influence on the language of English poetry over the past four centuries has been the beautifully cadenced prose of the King James Bible.

One story from the English tradition which has appealed to many writers is Bede's account of the conversion of the Anglo-Saxon King Edwin, in which one of the elders compares man's life to 'the swift flight of a single sparrow through the banqueting-hall where you are sitting at dinner on a winter's day... This sparrow flies swiftly through one door of the hall, and out through another. While he is inside, he is safe from the winter storms; but after a few moments of comfort, he vanishes from sight into the wintry world from which he came. Even so, man appears on earth for a little while; but of what went before this life and what follows, we know nothing.' Stephen Dobyns revisits the tale in 'Where We Are' (52), while Carol Rumens recalls it in her poem 'Jarrow' (51) about a visit to the monastery where Bede lived in the 8th century. The same image of the soul's journey through life compared to a sparrow's flight recurs later in the extract from Peter Reading's *Evagatory* in his Alcaic line 'flight of a sparrow brief through the feasting hall' (312).

The visionary Austrian poet Rainer Maria Rilke spent the winter of 1912 alone in a castle at Duino near Trieste. The trigger for his sequence of ten *Duino Elegies* – which took him ten years to complete – came as he paced the bastions in a restless mood, hearing a voice in the roaring wind calling 'Who, if I cried, would hear me among the angelic orders?' Rilke's poetry uses what he called 'external' or symbolic equivalents for inward experiences, so that Nature and all the visible works of man become a kind of externalised and visible consciousness, and consciousness a kind of internalised and visible nature. The Tenth Elegy (44) is a paradoxical affirmation of sorrow and suffering as well as life and joy which makes what he called 'full use of the strings of lamentation'. The writing-pad in which he drafted this poem includes this note: 'Art cannot be helpful through our trying to help and specially concerning ourselves with the distresses of others, but in so far as we bear our own distresses more passionately, give, now and then, a perhaps clearer meaning to endurance, and develop for ourselves the means of expressing the suffering within us and its conquest more precisely and clearly than is possible to those who have to apply their powers to something else.'

There has been much discussion about whether great artists should suffer for their work. Osip Mandelstam was persecuted under Stalin, who took a personal interest in the poet's fate. Imprisoned for a poem comparing the dictator's moustache to a cockroach, he died in a Siberian labour camp in 1938. 'The Eyesight of Wasps' (49) was written in exile a year earlier: 'I feel everything that ever happened to me,/ And I memorise it, but it's all in vain.' The poem has even greater power in the Russian original, which plays with the sound '*os*': *os* means axis (or axle), *osy* are wasps, *sosut* is sip or suck, and *os* is the same sound element in *Os*ip Mandelstam and *Ios*if Stalin.

Living

The fire in leaf and grass
so green it seems
each summer the last summer.

The wind blowing, the leaves
shivering in the sun,
each day the last day.

A red salamander
so cold and so
easy to catch, dreamily

moves his delicate feet
and long tail. I hold
my hand open for him to go.

Each minute the last minute.

DENISE LEVERTOV

Orkney / This Life

It is big sky and its changes,
the sea all round and the waters within.
It is the way sea and sky
work off each other constantly,
like people meeting in Alfred Street,
each face coming away with a hint
of the other's face pressed in it.
It is the way a week-long gale
ends and folk emerge to hear
a single bird cry way high up.

It is the way you lean to me
and the way I lean to you, as if
we are each other's prevailing;
how we connect along our shores,
the way we are tidal islands

joined for hours then inaccessible,
I'll go for that, and smile when I
pick sand off myself in the shower.
The way I am an inland loch to you
when a clatter of white whoops and rises...

It is the way Scotland looks to the South,
the way we enter friends' houses
to leave what we came with, or flick
the kettle's switch and wait.
This is where I want to live,
close to where the heart gives out,
ruined, perfected, an empty arch against the sky
where birds fly through instead of prayers
while in Hoy Sound the ferry's engines thrum
this life this life this life.

ANDREW GREIG

A Northern Morning

It rained from dawn. The fire died in the night.
I poured hot water on some foreign leaves;
I brought the fire to life. Comfort
spread from the kitchen like a taste of chocolate
through the head-waters of a body,
accompanied by that little-water-music.
The knotted veins of the old house tremble and carry
a louder burden: the audience joining in.

People are peaceful in a world so lavish
with the ingredients of life:
the world of breakfast easy as Tahiti.
But we must leave. Head down in my new coat
I dodge to the High Street conscious of my fellows
damp and sad in their vegetable fibres.
But by the bus-stop I look up: the spring trees
exult in the downpour, radiant, clean for hours:
This is the life! This is the only life!

ALISTAIR ELLIOT

Happiness

So early it's still almost dark out.
I'm near the window with coffee,
and the usual early morning stuff
that passes for thought.
When I see the boy and his friend
walking up the road
to deliver the newspaper.
They wear caps and sweaters,
and one boy has a bag over his shoulder.
They are so happy
they aren't saying anything, these boys.
I think if they could, they would take
each other's arm.
It's early in the morning,
and they are doing this thing together.
They come on, slowly.
The sky is taking on light,
though the moon still hangs pale over the water.
Such beauty that for a minute
death and ambition, even love,
doesn't enter into this.
Happiness. It comes on
unexpectedly. And goes beyond, really,
any early morning talk about it.

RAYMOND CARVER

My Father's Irish Setters

Always throughout his life
(The parts of it I knew)
Two or three would be racing
Up stairs and down hallways,
Whining to take us walking,
Or caked with dirt, resigning
Keen ears to bouts of talk —
Until his third, last wife

Put down her little foot.
That splendid, thoroughbred
Lineage was penned
Safely out of earshot:
Fed, of course, and watered,
But never let out to run.
'Dear God,' the new wife simpered,
Tossing her little head,
'Suppose they got run over –
Wouldn't *that* be the end?'

Each time I visited
(Once or twice a year)
I'd slip out, giving my word
Not to get carried away.
At the dogs' first sight of me
Far off – of anyone –
Began a joyous barking,
A russet-and-rapid-as-flame
Leaping, then whimpering lickings
Of face and hands through wire.
Like fire, like fountains leaping
With love and loyalty,
Put, were they, in safekeeping
By love, or for love's sake?
Dear heart, to love's own shame.
But loyalty transferred
Leaves famously slim pickings,
And no one's left to blame.

Divorced again, my father
(Hair white, face deeply scored)
Looked round and heaved a sigh.
The setters were nowhere.
Fleet muzzle, soulful eye
Dead lo! these forty winters?
Not so. Tonight in perfect
Lamplit stillness begin
With updraft from the worksheet,
Leaping and tongues, far-shining
Hearths of our hinterland:
Dour chieftain, maiden pining
Away for that lost music,
Her harpist's wild red hair...

Dear clan of Ginger and Finn,
As I go through your motions
(As they go through me, rather)
Love follows, pen in hand.

JAMES MERRILL

Legs

Of well-fed babies activate
Digestive juices, yet I'm no cannibal.
It is my metaphysical teeth that wait
Impatiently to prove those goodies edible.
The pink or creamy bonelessness, as soft
As dough or mashed potato, does not show
A hint of how each pair of limbs will grow.
Schoolboys' are badged with scabs and starred with scars,
Their sisters', in white ankle-socks, possess
No calves as yet. They will, and when they do
Another kind of hunger will distress
Quite painfully, but pleasurably too.
Those lovely double stalks of girls give me
So much delight: the brown expensive ones,
Like fine twin creatures of rare pedigree,
Seem independent of their owners, so
Much themselves are they. Even the plain
Or downright ugly, the veined and cruelly blotched
That look like marble badly stained, I've watched
With pity and revulsion, yet something more –
A wonder at the variousness of things
Which share a name: the podgy oatmeal knees
Beneath the kilt, the muscled double weapons above boots,
Eloquence of dancers', suffering of chars',
The wiry goatish, the long and smooth as milk –
The joy when these embrace like arms and cling!
O human legs, whose strangenesses I sing,
You more than please, though pleasure you have brought me,
And there are often times when you transport me.

VERNON SCANNELL

Homage to My Hips

these hips are big hips
they need space to
move around in.
they don't fit into little
petty places. these hips
are free hips.
they don't like to be held back.
these hips have never been enslaved,
they go where they want to go
they do what they want to do.
these hips are mighty hips.
these hips are magic hips.
i have known them
to put a spell on a man and
spin him like a top!

LUCILLE CLIFTON

Naked Vision

I was sent to fetch an eye
promised for a fresh corneal graft.
At the doctor's rooms nurse gave me
a common paper bag;
in that, a sterile jar;
in that, the disembodied eye.

I sat in Davey Street
on a low brick garden wall
and looked. The eye looked back.
It gazed, lucid and whole,
from its colourless solution.
The window of whose soul?

Trees in St David's Park
refreshed the lunchtime lovers:
riesling gold, claret dark;
late flowers flaunted all colours.
But my friend and I had eyes
only for one another.

GWEN HARWOOD

The Hug

It was your birthday, we had drunk and dined
    Half of the night with our old friend
      Who'd showed us in the end
    To a bed I reached in one drunk stride.
      Already I lay snug,
    And drowsy with the wine dozed on one side.

I dozed, I slept. My sleep broke on a hug,
    Suddenly, from behind,
In which the full lengths of our bodies pressed:
    Your instep to my heel,
    My shoulder-blades against your chest.
    It was not sex, but I could feel
    The whole strength of your body set,
      Or braced, to mine,
      And locking me to you
    As if we were still twenty-two
    When our grand passion had not yet
      Become familial.
    My quick sleep had deleted all
    Of intervening time and place.
      I only knew
The stay of your secure firm dry embrace.

THOM GUNN

The Hug

A woman is reading a poem on the street
and another woman stops to listen. We stop too,
with our arms around each other. The poem
is being read and listened to out here
in the open. Behind us
no one is entering or leaving the houses.

Suddenly a hug comes over me and I'm
giving it to you, like a variable star shooting light
off to make itself comfortable, then
subsiding. I finish but keep on holding
you. A man walks up to us and we know he hasn't
come out of nowhere, but if he could, he
would have. He looks homeless because of how
he needs. 'Can I have one of those?' he asks you,
and I feel you nod. I'm surprised,
surprised you don't tell him how
it is – that I'm yours, only
yours, etc., exclusive as a nose to
its face. Love – that's what we're talking about, love
that nabs you with 'for me
only' and holds on.

So I walk over to him and put my
arms around him and try to
hug him like I mean it. He's got an overcoat on
so thick I can't feel
him past it. I'm starting the hug
and thinking, 'How big a hug is this supposed to be?
How long shall I hold this hug?' Already
we could be eternal, his arms falling over my
shoulders, my hands not
meeting behind his back, he is so big!

I put my head into his chest and snuggle
in. I lean into him. I lean my blood and my wishes
into him. He stands for it. This is his
and he's starting to give it back so well I know he's
getting it. This hug. So truly, so tenderly
we stop having arms and I don't know if

my lover has walked away or what, or
if the woman is still reading the poem, or the houses –
what about them? – the houses.

Clearly, a little permission is a dangerous thing.
But when you hug someone you want it
to be a masterpiece of connection, the way the button
on his coat will leave the imprint of
a planet in my cheek
when I walk away. When I try to find some place
to go back to.

TESS GALLAGHER

Chemin de Fer

Alone on the railroad track
   I walked with pounding heart.
The ties were too close together
   or maybe too far apart.

The scenery was impoverished:
   scrub-pine and oak; beyond
its mingled gray-green foliage
   I saw the little pond

where the dirty hermit lives,
   lie like an old tear
holding onto its injuries
   lucidly year after year.

The hermit shot off his shot-gun
   and the tree by his cabin shook.
Over the pond went a ripple.
   The pet hen went chook-chook.

'Love should be put into action!'
   screamed the old hermit.
Across the pond an echo
   tried and tried to confirm it.

ELIZABETH BISHOP

He Sits Down on the Floor of a School
for the Retarded

I sit down on the floor of a school for the retarded,
a writer of magazine articles accompanying a band
that was met at the door by a child in a man's body
who asked them, 'Are you the surprise they promised us?'

It's Ryan's Fancy, Dermot on guitar,
Fergus on banjo, Denis on penny-whistle.
In the eyes of this audience, they're everybody
who has ever appeared on TV. I've been telling lies
to a boy who cried because his favourite detective
hadn't come with us; I said he had sent his love
and, no, I didn't think he'd mind if I signed his name
to a scrap of paper: when the boy took it, he said,
'Nobody will ever get this away from me,'
in the voice, more hopeless than defiant,
of one accustomed to finding that his hiding places
have been discovered, used to having objects snatched
out of his hands. Weeks from now I'll send him
another autograph, this one genuine
in the sense of having been signed by somebody
on the same payroll as the star.
Then I'll feel less ashamed. Now everyone is singing,
'Old MacDonald had a farm,' and I don't know what to do

about the young woman (I call her a woman
because she's twenty-five at least, but think of her
as a little girl, she plays that part so well,
having known no other), about the young woman who
sits down beside me and, as if it were the most natural
thing in the world, rests her head on my shoulder.

It's nine o'clock in the morning, not an hour for music.
And, at the best of times, I'm uncomfortable
in situations where I'm ignorant
of the accepted etiquette: it's one thing
to jump a fence, quite another to blunder
into one in the dark. I look around me
for a teacher to whom to smile out my distress.
They're all busy elsewhere. 'Hold me,' she whispers. 'Hold me.'

I put my arm round her. 'Hold me tighter.'
I do, and she snuggles closer. I half-expect
someone in authority to grab her
or me; I can imagine this being remembered
for ever as the time the sex-crazed writer
publicly fondled the poor retarded girl.
'Hold me,' she says again. What does it matter
what anybody thinks? I put my other arm around her,
rest my chin in her hair, thinking of children
real children, and of how they say it, 'Hold me,'
and of a patient in a geriatric ward
I once heard crying out to his mother, dead
for half a century, 'I'm frightened! Hold me!'
and of a boy-soldier screaming it on the beach
at Dieppe, of Nelson in Hardy's arms,
of Frieda gripping Lawrence's ankle
until he sailed off in his Ship of Death.

It's what we all want, in the end,
to be held, merely to be held,
to be kissed (not necessarily with the lips,
for every touching is a kind of kiss).

She hugs me now, this retarded woman, and I hug her.
We are brother and sister, father and daughter,
mother and son, husband and wife.
We are lovers. We are two human beings
huddled together for a little while by the fire
in the Ice Age, two hundred thousand years ago.

ALDEN NOWLAN

An Absolutely Ordinary Rainbow

The word goes round Repins,
the murmur goes round Lorenzinis,
at Tattersalls, men look up from sheets of numbers,
the Stock Exchange scribblers forget the chalk in their hands
and men with bread in their pockets leave the Greek Club:
There's a fellow crying in Martin Place. They can't stop him.

The traffic in George Street is banked up for half a mile
and drained of motion. The crowds are edgy with talk
and more crowds come hurrying. Many run in the back streets
which minutes ago were busy main streets, pointing:
There's a fellow weeping down there. No one can stop him.

The man we surround, the man no one approaches
simply weeps, and does not cover it, weeps
not like a child, not like the wind, like a man
and does not declaim it, nor beat his breast, nor even
sob very loudly – yet the dignity of his weeping

holds us back from his space, the hollow he makes about him
in the midday light, in his pentagram of sorrow,
and uniforms back in the crowd who tried to seize him
stare out at him, and feel, with amazement, their minds
longing for tears as children for a rainbow.

Some will say, in the years to come, a halo
or force stood around him. There is no such thing.
Some will say they were shocked and would have stopped him
but they will not have been there. The fiercest manhood,
the toughest reserve, the slickest wit amongst us

trembles with silence, and burns with unexpected
judgements of peace. Some in the concourse scream
who thought themselves happy. Only the smallest children
and such as look out of Paradise come near him
and sit at his feet, with dogs and dusty pigeons.

Ridiculous, says a man near me, and stops
his mouth with his hands, as if it uttered vomit –
and I see a woman, shining, stretch her hand
and shake as she receives the gift of weeping;
as many as follow her also receive it

and many weep for sheer acceptance, and more
refuse to weep for fear of all acceptance,
but the weeping man, like the earth, requires nothing,
the man who weeps ignores us, and cries out
of his writhen face and ordinary body

42

not words, but grief, not messages, but sorrow,
hard as the earth, sheer, present as the sea –
and when he stops, he simply walks between us
mopping his face with the dignity of one
man who has wept, and now has finished weeping.

Evading believers, he hurries off down Pitt Street.

LES MURRAY

A Prayer

In our country they are desecrating churches.
May the rain that pours in pour into the font.
Because no snowflake ever falls into the wrong place,
May snow lie on the altar like an altar cloth.

MICHAEL LONGLEY

Prayer

Some days, although we cannot pray, a prayer
utters itself. So, a woman will lift
her head from the sieve of her hands and stare
at the minims sung by a tree, a sudden gift.

Some nights, although we are faithless, the truth
enters our hearts, that small familiar pain;
then a man will stand stock-still, hearing his youth
in the distant Latin chanting of a train.

Pray for us now. Grade I piano scales
console the lodger looking out across
a Midlands town. Then dusk, and someone calls
a child's name as though they named their loss.

Darkness outside. Inside, the radio's prayer –
Rockall. Malin. Dogger. Finisterre.

CAROL ANN DUFFY

Encounter

We were riding through frozen fields in a wagon at dawn.
A red wing rose in the darkness.

And suddenly a hare ran across the road.
One of us pointed to it with his hand.

That was long ago. Today neither of them is alive,
Not the hare, nor the man who made the gesture.

O my love, where are they, where are they going
The flash of a hand, streak of movement, rustle of pebbles.
I ask not out of sorrow, but in wonder.

CZESLAW MILOSZ
translated by from the Polish by Czeslaw Milosz & Lillian Vallee

from The Tenth Duino Elegy

But how alien, alas, at the streets of the city of grief,
where, in the false silence formed of continual uproar,
the figure cast from the mold of emptiness stoutly
swaggers: the gilded noise, the bursting memorial.
Oh how completely an angel would stamp out their market of solace,
bounded by the church with its ready-made consolations:
clean and disenchanted and shut as a post-office on Sunday.
Farther out, though, the city's edges are curling with carnival.
Swings of freedom! Divers and jugglers of zeal!
And the shooting-gallery's targets of prettified happiness,
which jump and kick back with a tinny sound
when hit by some better marksman...

       ...Oh, but a little farther,
beyond the last of the billboards, plastered with signs for 'Deathless',
that bitter beer which seems so sweet to its drinkers
as long as they chew fresh distractions in between sips...,
just in back of the billboard, just behind, the view becomes real.
Children are playing, and lovers are holding hands, to the side,

solemnly in the meagre grass, and dogs are doing what is natural.
Lament... He comes out behind her, into the meadows. She says:
– It's a long walk. We live way out there... [...]

But there, in the valley, where they live, one of the elder Laments
answers the youth when he questions her: – Long ago,
she says, we Laments were a powerful race, Our forefathers worked
the mines, up there in the mountain-range; sometimes even
among men you can find a polished nugget of primal grief
or a chunk of petrified rage from the slag of an ancient volcano.
Yes, that came from up there. We used to be rich. –

And gently she guides him through the vast landscape of Lament,
shows him the pillars of the temples, and the ruined walls
of those castles from which, long ago, the princes of Lament
wisely ruled the land, Shows him the tall
trees of tears and the fields of blossoming grief
(the living know it just as a mild green shrub);
shows him the herds of sorrow, grazing, – and sometimes
a startled bird, flying low through their upward gaze,
far away trace the image of its solitary cry. – [...]

RAINER MARIA RILKE
translated from the German by Stephen Mitchell

Variation on a Theme by Rilke
(The Book of Hours, Book 1, Poem 1, Stanza 1)

A certain day became a presence to me;
there it was, confronting me – a sky, air, light:
a being. And before it started to descend
from the height of noon, it leaned over
and struck my shoulder as if with
the flat of a sword, granting me
honor and a task. The day's blow
rang out, metallic or it was I, a bell awakened,
and what I heard was my whole self
saying and singing what it knew: *I can.*

DENISE LEVERTOV

45

from A Gilded Lapse of Time

Then Gabriel sent down a dream that I stood
Holding a broken-off branch in the wood's heart,
And turning around, I saw the gate built with mud

From the other side, and flights of stairs above my head –
I had passed through it, and the branch I found myself
Holding shrank in my arms and withered away.

Fastened above the gate, a broken honeycomb
Like the concave interior of a death mask
Knocked from an ancestral frieze

Gaped: I had struck it – I had meant only
To open your book, to study poetry's empty beauty,
Not to rest my hand on two featureless tablets of wax

Fashioned with honeycombs in the age of kings,
The combs a poet touches to his lips,
Seeking to cross the threshold, to signify

A sacred conversation. I had broken
The reliquary of the bee, where she had sifted
Her yellow powder through melismatic generations,

Worlds, numberless lifetimes, seeking to finish
Her combs, to mix a flower-dust paste and fix
One drop to the blank mask of her catacomb,

To the brink of a miniature chasm – we are meant
To open a hive with reverence, but instead
I had broken the hive apart with a branch, and worse,

I had left the honeycomb dripping on the ground
In the wood's heart, a profanity
Of waste, and the bees whirled into my ears

Their endless sequences, their burning rhymes
I groped among for what I meant to say.
Angels were there, and one of them turned

And struck me when I spoke, and I lifted my hand
And touched blood on my mouth, and then I saw
They were holding an impression from your face –

Or rather a heavy honeycomb, and your words
Were a stream of bees floating toward me in sunlight.
When I opened your book I thought you spoke,

Or else it was Gabriel lifting to my lips
A tablespoon of golden, boiling smoke
So wounding to my mouth I turned my back

On the source of poetry, and then I woke.

GJERTRUD SCHNACKENBERG

Dark Angel

It was the sound of darkness, mother said,
But still I heard you calling in the night.
It was our old poinciana, straight from hell,
Its full-moon perfume wafting through the house...

Or fine mosquitoes, rising from the river
Just coiling in the dark there, down the road;
It was that sound, of water and the trees,
That somehow found a way into my sleep.

At night, between poinciana and the river,
Something of me walked round and round and round
Near that black water with its snags and snakes
And long low sounds that keep the grass alive,

And you were there as well, a touch away,
Always about to pull the darkness back,
And there were always branches rustling hard
And tall reeds bending. Never any wind.

KEVIN HART

Temptation

Call yourself alive? Look, I promise you
that for the first time you'll feel your pores opening
like fish mouths, and you'll actually be able to hear
your blood surging through all those lanes,
and you'll feel light gliding across the cornea
like the train of a dress. For the first time
you'll be aware of gravity
like a thorn in your heel,
and your shoulder blades will ache for want of wings.
Call yourself alive? I promise you
you'll be deafened by dust falling on the furniture,
you'll feel your eyebrows turning to two gashes,
and every memory you have – will begin
at Genesis.

NINA CASSIAN
translated from the Romanian by Brenda Walker & Andrea Deletant

Poppies in October

Even the sun-clouds this morning cannot manage such skirts.
Nor the woman in the ambulance
Whose red heart blooms through her coat so astoundingly —

A gift, a love gift
Utterly unasked for
By a sky

Palely and flamily
Igniting its carbon monoxides, by eyes
Dulled to a halt under bowlers.

O my God, what am I
That these late mouths should cry open
In a forest of frost, in a dawn of cornflowers.

SYLVIA PLATH

'Eyesight of Wasps'

Armed with the eyesight of slender wasps,
sucking at the earth's axis, the earth's axis,
I feel everything that ever happened to me,
and I memorise it, but it's all in vain.

I don't draw and I don't sing,
and I don't play the violin with a black-voiced bow.
I drive my sting only into life, and love
to envy the powerful, cunning wasps.

Oh, if I could be compelled
by the sting of the air and the summer warmth
to pass through the worlds of dreams and death,
to sense the earth's axis, the earth's axis...

OSIP MANDELSTAM
translated from the Russian by Richard & Elizabeth McKane

The Wasps

The apples on the tree are full of wasps;
Red apples, racing like hearts. The summer pushes
Her tongue into the winter's throat.

But at six today, like rain, like the first drops,
The wasps came battering softly at the black glass.
They want the light, the cold is at their backs.

That morning last year when the light had been left on
The strange room terrified the heart in me,
I could not place myself, didn't know my own

Insect scribble: then saw the whole soft
Pelt of wasps, its underbelly, the long black pane
Yellow with visitants, it seethed, the glass sounded.

I bless my life: that so much wants in.

DAVID CONSTANTINE

The Old World

I believe in the soul; so far
It hasn't made much difference.
I remember an afternoon in Sicily.
The ruins of some temple.
Columns fallen in the grass like naked lovers.

The olives and goat cheese tasted delicious
And so did the wine
With which I toasted the coming night,
The darting swallows,
The Saracen wind and moon.

It got darker. There was something
Long before there were words:
The evening meal of shepherds...
A fleeting whiteness among the trees...
Eternity eavesdropping on time.

The goddess going to bathe in the sea.
She must not be followed.
These rocks, these cypress trees,
May be her old lovers.
Oh to be one of them, the wine whispered to me.

CHARLES SIMIC

Watering the Horse

How strange to think of giving up all ambition!
Suddenly I see with such clear eyes
The white flake of snow
That has just fallen on the horse's mane!

ROBERT BLY

Saint Animal

Suddenly it was clear to me –
I was something I hadn't been before.
It was as if the animal part of my being

had reached some kind of maturity that gave it
authority, and had begun to use it.

I thought about death for two years.
My animal flailed and tore at its cage
till I let it go. I watched it

drift out into the easy eddies of twilight
and then veer off, not knowing me.

I'm not a bird but I'm inhabited by a spirit
that's uplifting me. It's my animal, my saint
and soldier, my flame of yearning,

come back to tell me
what it was like to be without me.

CHASE TWICHELL

Jarrow

Nothing is left to dig, little to make.
Night has engulfed both firelit hall and sparrow.
Wind and car-noise pour across the Slake.
Nothing is left to dig, little to make
A stream of rust where a great ship might grow.
And where a union-man was hung for show
Nothing is left to dig, little to make.
Night has engulfed both firelit hall and sparrow.

CAROL RUMENS

Where We Are
(after Bede)

A man tears a chunk of bread off the brown loaf,
then wipes the gravy from his plate. Around him
at the long table, friends fill their mouths
with duck and roast pork, fill their cups from
pitchers of wine. Hearing a high twittering, the man

looks to see a bird – black with a white patch
beneath its beak – flying the length of the hall,
having flown in by a window over the door. As straight
as a taut string, the bird flies beneath the roofbeams,
as firelight flings its shadow against the ceiling.

The man pauses – one hand holds the bread, the other
rests upon the table – and watches the bird, perhaps
a swift, fly toward the window at the far end of the room.
He begins to point it out to his friends, but one is
telling hunting stories, as another describes the best way

to butcher a pig. The man shoves the bread in his mouth,
then slaps his hand down hard on the thigh of the woman
seated beside him, squeezes his fingers to feel the firm
muscles and tendons beneath the fabric of her dress.
A huge dog snores on the stone hearth by the fire.

From the window comes the clicking of pine needles
blown against it by an October wind. A half moon
hurries along behind scattered clouds, while the forest
of black spruce and bare maple and birch surrounds
the long hall the way a single rock can be surrounded

by a river. This is where we are in history – to think
the table will remain full; to think the forest will
remain where we have pushed it; to think our bubble of
good fortune will save us from the night – a bird flies in
from the dark, flits across a lighted hall and disappears.

STEPHEN DOBYNS

2

Roads

World is crazier and more of it than we think,
Incorrigibly plural. I peel and portion
A tangerine and spit the pips and feel
The drunkenness of things being various.

LOUIS MacNEICE
'Snow'

MANY OF THESE POEMS dramatise important life decisions: the journeys we
take, the roads we choose or have chosen for us. Robert Frost's 'The Road
Not Taken' (55) became America's favourite modern poem because it encap-
sulates everyone's anxieties about roads we might take in life. Stevie Smith's
'Not Waving but Drowning' (57) contrasts passive and proactive approaches,
while Simon Armitage's account of his character's moral choices in 'Poem'
(57) is not unlike the Frank Sinatra song 'My Way', ending with 'sometimes
he did this, sometimes he did that'. This modern condition is all about open-
ness to experience: 'Plurality is all', wrote Weldon Kees, the American poet
who disappeared in 1955 and was never seen again. The world is 'incorrigibly
plural', says Louis MacNeice in 'Snow' (74), and many other modern poems
celebrate what he calls 'the drunkenness of things being various'.

   Those journeys and roads can be both literal and metaphorical. Poems
about driving, especially at night, are as typical of modern poetry as the road
movie is of contemporary cinema. The crucial revelation in these quests for
wisdom often involves an encounter of some kind. William Stafford does no
actual driving in 'Traveling through the Dark' (84). He has already halted for
the deer; this is clearly a stop for decision-making on life's journey. The poet
was an American conscientious objector during the War, and the poem raises
questions about individual responsibility. John Burnside's car actually hits his
deer in 'Penitence' (84), but he cannot confront the consequences of his action,
feeling the body of the animal in his own flesh, like Galway Kinnell's hunter
in his shamanistic poem 'The Bear' (63). As Kinnell has said: 'If you could
keep going deeper and deeper, you'd finally not be a person…you'd be a blade
of grass or ultimately perhaps a stone. And if a stone could speak, poetry would
be its words.' Through the medium of the poem, Kinnell throws off the 'sticky
infusion' of speech, becoming one with the natural world, sharing the primal
experiences of birth and death with his hunter.

Elizabeth Bishop started writing 'The Moose' (87) after a journey from Brazil to her childhood home in Nova Scotia in August 1946, and it took her over 25 years to get the poem right; she describes the problems of handling its trimeter line in letters written over many years. The poem is a subtle master-piece as well as one of Bishop's most revised poems: note the unobtrusive brilliance of its intricate rhymes, the apparent ease of its present tense narra-tion (giving the poem immediacy but also a sense of timelessness), and that opening sentence meandering with the bus through the first six stanzas. There was also the problem of how to write the poem, her worries about 'mixing fact and fiction', for the original description she gave at the time in a letter to her friend, the poet Marianne Moore, included the meeting with the 'grand, other-worldly' cow moose, but the fog and the animal's behaviour – sniffing 'at the bus's hot hood' – were witnessed by her driver and with a different group of passengers on an earlier trip in which the encounter was with an even bigger and presumably more frightening bull moose.

A few months before Bishop finished 'The Moose', another American poet, John Berryman, jumped to his death from a Mississippi bridge. All Berryman's work is haunted by his own father's supposed suicide, and his *Dream Songs*, a sequence of 385 poems, present a running minstrel show in several voices, including the Henry mentioned in Tracey Herd's title (67), his often blacked-up alter ago, also called Pussy-cat or Mr Bones. Ten of *The Dream Songs* (67) lament the death of his friend and fellow alcoholic poet Delmore Schwartz, who imagines his other self in 'The Heavy Bear Who Goes with Me' (66) as a clownish, inescapable animal 'in love with candy, anger, and sleep'.

Robert Frost's 'Directive' (71) is a quest poem which parodies the medieval legend of the Grail. The melancholic Randall Jarrell called it 'hard to under-stand, but easy to love'. He found the poem consoling as well as heart-breaking, moved by its evocation of 'so much longing, tenderness, and passive sadness' as well by Frost's perception that 'each life is pathetic because it wears away into the death that it at last half-welcomes – that even its salvation, far back at the cold root of things, is make-believe, a plaything hidden among the ruins of the lost cultures...Its humour and acceptance and humanity, its familiarity and elevation, give it a composed matter-of-fact magnificence.'

It is illuminating to compare Jarrell's response with Seamus Heaney's, keep-ing in mind his notion of the 'redress of poetry' (22), for Heaney views the poem as 'in some oblique or important way an apologia for all art'. For him, as for the Grail knights, the site of the poem is a 'locus of knowledge, a scene of instruction and revelation', and 'the games of make-believe which the chil-dren played in the playhouse were a kind of freely invented answer to every-thing experienced in the "house in earnest" where (the tone makes this clear) life was lived in sorrow and anger. Frost suggests, in fact, that the life endured by the occupants of the actual house finds its best memorial and expression in the "house of make-believe"...the imaginative transformation of human life is the means by which we can most truly grasp and comprehend it...The poem provides a draught of the clear water of transformed understanding and fills the reader with a momentary sense of freedom and wholeness.'

Mark Strand and Eavan Boland have noted how Frost's blank verse in this much discussed poem is 'deceptively driven by a vernacular narrative tone' and intensely stylised, as in the first line's 'rare iambic rush of monosyllables'.

The Road Not Taken

Two roads diverged in a yellow wood,
And sorry I could not travel both
And be one traveler, long I stood
And looked down one as far as I could
To where it bent in the undergrowth;

Then took the other, as just as fair,
And having perhaps the better claim,
Because it was grassy and wanted wear;
Though as for that, the passing there
Had worn them really about the same,

And both that morning equally lay
In leaves no step had trodden black.
Oh, I kept the first for another day!
Yet knowing how way leads on to way,
I doubted if I should ever come back.

I shall be telling this with a sigh
Somewhere ages and ages hence:
Two roads diverged in a wood, and I –
I took the one less traveled by,
And that has made all the difference.

ROBERT FROST

The Bay

On the road to the bay was a lake of rushes
Where we bathed at times and changed in the bamboos.
Now it is rather to stand and say:
How many roads we take that lead to Nowhere,
The alley overgrown, no meaning now but loss:
Not that veritable garden where everything comes easy.

And by the bay itself were cliffs with carved names
And a hut on the shore beside the Maori ovens.
We raced boats from the banks of the pumice creek
Or swam in those autumnal shallows
Growing cold in amber water, riding the logs
Upstream, and waiting for the taniwha.

So now I remember the bay and the little spiders
On driftwood, so poisonous and quick.
The carved cliffs and the great outcrying surf
With currents round the rocks and the birds rising.
A thousand times an hour is torn across
And burned for the sake of going on living.
But I remember the bay that never was
And stand like stone and cannot turn away.

JAMES K. BAXTER

Tyranny of Choice

Pick a card, any card
You'll say. I love this trick –
The tease and tyranny of choice –
The dove's tail tender
On your fine and hidden fingers,
And the thumb I'm under.

You know my Queen of Hearts
By the dog-ear on her top-left
Bottom-right corner;
By the voluptuous sad mouth
Which will not smile,
Whichever way you turn her.

ELIZABETH GARRETT

Not Waving but Drowning

Nobody heard him, the dead man,
But still he lay moaning:
I was much further out than you thought
And not waving but drowning.

Poor chap, he always loved larking
And now he's dead
It must have been too cold for him his heart gave way,
They said.

Oh, no no no, it was too cold always
(Still the dead one lay moaning)
I was much too far out all my life
And not waving but drowning.

STEVIE SMITH

Poem

And if it snowed and snow covered the drive
he took a spade and tossed it to one side.
And always tucked his daughter up at night.
And slippered her the one time that she lied.

And every week he tipped up half his wage.
And what he didn't spend each week he saved.
And praised his wife for every meal she made.
And once, for laughing, punched her in the face.

And for his mum he hired a private nurse.
And every Sunday taxied her to church.
And he blubbed when she went from bad to worse.
And twice he lifted ten quid from her purse.

Here's how they rated him when they looked back:
sometimes he did this, sometimes he did that.

SIMON ARMITAGE

Choose

The single clenched fist lifted and ready,
Or the open asking hand held out and waiting.
Choose:
For we meet by one or the other.

CARL SANDBURG

Meeting in a Lift

We stepped into the lift. The two of us, alone.
We looked at each other and that was all.
Two lives, a moment, fullness, bliss.
At the fifth floor she got out and I went on up
knowing I would never see her again,
that it was a meeting once and for all,
that if I followed her I would be like a dead man in her tracks
and that if she came back to me
it would only be from the other world.

VLADIMÍR HOLAN
translated from the Czech by Ian & Jarmila Milner

'i thank You God for most this amazing'

i thank You God for most this amazing
day:for the leaping greenly spirits of trees
and a blue true dream of sky;and for everything
which is natural which is infinite which is yes

(i who have died am alive again today,
and this is the sun's birthday;this is the birth
day of life and of love and wings:and of the gay
great happening illimitably earth)

how should tasting touching hearing seeing
breathing any—lifted from the no
of all nothing—human merely being
doubt unimaginable You?

(now the ears of my ears awake and
now the eyes of my eyes are opened)

E.E. CUMMINGS

You

Be yourself: show your flyblown eyes
to the world, give no cause for concern,
wash the paunchy body whose means you
live within, suffer the illnesses
that are your prerogative alone –

the prognosis refers to nobody but you;
you it is who gets up every morning
in your skin, you who chews your dinner
with your mercury-filled teeth, gaining
garlic breath or weight, you dreading,

you hoping, you regretting, you interloping.
The earth has squeezed you in, found you space;
any loss of face you feel is solely yours –
you with the same old daily moods, debts,
intuitions, food fads, pet hates, Achilles' heels.

You carry on as best you can the task of being,
whole-time, you; you in wake and you in dream,
at all hours, weekly, monthly, yearly, life,
full of yourself as a tallow candle is of fat,
wallowing in self-denial, self-esteem.

DENNIS O'DRISCOLL

Begin

Begin again to the summoning birds
to the sight of light at the window,
begin to the roar of morning traffic
all along Pembroke Road.
Every beginning is a promise
born in light and dying in dark
determination and exaltation of springtime
flowering the way to work.
Begin to the pageant of queuing girls
the arrogant loneliness of swans in the canal
bridges linking the past and future
old friends passing though with us still.
Begin to the loneliness that cannot end
since it perhaps is what makes us begin,
begin to wonder at unknown faces
at crying birds in the sudden rain
at branches stark in the willing sunlight
at seagulls foraging for bread
at couples sharing a sunny secret
alone together while making good.
Though we live in a world that dreams of ending
that always seems about to give in
something that will not acknowledge conclusion
insists that we forever begin.

BRENDAN KENNELLY

Entirely

If we could get the hang of it entirely
    It would take too long;
All we know is the splash of words in passing
    and falling twigs of song,
And when we try to eavesdrop on the great
    Presences it is rarely
That by a stroke of luck we can appropriate
    Even a phrase entirely.

If we could find our happiness entirely
    In somebody else's arms
We should not fear the spears of the spring nor the city's
    Yammering fire alarms
But, as it is, the spears each year go through
    Our flesh and almost hourly
Bell or siren banishes the blue
    Eyes of Love entirely.

And if the world were black or white entirely
    And all the charts were plain
Instead of a mad weir of tigerish waters,
    A prism of delight and pain,
We might be surer where we wished to go
    Or again we might be merely
Bored but in brute reality there is no
    Road that is right entirely.

LOUIS MacNEICE

Integrity

> *the quality or state of being complete;*
> *unbroken condition; entirety*
> WEBSTER

A wild patience has taken me this far

as if I had to bring to shore
a boat with a spasmodic outboard motor
old sweaters, nets, spray-mottled books
tossed in the prow
some kind of sun burning my shoulder-blades.
Splashing the oarlocks. Burning through.
Your forearms can get scalded, licked with pain
in a sun blotted like unspoken anger
behind a casual mist.

The length of daylight
this far north, in this
forty-ninth year of my life
is critical.

The light is critical: of me, of this
long-dreamed, involuntary landing
on the arm of an inland sea.
The glitter of the shoal
depleting into shadow
I recognise: the stand of pines
violet-black really, green in the old postcard
but really I have nothing but myself
to go by; nothing
stands in the realm of pure necessity
except what my hands can hold.

Nothing but myself?...My selves.
After so long, this answer.
As if I had always known
I steer the boat in, simply.
The motor dying on the pebbles
cicadas taking up the hum
dropped in the silence.

Anger and tenderness: my selves.
And now I can believe they breathe in me
as angels, not polarities.
Anger and tenderness: the spider's genius
to spin and weave in the same action
from her own body, anywhere –
even from a broken web.

The cabin in the stand of pines
is still for sale. I know this. Know the print
of the last foot, the hand that slammed and locked that door,
then stopped to wreathe the rain-smashed clematis
back on the trellis
for no one's sake except its own.
I know the chart nailed to the wallboards
the icy kettle squatting on the burner.
The hands that hammered in those nails
emptied that kettle one last time
are these two hands
and they have caught the baby leaping
from between trembling legs
and they have worked the vacuum aspirator
and stroked the sweated temples

and steered the boat here through this hot
misblotted sunlight, critical light
imperceptibly scalding
the skin these hands will also salve.

ADRIENNE RICH

The Bear

1

In late winter
I sometimes glimpse bits of steam
coming up from
some fault in the old snow
and bend close and see it is lung-colored
and put down my nose
and know
the chilly, enduring odor of bear.

2

I take a wolf's rib and whittle
it sharp at both ends
and coil it up
and freeze it in blubber and place it out
on the fairway of the bears.

And when it has vanished
I move out on the bear tracks,
roaming in circles
until I come to the first, tentative, dark
splash on the earth.

And I set out
running, following the splashes
of blood wandering over the world.
At the cut, gashed resting places
I stop and rest,
at the crawl-marks
where he lay out on his belly

to overpass some stretch of bauchy ice
I lie out
dragging myself forward with bear-knives in my fists.

3

On the third day I begin to starve,
at nightfall I bend down as I knew I would
at a turd sopped in blood,
and hesitate, and pick it up,
and thrust it in my mouth, and gnash it down,
and rise
and go on running.

4

On the seventh day,
living by now on bear blood alone,
I can see his upturned carcass far out ahead, a scraggled,
steamy hulk,
the heavy fur riffling in the wind.

I come up to him
and stare at the narrow-spaced, petty eyes,
the dismayed
face laid back on the shoulder, the nostrils
flared, catching
perhaps the first taint of me as he
died.

I hack
a ravine in his thigh, and eat and drink,
and tear him down his whole length
and open him and climb in
and close him up after me, against the wind,
and sleep.

5

And dream
of lumbering flatfooted
over the tundra,
stabbed twice from within,
splattering a trail behind me,
splattering it out no matter which way I lurch,

no matter which parabola of bear-transcendence,
which dance of solitude I attempt,
which gravity-clutched leap,
which trudge, which groan.

6

Until one day I totter and fall –
fall on this
stomach that has tried so hard to keep up,
to digest the blood as it leaked in,
to break up
and digest the bone itself: and now the breeze
blows over me, blows off
the hideous belches of ill-digested bear blood
and rotted stomach
and the ordinary, wretched odor of bear,

blows across
my sore, lolled tongue a song
or screech, until I think I must rise up
and dance. And I lie still.

7

I awaken I think. Marshlights
reappear, geese
come trailing again up the flyway.
In her ravine under old snow the dam-bear
lies, licking
lumps of smeared fur
and drizzly eyes into shapes
with her tongue. And one
hairy-soled trudge stuck out before me,
the next groaned out,
the next,
the next,
the rest of my days I spend
wandering: wondering
what, anyway,
was that sticky infusion, that rank flavor of blood, that poetry,
        by which I lived?

GALWAY KINNELL

65

The Heavy Bear Who Goes With Me

'the withness of the body'

The heavy bear who goes with me,
A manifold honey to smear his face,
Clumsy and lumbering here and there,
The central ton of every place,
The hungry beating brutish one
In love with candy, anger, and sleep,
Crazy factotum, dishevelling all,
Climbs the building, kicks the football,
Boxes his brother in the hate-ridden city.

Breathing at my side, that heavy animal,
That heavy bear who sleeps with me,
Howls in his sleep for a world of sugar,
A sweetness intimate as the water's clasp,
Howls in his sleep because the tight-rope
Trembles and shows the darkness beneath,
– The strutting show-off is terrified,
Dressed in his dress-suit, bulging his pants,
Trembles to think that his quivering meat
Must finally wince to nothing at all.

That inescapable animal walks with me,
Has followed me since the black womb held,
Moves where I move, distorting my gesture,
A caricature, a swollen shadow,
A stupid clown of the spirit's motive,
Perplexes and affronts with his own darkness,
The secret life of belly and bone,
Opaque, too near, my private, yet unknown,
Stretches to embrace the very dear
With whom I would walk without him near,
Touches her grossly, although a word
Would bare my heart and make me clear,
Stumbles, flounders, and strives to be fed
Dragging me with him in his mouthing care,
Amid the hundred million of his kind,
The scrimmage of appetite everywhere.

DELMORE SCHWARTZ

from Dream Songs (157)

Ten Songs, one solid block of agony,
I wrote for him, and then I wrote no more.
His sad ghost must aspire
free of my love to its own post, that ghost,
among its fellows, Mozart's, Bach's, Delmore's
free of its careful body

high in the shades which line that avenue
where I will gladly walk, beloved of one,
and listen to the Buddha.
His work downhill, I don't conceal from you,
ran and ran out. The brain shook as if stunned,
I hope he's over that,

flame may his glory in that other place,
for he was fond of fame, devoted to it,
and every first-rate soul
has sacrifices which it puts in play,
I hope he's sitting with his peers: sit, sit,
& recover and be whole.

JOHN BERRYMAN

from Some mangled Dream Songs for Henry who is twenty-eight years dead and past caring

Shadowed by your father
in his terrible pose, the shotgun crammed
into his mouth, and inside the house
the bewildered little boy who heard
the echo of that shotgun blast
through every dawn that ever rose

far off in the reddening east
as each bright morning rose.
Your lover's face turns briefly

on the crumpled pillow, her cheeks warm,
her sweet, delicious lips, pouting
and closed just like a morning rose.

Yes, you'll ruin her too, tear her root and limb
from the soil that nourished her
and try to cram her in the glass
that sits clearly on your windowsill,
cursing when her sharp claws scratch you
and crying like a little boy

when night comes and she's gone home.

TRACEY HERD

Window

End of season, end of play – no one left
But a boy playing with the lonely sea
On the rain-wet shore below that runs
Helplessly on and on into advancing dusk.
Pushed under the cliff, houses look to themselves,
Look blindly away from the darkening game
In which the boy runs purposefully
Seawards and shorewards at the tide's edge
Like someone bearing a message no one
Wishes to receive – something written long ago
In his head, now overgrown with hair.
He never will stop running, for his limbs
Are oiled, his skill increases mysteriously
And the sea has become hopelessly attached.
When he runs shorewards feigning fear,
Like a father being chased by his own child,
The sea rushes after him, monstrously grey;
But when he turns, it whitens and retreats.

And while this goes on, here in the house –
As if by special arrangement –
Someone very quietly plays Reynaldo Hahn.
The boy does not know this; he is only human.

Soon the game must end unaccompanied.
But no, he is turning and running again
To hidden music, as if for the first time.

FREDA DOWNIE

The door

Go and open the door.
   Maybe outside there's
   a tree, or a wood,
   a garden,
   or a magic city.

Go and open the door.
   Maybe a dog's rummaging.
   Maybe you'll see a face,
or an eye,
or the picture
         of a picture.

Go and open the door.
   If there's a fog
   it will clear.

Go and open the door.
   Even if there's only
   the darkness ticking,
   even if there's only
   the hollow wind,
   even if
       nothing
          is there,
go and open the door.

At least
there'll be
a draught.

MIROSLAV HOLUB
translated from the Czech by Ian Milner

The Door

One day you'll see:
you've been knocking on a door
without a house.
You've been waiting, shivering, yelling
words of daring and hope.

One day you'll see:
there is no one on the other side
except as ever, the jubilant ocean
that won't shatter ceramically like a dream
when you and I shatter.

But not yet. Now
you wait outside, watching
the blue arches of mornings
that will break
but are now perfect.

Underneath on tiptoe
pass the faces, speaking to you,
saying 'you', 'you', 'you',
smiling, waving, arriving
in unfailing chronology.

One day you'll doubt your movements,
you will shudder
at the accuracy of your sudden age.
You will ache for slow beauty
to save you from your quick, quick life.

But not yet. Hope
fills the yawn of time.
Blue surrounds you. Now let's say
you see a door and knock,
and wait for someone to hear.

KAPKA KASSABOVA

Directive

Back out of all this now too much for us,
Back in a time made simple by the loss
Of detail, burned, dissolved, and broken off
Like graveyard marble sculpture in the weather,
There is a house that is no more a house
Upon a farm that is no more a farm
And in a town that is no more a town.
The road there, if you'll let a guide direct you
Who only has at heart your getting lost,
May seem as if it should have been a quarry –
Great monolithic knees the former town
Long since gave up pretense of keeping covered.
And there's a story in a book about it:
Besides the wear of iron wagon wheels
The ledges show lines ruled southeast-northwest,
The chisel work of an enormous Glacier
That braced his feet against the Arctic Pole.
You must not mind a certain coolness from him
Still said to haunt this side of Panther Mountain.
Nor need you mind the serial ordeal
Of being watched from forty cellar holes
As if by eye pairs out of forty firkins.
As for the woods' excitement over you
That sends light rustle rushes to their leaves,
Charge that to upstart inexperience.
Where were they all not twenty years ago?
They think too much of having shaded out
A few old pecker-fretted apple trees.
Make yourself up a cheering song of how
Someone's road home from work this once was,
Who may be just ahead of you on foot
Or creaking with a buggy load of grain.
The height of the adventure is the height
Of country where two village cultures faded
Into each other. Both of them are lost.
And if you're lost enough to find yourself
By now, pull in your ladder road behind you
And put a sign up CLOSED to all but me.
Then make yourself at home. The only field
Now left's no bigger than a harness gall.

71

First there's the children's house of make-believe,
Some shattered dishes underneath a pine,
The playthings in the playhouse of the children.
Weep for what little things could make them glad.
Then for the house that is no more a house,
But only a belilaced cellar hole,
Now slowly closing like a dent in dough.
This was no playhouse but a house in earnest.
Your destination and your destiny's
A brook that was the water of the house,
Cold as a spring as yet so near its source,
Too lofty and original to rage.
(We know the valley streams that when aroused
Will leave their tatters hung on barb and thorn.)
I have kept hidden in the instep arch
Of an old cedar at the waterside
A broken drinking goblet like the Grail
Under a spell so the wrong ones can't find it,
So can't get saved, as Saint Mark says they mustn't.
(I stole the goblet from the children's playhouse.)
Here are your waters and your watering place.
Drink and be whole again beyond confusion.

ROBERT FROST

The Road Home

It is the road to God
that matters now, the ragged road, the wood.

And if you will, drop pebbles here and there
like Hansel, Gretel, right where

they'll shine
in the wilful light of the moon.

You won't be going back to the hut
where father, mother plot

the *cul de sac* of the world
in a field

that's permanently full
of people

looking for a festival
of literature, a fairy tale,

a feathered
nest of brothers, sisters. Would

that first world, bared now to the word
God, wade

with you, through wood, into the weald and weather
of the stars?

GILLIAN ALLNUTT

Stopping by Woods on a Snowy Evening

Whose woods these are I think I know.
His house is in the village, though;
He will not see me stopping here
To watch his woods fill up with snow.

My little horse must think it queer
To stop without a farmhouse near
Between the woods and frozen lake
The darkest evening of the year.

He gives his harness bells a shake
To ask if there is some mistake.
The only other sound's the sweep
Of easy wind and downy flake.

The woods are lovely, dark and deep,
But I have promises to keep,
And miles to go before I sleep,
And miles to go before I sleep.

ROBERT FROST

Snow

The room was suddenly rich and the great bay-window was
Spawning snow and pink roses against it
Soundlessly collateral and incompatible:
World is suddener than we fancy it.

World is crazier and more of it than we think,
Incorrigibly plural. I peel and portion
A tangerine and spit the pips and feel
The drunkenness of things being various.

And the fire flames with a bubbling sound for world
Is more spiteful and gay than one supposes –
On the tongue on the eyes on the ears in the palms of one's hands –
There is more than glass between the snow and the huge roses.

LOUIS MacNEICE

History

Where and when exactly did we first have sex?
Do you remember? Was it Fitzroy Avenue,
Or Cromwell Road, or Notting Hill?
Your place or mine? Marseilles or Aix?
Or as long ago as that Thursday evening
When you and I climbed through the bay window
On the ground floor of Aquinas Hall
And into the room where MacNeice wrote 'Snow',
Or the room where they say he wrote 'Snow'.

PAUL MULDOON

History

It's only a week but already you are slipping
down the cold black chute of history. Postcards.
Phonecalls. It's like never having seen the Wall,
except in pieces on the dusty shelves of friends.

Once I queued for hours to see the moon in a box
inside a museum, so wild it should have been kept
in a zoo at least but there it was, unremarkable,
a pile of dirt some god had shaken down.

I wait for your letters now: a fleet of strange cargo
with news of changing borders, a heart's small
journeys. They're like the relics of a saint.
Opening the dry white papers is kissing a bone.

MAURA DOOLEY

Snow

It began to snow at midnight. And certainly
the kitchen is the best place to sit,
even the kitchen of the sleepless.
It's warm there, you cook yourself something, drink wine
and look out of the window at your friend eternity.
Why care whether birth and death are merely points
when life is not a straight line.
Why torment yourself eyeing the calendar
and wondering what is at stake.
Why confess you don't have the money
to buy Saskia shoes?
And why brag
that you suffer more than others.

If there were no silence here
the snow would have dreamed it up.
You are alone.
Spare the gestures. Nothing for show.

VLADIMÍR HOLAN
translated from the Czech by Ian & Jarmila Milner

The Cablecar

The silver box rose lightly up from the valley,
ape-easy, hanging on by its one arm;
in minutes, it had shrunk the town to a diagram,
the leaping river to a sluggish leat of kaolin,
the fletched forests to points it overrode.
It had you in its web of counterweights,
of circles evolved to parallel straight lines.

Riding the long slurs, it whisked you over
the moraine's hopeless rubble. It had your heart
in your mouth at every pylon, where it sagged,
leaned back, swooped on. It had you hear how ice
cracked on the cable. It had you watch it throw
an already crumpled shadow of bent steel
onto the seracs. It made you think of falling.

By the time it lowered you back to the spread valley,
to the broad-roofed houses decorated with lights,
you could think only of what it was like to step
out, at the top, onto the giddy edge
of snowfields still unprinted, that pure blaze;
to be robbed of your breath by the thin air, by a glimpse
of the moon's daytime ghost on solid blue.

LAWRENCE SAIL

That Silent Evening

I will go back to that silent evening
when we lay together and talked in low, silent voices,
while outside slow lumps of soft snow
fell, hushing as they got near the ground,
with a fire in the room, in which centuries
of tree went up in continuous ghost-giving-up,
without a crackle, into morning light.
Not until what hastens went slower did we sleep.
When we got home we turned and looked back
at our tracks twining out of the woods,
where the branches we brushed against let fall
puffs of sparkling snow, quickly, in silence,
like stolen kisses, and where the *scritch scritch scritch*
among the trees, which is the sound that dies
inside the sparks from the wedge when the sledge
hits it off center telling everything inside
it is fire, jumped to a black branch, puffed up
but without arms and so to our eyes lonesome,
and yet also – how could we know this? – *happy!*
in shape of chickadee. Lying still in snow,
not iron-willed, like railroad tracks, willing
not to meet until heaven, but here and there
making slubby kissing stops in the field,
our tracks wobble across the snow their long scratch.
Everything that happens here is really little more,
if even that, than a scratch, too. Words, in our mouths,
are almost ready, already, to bandage the one
whom the *scritch scritch scritch*, meaning *if how when*
we might lose each other, scratches scratches scratches
from this moment to that. Then I will go back
to that silent evening, when the past just managed
to overlap the future, if only by a trace,
and the light doubles and shines
through the dark the sparkling that heavens the earth.

GALWAY KINNELL

The Journey

One day you finally knew
what you had to do, and began,
though the voices around you
kept shouting
their bad advice –
though the whole house
began to tremble
and you felt the old tug
at your ankles.
'Mend my life!'
each voice cried.
But you didn't stop.
You knew what you had to do,
though the wind pried
with its stiff fingers
at the very foundations,
though their melancholy
was terrible.
It was already late
enough, and a wild night,
and the road full of fallen
branches and stones.
But little by little,
as you left their voices behind,
the stars began to burn
through the sheets of clouds,
and there was a new voice
which you slowly
recognised as your own,
that kept you company
as you strode deeper and deeper
into the world,
determined to do
the only thing you could do –
determined to save
the only life you could save.

MARY OLIVER

When You've Got

When you've got the plan of your life
matched to the time it will take
but you just want to press SHIFT / BREAK
and print over and over
this is not what I was after
this is not what I was after,

when you've finally stripped out the house
with its iron-cold fireplace,
its mouldings, its mortgage,
its single-skin walls
but you want to write in the plaster
'This is not what I was after,'

when you've got the rainbow-clad baby
in his state-of-the-art pushchair
but he arches his back at you
and pulps his Activity Centre
and you just want to whisper
'This is not what I was after,'

when the vacuum seethes and whines in the lounge
and the waste-disposal unit blows,
when tenners settle in your account
like snow hitting a stove,
when you get a chat from your spouse
about marriage and personal growth,

when a wino comes to sleep in your porch
on your Citizen's Charter
and you know a hostel's opening soon
but your headache's closer
and you really just want to torch
the bundle of rags and newspaper

and you'll say to the newspaper
'This is not what we were after,
this is not what we were after.'

HELEN DUNMORE

Yes

It's like a tap-dance
Or a new pink dress,
A shit-naive feeling
Saying Yes.

Some say Good morning
Some say God bless –
Some say Possibly
Some say Yes.

Some say Never
Some say Unless
It's stupid and lovely
To rush into Yes.

What can it mean?
It's just like life,
One thing to you
One to your wife.

Some go local
Some go express
Some can't wait
To answer Yes.

Some complain
Of strain and stress
The answer may be
No for Yes.

Some like failure
Some like success
Some like Yes Yes
Yes Yes Yes.

Open your eyes,
Dream but don't guess.
Your biggest surprise
Comes after Yes.

MURIEL RUKEYSER

Happiness

A state you must dare not enter
    with hopes of staying,
quicksand in the marshes, and all

the roads leading to a castle
    that doesn't exist.
But there it is, as promised,

with its perfect bridge above
    the crocodiles,
and its doors forever open.

STEPHEN DUNN

Machines

Dearest, note how these two are alike:
This harpsichord pavane by Purcell
And the racer's twelve-speed bike.

The machinery of grace is always simple.
This chrome trapezoid, one wheel connected
To another of concentric gears,
Which Ptolemy dreamt of and Schwinn perfected,
Is gone. The cyclist, not the cycle, steers.
And in the playing, Purcell's chords are played away.

So this talk, or touch if I were there,
Should work its effortless gadgetry of love,
Like Dante's heaven, and melt into the air.

If it doesn't, of course, I've fallen. So much is chance,
So much agility, desire, and feverish care,
As bicyclists and harpsichordists prove

Who only by moving can balance,
Only by balancing move.

MICHAEL DONAGHY

Alone

I

One evening in February I came near to dying here.
The car skidded sideways on the ice, out
on the wrong side of the road. The approaching cars –
their lights – closed in.

My name, my girls, my job
broke free and were left silently behind
further and further away. I was anonymous
like a boy in a playground surrounded by enemies.

The approaching traffic had huge lights.
They shone on me while I pulled at the wheel
in a transparent terror that floated like egg white.
The seconds grew – there was space in them –
they grew as big as hospital buildings.

You could almost pause
and breathe out for a while
before being crushed.

Then something caught: a helping grain of sand
or a wonderful gust of wind. The car broke free
and scuttled smartly right over the road.
A post shot up and cracked – a sharp clang – it
flew away in the darkness.

Then – stillness. I sat back in my seat-belt
and saw someone coming through the whirling snow
to see what had become of me.

II

I have been walking for a long time
on the frozen Östergötland fields.
I have not seen a single person.

In other parts of the world
there are people who are born, live and die
in a perpetual crowd.

82

To be always visible – to live
in a swarm of eyes –
a special expression must develop.
Face coated with clay.

The murmuring rises and falls
while they divide up among themselves
the sky, the shadows, the sand grains.

I must be alone
ten minutes in the morning
and ten minutes in the evening.
– Without a programme.

Everyone is queuing at everyone's door.

Many.

One.

TOMAS TRANSTRÖMER
translated from the Swedish by Robin Fulton

Couplings

Life is a house in ruins. And we mean to fix it up
and make it snug. With our hands we knock it into shape

to the very top. Till beneath this we fasten a roofbeam
that will watch the coming and going of our skyless life,

two crooked segments. They are fitted together,
timbers in concord. Smooth beams, and wide.

Two in touch. That's the craft we nurture in folding
doubled flesh on a frame. Conjoining the smooth couplings

that sometimes arch into one. Aslant above a cold world,
hollow wood wafting passion. Then stock still for a time.

And how clear-cut the roof, creaking love at times,
as it chides the worm to keep off and await its turn.

MENNA ELFYN
translated from the Welsh by Joseph Clancy

Traveling through the Dark

Traveling through the dark I found a deer
dead on the edge of the Wilson River road.
It is usually best to roll them into the canyon:
that road is narrow; to swerve might make more dead.

By glow of the tail-light I stumbled back of the car
and stood by the heap, a doe, a recent killing;
she had stiffened already, almost cold.
I dragged her off; she was large in the belly.

My fingers touching her side brought me the reason –
her side was warm; her fawn lay there waiting,
alive, still, never to be born.
Beside that mountain road I hesitated.

The car aimed its lowered parking lights;
under the hood purred the steady engine.
I stood in the glare of the warm exhaust turning red;
around our group I could hear the wilderness listen.

I thought hard for us all – my only swerving –
then pushed her over the edge into the river.

WILLIAM STAFFORD

Penitence

I was driving into the wind
on a northern road,
the redwoods swaying around me like a black
ocean.
        I'd drifted off: I didn't see the deer
till it bounced away,
the back legs swinging outwards as I braked
and swerved into the tinder
of the verge.

Soon as I stopped
the headlamps filled with moths
and something beyond the trees was tuning in,
a hard attention
boring through my flesh
to stroke the bone.
That shudder took so long
to end, I thought the animal had slipped
beneath the wheels, and lay there
quivering.
I left the engine running; stepped outside;
away, at the edge of the light, a body
shifted amongst the leaves
and I wanted to go, to help, to make it well,
but every step I took
pushed it away.
Or – no; that's not the truth,
or all the truth:
now I admit my own fear held me back,
not fear of the dark, or that presence
bending the trees;
not even fear, exactly, but the dread
of touching, of colliding with that pain.
I stood there, in the river of the wind,
for minutes; then I walked back to the car
and drove away.
I want to think that deer
survived; or, if it died,
it slipped into the blackness unawares.
But now and then I drive out to the woods
and park the car: the headlamps fill with moths;
the woods tune in; I listen to the night
and hear an echo, fading through the trees,
my own flesh in the body of the deer
still resonant, remembered through the fender.

JOHN BURNSIDE

Slow Animals Crossing

Lemurs somehow, at that lilt of the road
up and sideways at the trees, stooping through
the farmyard on the way to Derrybeg.
Surely there are slower creatures who could cross:
turtles with their solemn wiping gait
or sloths who swim as though to sink
is no disgrace, such aqualungs of air would be
trapped among their matted spider hair.
I think of water since that night was full of it
and white frogs leapt into my lights
like chewing gum attempting
to free itself from tarmac. And I think of lemurs
whenever I see that sign with its red letters
because of the night, and the story
of the three men walking home, and the man
on the left said 'goodnight' to someone, and
the man on the right, 'goodnight' to someone else
and the man in the middle asked who
were they talking to? And one had seen a man
and one had seen a woman, and both
described the third man's parents, turning off
at the road to the graveyard. And when I thought
of lemurs I'd forgotten they were named
for the Latin word for spirits, and I only saw,
crawling slowly in my mind across the night road
back to my parents' house and my daughter,
the bandit eyes and banded tails and soft grey backs
and the white hands of lemurs, delicately placed
upon the twist and the shrug of the road.

W.N. HERBERT

The Moose

From narrow provinces
of fish and bread and tea,
home of the long tides
where the bay leaves the sea
twice a day and takes
the herrings long rides,

where if the river
enters or retreats
in a wall of brown foam
depends on if it meets
the bay coming in,
the bay not at home;

where, silted red,
sometimes the sun sets
facing a red sea,
and others, veins the flats'
lavender, rich mud
in burning rivulets;

on red, gravelly roads,
down rows of sugar maples,
past clapboard farmhouses
and neat, clapboard churches,
bleached, ridged as clamshells,
past twin silver birches,

through late afternoon
a bus journeys west,
the windshield flashing pink,
pink glancing off of metal,
brushing the dented flank
of blue, beat-up enamel;

down hollows, up rises,
and waits, patient, while
a lone traveller gives
kisses and embraces
to seven relatives
and a collie supervises.

Goodbye to the elms,
to the farm, to the dog.
The bus starts. The light
grows richer; the fog,
shifting, salty, thin,
comes closing in.

Its cold, round crystals
form and slide and settle
in the white hens' feathers,
in gray glazed cabbages,
on the cabbage roses
and lupins like apostles;

the sweet peas cling
to their wet white string
on the whitewashed fences;
bumblebees creep
inside the foxgloves,
and evening commences.

One stop at Bass River.
Then the Economies –
Lower, Middle, Upper;
Five Islands, Five Houses,
where a woman shakes a tablecloth
out after supper.

A pale flickering. Gone.
The Tantramar marshes
and the smell of salt hay.
An iron bridge trembles
and a loose plank rattles
but doesn't give way.

On the left, a red light
swims through the dark:
a ship's port lantern.
Two rubber boots show,
illuminated, solemn.
A dog gives one bark.

A woman climbs in
with two market bags,
brisk, freckled, elderly.
'A grand night. Yes, sir,
all the way to Boston.'
She regards us amicably.

Moonlight as we enter
the New Brunswick woods,
hairy, scratchy, splintery;
moonlight and mist
caught in them like lamb's wool
on bushes in a pasture.

The passengers lie back.
Snores. Some long sighs.
A dreamy divagation
begins in the night,
a gentle, auditory,
slow hallucination....

In the creakings and noises,
an old conversation
– not concerning us,
but recognisable,
somewhere, back in the bus:
Grandparents' voices

uninterruptedly
talking, in Eternity:
names being mentioned,
things cleared up finally;
what he said, what she said,
who got pensioned;

deaths, deaths and sicknesses;
the year he remarried;
the year (something) happened.
She died in childbirth.
That was the son lost
when the schooner foundered.

He took to drink. Yes.
She went to the bad.
When Amos began to pray
even in the store and
finally the family had
to put him away.

'Yes…' that peculiar
affirmative. 'Yes…'
A sharp, indrawn breath,
half groan, half acceptance,
that means 'Life's like that.
We know it (also death).'

Talking the way they talked
in the old featherbed,
peacefully, on and on,
dim lamplight in the hall,
down in the kitchen,
the dog tucked in her shawl.

Now, it's all right now
even to fall asleep
just as on all those nights.
– Suddenly the bus driver
stops with a jolt,
turns off his lights.

A moose has come out of
the impenetrable wood
and stands there, looms, rather,
in the middle of the road.
It approaches; it sniffs
at the bus's hot hood.

Towering, antlerless,
high as a church,
homely as a house
(or, safe as houses).
A man's voice assures us
'Perfectly harmless…'

Some of the passengers
exclaim in whispers,
childishly, softly,
'Sure are big creatures.'
'It's awful plain.'
'Look! It's a she!'

Taking her time,
she looks the bus over,
grand, otherworldly.
Why, why do we feel
(we all feel) this sweet
sensation of joy?

'Curious creatures,'
says our quiet driver,
rolling his r's.
'Look at that, would you.'
Then he shifts gears.
For a moment longer,

by craning backward,
the moose can be seen
on the moonlit macadam;
then there's a dim
smell of moose, an acrid
smell of gasoline.

ELIZABETH BISHOP

Wife Hits Moose

Sometime around dusk moose lifts
his heavy, primordial jaw, dripping, from pondwater
and, without psychic struggle,
decides the day, for him, is done: time
to go somewhere else. Meanwhile, wife
drives one of those roads that cut straight north,
a highway dividing the forests

not yet fat enough for the paper companies.
This time of year full dark falls
about eight o'clock – pineforest and blacktop
blend. Moose reaches road, fails
to look both ways, steps
deliberately, ponderously... Wife
hits moose, hard,

at a slight angle (brakes slammed, car
spinning) and moose rolls over hood, antlers –
as if diamond-tipped – scratch windshield, car
damaged: rib-of-moose imprint
on fender, hoof shatters headlight.
Annoyed moose lands on feet and walks away.
Wife is shaken, unhurt, amazed.

– Does moose believe in a Supreme Intelligence?
Speaker does not know.
– Does wife believe in a Supreme Intelligence?
Speaker assumes as much: spiritual intimacies
being between the spirit and the human.
– Does speaker believe in a Supreme Intelligence?
Yes. Thank You.

THOMAS LUX

92

3

Dead or alive

What's writing really about? It's about trying to take
fuller possession of the reality of your life.

TED HUGHES

A writer is not interested in explaining reality;
he's interested in capturing it.

BRENDAN KENNELLY

DEAD OR ALIVE takes you from low ebb to high hope, from wasted time to reawakening. The poems include some relating to depression whose effect is very different from the songs of Leonard Cohen or Joy Division, for these are songs not of wallowing but of renewal, as emotionally charged as a Greek drama or a powerfully written crime thriller. Aristotle wrote of this kind of *catharsis* as a purification of the emotions, and psychologists have taken this to mean the purging of the effects of pent-up emotion and repressed thoughts by bringing them to the surface of consciousness. Poetry can jolt the reader into recognition because everything superfluous is cut out, the whole experience concentrated into a single well-wrought poem whose effect is intensified each time it is re-read. Committed to memory the poem becomes even more personal, with single lines brought to mind often years later exactly when they have a direct bearing on the person's own situation.

But my heading signposts both poles, *dead* or *alive*, for there are exultant poems here which sing with the rediscovery of life and living. Everyone swings between negative and positive, and I've selected poems which contradict one another, and set them side by side, so that poems about hitting rock bottom are immediately followed by others which lift you out of sadness into assertion. George Seferis said poetry should be 'strong enough to help' (21): this kind of poetry isn't about self-help, but I think *experiencing* the poem is helpful because poetry as strong as this helps keep us connected with our humanity.

Anne Sexton was one of several modern American poets who committed suicide. She wrote harrowing poems about mental breakdown, emotional difficulties, and addiction, but with extraordinary verve and stinging wit. Her fascination with death is evident from book titles like *Live or Die*, *The Death Notebooks* and *The Awful Rowing Toward God*, and from the poem 'Her Kind' (125). Tracey Herd's monologue (126) draws on Sexton's self-conscious writing and persona: she gave flamboyant readings, sometimes appearing on stage with a rock band as 'Anne Sexton and Her Kind'. Brecht's 'Epistle on suicide' (124) is equally provocative, ironically exploiting difficult feelings about self-worth to draw a protest from the reader, disagreement with the poem prompting a revaluing of the act itself.

Hermione Lee calls Stevie Smith's 'Harold's Leap' (124) 'a dignified tribute to a brave failure', adding that she likes these kinds of poems about death or suicide because 'like a biography or a love-letter, they tell the story of a relationship between the writer and the lost subject, who is re-found in the poem; and because of the problem they all confront, of turning a grief into a shape'. One shape particularly well suited to dealing with loss or desolation is the villanelle, which works through formalised repetition (see glossary, 470), as in the examples here by William Empson (101), Weldon Kees (101), Theodore Roethke (106) and Elizabeth Bishop (118), and later in the book, Dylan Thomas's 'Do Not Go Gentle into That Good Night' (379) and Derek Mahon's 'Antarctica' (407). As Mark Strand and Eavan Boland observe in *The Making of a Poem*, the villanelle repudiates forward motion, temporality and dissolution through a series of retrievals: 'It circles around and around, refusing to go forward in any kind of linear development, and so suggesting at the deeper level, powerful recurrences of mood and emotion and memory.'

Robert Frost wrote that 'Poetry provides the one permissible way of saying one thing and meaning another'. A prime example of that would be Elizabeth Bishop's villanelle 'One Art' (118), which claims 'The art of losing isn't hard to master' but the effect of its repeatedly rhymed assertions is to assert the opposite, with the parenthesised interjection ('*Write* it!') brilliantly disrupting the clinching last line. Indirection and understatement can often provide a stronger means of expressing and confronting a conflict between thought and feeling than open lament or direct description.

William Empson's poetry and criticism influenced a whole generation of modern poets, from Eliot to Larkin. His passionately intelligent and questioning poetry is difficult but rewarding, owing much to the example of John Donne and later Metaphysical poets of the 17th century as well as to his early training as a mathematician and his immersion in science and philosophy. His villanelle 'Missing Dates' (101) is a parable of politics and the private life, suffused with foreboding on both levels. Empson said he felt compelled to 'learn a style from despair', striving through his poems to cope with the contradictory 'strangeness of the world, in which we are often tripped up and made helpless'.

Louise Glück won America's Pulitzer Prize for *The Wild Iris*, a remarkable sequence of poems written in the language of flowers in three kinds of interweaving voices, human, natural world and "external". Her book revisits and reinvigorates the myth of Persephone with poems in the "voice" of plants, such as the lily in 'Trillium' (95), the nettle in 'Lamium' (119), and 'The Wild Iris' (414). These are emblematic of the cycles of nature as well as the vicissitudes of human life, as if tuned to the rhythms of the Earth itself, from rebirth in spring to autumn decay. We must believe in the possibility of resurrection at the same time as we accept the inevitability of withdrawal: 'Human beings must be taught to love / silence and darkness.'

Maura Dooley's poem 'What Every Woman Should Carry' is one of a quartet of poems (114-16) which every woman should carry.

'To eat a pie and to have it...'

To eat a pie and to have it – I
sometimes succeed – I exchange
a piece of lived life for poetry, and then on
for roubles and kopecks – I live off that same
life, eat my own tail and shins
and they grow again, always anew
and the eagle of poetry rises again into flight
and tries to rise with me away from this world
towards a higher world, from which, once,
I was expelled. I remember it
and in my dreams I see it over and over again,
but in reality I do not know how to go there,
although I go on reading stories and folklore studies,
believing that one day I shall discover the way.
Then I shall still need wings. Only wings.
Perhaps my own.

JAAN KAPLINSKI
translated from the Estonian by Hildi Hawkins

Trillium

When I woke up I was in a forest. The dark
seemed natural, the sky through the pine trees
thick with many lights.

I knew nothing; I could do nothing but see.
And as I watched, all the lights of heaven
faded to make a single thing, a fire
burning through the cool firs.
Then it wasn't possible any longer
to stare at heaven and not be destroyed.

Are there souls that need
death's presence, as I require protection?
I think if I speak long enough

I will answer that question, I will see
whatever they see, a ladder
reaching through the firs, whatever
calls them to exchange their lives –

Think what I understand already.
I woke up ignorant in a forest;
only a moment ago, I didn't know my voice
if one were given me
would be so full of grief, my sentences
like cries strung together.
I didn't even know I felt grief
until that word came, until I felt
rain streaming from me.

LOUISE GLÜCK

'I saw the daughter of the sun...'

I saw the daughter of the sun; she stood
Under the north rise of the copse, where now
The shade-hoar faded, where began to show
Pale primrose-heads, fresh as her own pale hood
Of straight hair, groups of early mercury
No greener than her own plain sheeny gown –
Long had I wandered in the winter-town
Of smoke-grey fog, of stone-grey field and tree.

Nor girl she seemed, nor goddess; her grave face,
Soft as a child's, yet wise, brighter than spring,
More warm than summer, had strange shadowing,
Than mundane lustre held both more and less;

No mirth was there, no glee, no eagerness,
No love, save love for every living thing.

ELIZABETH DARYUSH

Stonepicker

She is scooped out and bow-like,
As if her string
Has been drawn tight.

But really, she is
Plucking stones from the dirt
For her shoulder-bag.

It is her dead albatross,
Her cross, her choice,
In it lie her weapons.

Each granite sphere
Or sea-worn flint
Has weight against your sin,

You cannot win.
She calls you close,
But not to let you in, only

For a better aim.

FRIEDA HUGHES

The arrow

Wounded, he'd have
been lost in the forest
had he not followed the arrow.

More than half
of it
protruded from his chest
and showed him the way.

The arrow
had struck him in the back
and pierced his body.
Its bloody tip
was a signpost.

What a blessing
to have it point
a path
between the trees!

Now he knew
he'd never again
go wrong

and he
wasn't far
from the mark.

MARIN SORESCU
translated from the Romanian
by John Hartley Williams & Hilde Ottschofski

Be Not Too Hard

Be not too hard for life is short
And nothing is given to man;
Be not too hard when he is sold and bought
For he must manage as best he can;
Be not too hard when he gladly dies
Defending things he does not own;
Be not too hard when he tells lies
And if his heart is sometimes like a stone
Be not too hard – for soon he dies,
Often no wiser than he began;
Be not too hard for life is short
And nothing is given to man.

CHRISTOPHER LOGUE

Modern Sorcery

You could have been just another maggot
Squirming over history's roadkill.
Instead a witch took pity on you, lucky fellow,
Made you say abracadabra, and much else
You didn't understand
While you held on to the hem of her skirt.

You know neither the place nor the hour
Of your transfiguration.
A kitten lapping a drop of milk
Fallen from the Blessed Virgin's breast
In a church at dawn. That's how it felt:
The two of you kneeling there.

Outside, there was a flash of lightning
Like a tongue passing over a bloody knife,
But you were safe.
Hexed once and for all in her open arms,
Giddy and tickled pink with her sorcery.

CHARLES SIMIC

Tonight of Yesterday

The evening slips you into it, has kept a place for you
and those wildwood limbs that have already settled on
the morning. The words you have for it are flyblown now
as the dandelion you'll whistle tomorrow into a lighter air.
But tonight, your sleep will be as round as your mouth,
berried with the story of sunlight finally run to ground.
You are all about tomorrow. The moon has your name
memorised: the curl of your back, your face, an open book.

VONA GROARKE

Sonnet

Well, she told me I had an aura. 'What?' I said.
'An aura,' she said. 'I heered you,' I said, 'but
you ain't significating.' 'What I mean, you got
this fuzzy light like, all around your head,
same as Nell the epelectric when she's nigh read-
y to have a fit, only you ain't having no fit.'
'Why, that's a fact,' I said, 'and I ain't about
to neither. I reckon it's more like that dead
rotten fir stump by the edge of the swamp on misty
nights long about cucumber-blossoming time
when the foxfire's flickering round.' 'I be goddamn
if that's it,' she said. 'Why, you ain't but sixty-
nine, you ain't a-rotting yet. What I say
is you got a goddamn naura.' 'OK,' I said. 'OK.'

HAYDEN CARRUTH

Lying in a Hammock at William Duffy's Farm in Pine Island, Minnesota

Over my head, I see the bronze butterfly,
Asleep on the black trunk,
Blowing like a leaf in green shadow.
Down the ravine behind the empty house,
The cowbells follow one another
Into the distances of the afternoon.
To my right,
In a field of sunlight between two pines,
The droppings of last year's horses
Blaze up into golden stones.
I lean back as the evening darkens and comes on.
A chicken hawk floats over, looking for home.
I have wasted my life.

JAMES WRIGHT

Missing Dates

Slowly the poison the whole blood stream fills.
It is not the effort nor the failure tires.
The waste remains, the waste remains and kills.

It is not your system or clear sight that mills
Down small to the consequence a life requires;
Slowly the poison the whole blood stream fills.

They bled an old dog dry yet the exchange rills
Of young dog blood gave but a month's desires;
The waste remains, the waste remains and kills.

It is the Chinese tombs and the slag hills
Usurp the soil, and not the soil retires.
Slowly the poison the whole blood stream fills.

Not to have fire is to be a skin that shrills.
The complete fire is death. From partial fires
The waste remains, the waste remains and kills.

It is the poems you have lost, the ills
From missing dates, at which the heart expires.
Slowly the poison the whole blood stream fills.
The waste remains, the waste remains and kills.

WILLIAM EMPSON

Villanelle

The crack is moving down the wall.
Defective plaster isn't all the cause.
We must remain until the roof falls in.

It's mildly cheering to recall
That every building has its little flaws.
The crack is moving down the wall.

Here in the kitchen, drinking gin,
We can accept the damndest laws.
We must remain until the roof falls in.

And though there's no one here at all,
One searches every room because
The crack is moving down the wall.

Repairs? But how can one begin?
The lease has warnings buried in each clause.
We must remain until the roof falls in.

These nights one hears a creaking in the hall,
The sort of thing that gives one pause.
The crack is moving down the wall.
We must remain until the roof falls in.

WELDON KEES

Signs

Threading the palm, a web of little lines
Spells out the lost money, the heart, the head,
The wagging tongues, the sudden deaths, in signs
We would smooth out, like imprints on a bed,

In signs that can't be helped, geese heading south,
In signs read anxiously, like breath that clouds
A mirror held to a barely open mouth,
Like telegrams, the gathering of crowds –

The plane's X in the sky, spelling disaster:
Before the whistle and hit, a tracer flare;
Before rubble, a hairline crack in plaster
And a housefly's panicked scribbling on the air.

GJERTRUD SCHNACKENBERG

from When One Has Lived a Long Time Alone

When one has lived a long time alone,
one wants to live again among men and women,
to return to that place where one's ties with the human
broke, where the disquiet of death and now also
of history glimmers its firelight on faces,
where the gaze of the new baby looks past the gaze
of the great granny, and where lovers speak,
on lips blowsy from kissing, that language
the same in each mouth, and like birds at daybreak
blether the song that is both earth's and heaven's,
until the sun has risen, and they stand
in the daylight of being made one: kingdom come,
when one has lived a long time alone.

GALWAY KINNELL

My Dark Fathers

My dark fathers lived the intolerable day
Committed always to the night of wrong,
Stiffened at the hearthstone, the woman lay,
Perished feet nailed to her man's breastbone.
Grim houses beckoned in the swelling gloom
Of Munster fields where the Atlantic night
Fettered the child within the pit of doom,
And everywhere a going down of light.

And yet upon the sandy Kerry shore
The woman once had danced at ebbing tide
Because she loved flute music – and still more
Because a lady wondered at the pride
Of one so humble. That was long before
The green plant withered by an evil chance;
When winds of hunger howled at every door
She heard the music dwindle and forgot the dance.

Such mercy as the wolf receives was hers
Whose dance became a rhythm in a grave,
Achieved beneath the thorny savage furze
That yellowed fiercely in a mountain cave.
Immune to pity, she, whose crime was love,
Crouched, shivered, searched the threatening sky,
Discovered ready signs, compelled to move
Her to her innocent appalling cry.

Skeletoned in darkness, my dark fathers lay
Unknown, and could not understand
The giant grief that trampled night and day,
The awful absence moping through the land.
Upon the headland, the encroaching sea
Left sand that hardened after tides of Spring,
No dancing feet disturbed its symmetry
And those who loved good music ceased to sing.

Since every moment of the clock
Accumulates to form a final name,
Since I am come of Kerry clay and rock,
I celebrate the darkness and the shame
That could compel a man to turn his face
Against the wall, withdrawn from light so strong
And undeceiving, spancelled in a place
Of unapplauding hands and broken song.

BRENDAN KENNELLY

Hoping It Might Be So

There must be a place where the whole of it all comes right,
Where the little boy buggered and strangled in the wood
Is comforted by his parents, and comforts his parents,
And everything horrible ever is understood,

I say:

For at least six million reasons or else no light,
No light in the day.

104

There must be somewhere it doesn't happen like this,
Where reparation is made, *à tous compris*,
Where the drowned men rise, walk back from the boats in the
        evening,
And the lost child sings on her new-made father's knee,

I say:

For at least six million reasons or else no reason
And nothing to be.

KIT WRIGHT

Clear Night

Clear night, thumb-top of a moon, a back-lit sky.
Moon-fingers lay down their same routine
On the side deck and the threshold, the white keys and the
        black keys.
Bird hush and bird song. A cassia flower falls.

1 want to be bruised by God.
I want to be strung up in a strong light and singled out.
I want to be stretched, like music wrung from a dropped seed.
I want to be entered and picked clean.

And the wind says 'What?' to me.
And the castor beans, with their little earrings of death, say
        'What?' to me.
And the stars start out on their cold slide through the dark.
And the gears notch and the engines wheel.

CHARLES WRIGHT

Defeated

This burning behind my eyes as I open a door
Means that the blocky thing in my body has won.
The opaque sleep, heavy as October grass,
Grows stubbornly, triumphant even at midnight.

And another day disappears into the cliff
Eskimos come to greet it with sharp cries.
Black water swells up over the new hole.
The ape, alone in his bamboo cage, smells

The python, and cries, but no one hears him call.
The grave moves forward from its ambush,
Curling slowly, with sideways motion,
Passing under bushes and through leaf tunnels,

Leaving dogs and sheep murdered where it slept.
Some shining thing inside us, that has
Served us well, shakes its bamboo bars.
It may be gone before we wake.

ROBERT BLY

The Waking

I wake to sleep, and take my waking slow.
I feel my fate in what I cannot fear.
I learn by going where I have to go.

We think by feeling. What is there to know?
I hear my being dance from ear to ear.
I wake to sleep, and take my waking slow.

Of those so close beside me, which are you?
God bless the Ground! I shall walk softly there,
And learn by going where I have to go.

Light takes the Tree; but who can tell us how?
The lowly worm climbs up a winding stair;
I wake to sleep, and take my waking slow.

Great Nature has another thing to do
To you and me; so take the lively air,
And, lovely, learn by going where to go.

This shaking keeps me steady. I should know.
What falls away is always. And is near.
I wake to sleep, and take my waking slow.
I learn by going where I have to go.

THEODORE ROETHKE

Mirages

Waking up in the same skin isn't enough.
You need more and more evidence
of who it is that
wakes up in the same skin.

But what evidence?
Reality is unreliable: a whirlwind
of dust that appears
and disappears every day.

Your thirst stretches out its white dunes.

Every day in the dust
you distinguish

not islands but their darkness
heaped on the polished mirror of a sea.

Not doors but their shadows
slammed in the house of wind.

Not lighthouses but their half-second SOS
in red, green and yellow.

Not language but languages.

Not your hand closing a curtain
but a hand.

And the day is over,
not wiser than the night in which
you waited for someone
who came and wasn't what you waited for.

KAPKA KASSABOVA

How to kill a living thing

Neglect it
Criticise it to its face
Say how it kills the light
Traps all the rubbish
Bores you with its green

Continually
Harden your heart
Then
Cut it down close
To the root as possible

Forget it
For a week or a month
Return with an axe
Split it with one blow
Insert a stone

To keep the wound wide open

EIBHLÍN NIC EOCHAIDH

from Sublimation

Once you called at midnight
to talk about Hindemith,
to tell me how his overtones connect each bar,
invisible thread, sounds we can't hear.
These harmonics guide us through the music, resolve
the twelve tones like mist in a valley,
the reflection of sky in water,
the illusion that what's unnamed remains unformed.
Our voices connected by black wire,
words carried on waves.

We are the strain and stress of a line,
the poem's tension singing in each black wire
of words, and between the first line and the last.
We are the angle of light that burns water,
the point of intersection that creates perspective.

You have lived Brecht's parable of the Chalk Circle.
When I was caught in the middle, you let go
so I wouldn't be torn to pieces.
Your actions have taught me what it is to love –
that it's holding back, as well as holding.

For the first time I'm going
where you can't join me. I know that home
is the one place you won't come.
But you of all people must understand –
the need to hear my language in every mouth.
I can't think in America.

I've never let myself describe you
and now that there's no time left
your meaning spills out of me
like the essence of an atom cracking
on the edge of speed's bowl,
liquid in its longing to become part of something else,
transformed.

Flesh moves to become spirit.
You were the only one to understand my conversion.
Many people have asked me about God;
my proof is manifestation,
that God can be called
'getting over fear'.

I wanted badly that truth be a single thing;
now I know it won't be measured.

It wasn't Heisenberg or Hindemith, but you
who convinced me
that nothing can be unravelled to its core,
that truth is a field, a cage, a cloud of sound.
How else to reconcile the faces of those running away
with the faces of those turning away,
with the faces of those in uniform – that hair-shirt
that says more about a man than his eyes
because you can't tell the parts of his face
that are his.
How else to encompass both that crying and those
orders; the sound of my own voice
begging, and my voice telling jokes to the man
without shoes beside me on a train;
how else to encompass the moon's chilling scream
as it calls out in its bad sleep above the earth
and your voice on the phone,
waking me in Paris, Los Angeles, New York.

ANNE MICHAELS

Horse

I've never seen a soul detached from its gender,
but I'd like to. I'd like to see my own that way,
free of its female tethers. Maybe it would be like
riding a horse. The rider's the human one,
but everyone looks at the horse.

CHASE TWICHELL

Swineherd

When all this is over, said the swineherd,
I mean to retire, where
Nobody will have heard about my special skills
And conversation is mainly about the weather.

I intend to learn how to make coffee, at least as well
As the Portuguese lay-sister in the kitchen
And polish the brass fenders every day.
I want to lie awake at night
Listening to cream crawling to the top of the jug
And the water lying soft in the cistern.

I want to see an orchard where the trees grow in straight lines
And the yellow fox finds shelter between the navy-blue trunks,
Where it gets dark early in summer
And the apple-blossom is allowed to wither on the bough.

EILÉAN NÍ CHUILLEANÁIN

The way we live

Pass the tambourine, let me bash out praises
to the Lord God of movement, to Absolute
non-friction, flight, and the scarey side:
death by avalanche, birth by failed contraception.
Of chicken tandoori and reggae, loud, from tenements,
commitment, driving fast and unswerving
friendship. Of tee-shirts on pulleys, giros and Bombay,
barmen, dreaming waitresses with many fake-gold
bangles. Of airports, impulse, and waking to uncertainty,
to strip-lights, motorways, or that pantheon –
the mountains. To overdrafts and grafting

and the fit slow pulse of wipers as you're
creeping over Rannoch, while the God of moorland
walks abroad with his entourage of freezing fog,
his bodyguard of snow.

111

Of endless gloaming in the North, of Asiatic swelter,
to launderettes, anecdotes, passions and exhaustion,
Final Demands and dead men, the skeletal grip
of government. To misery and elation; mixed,
the sod and caprice of landlords.
To the way it fits, the way it is, the way it seems
to be: let me bash out praises – pass the tambourine.

KATHLEEN JAMIE

Apologia

My life is too dull and too careful –
even I can see that:
the orderly bedside table,
the spoilt cat.

Surely I should have been bolder.
What could biographers say?
*She got up, ate toast and went shopping
day after day?*

Whisky and gin are alarming,
Ecstasy makes you drop dead.
Toy boys make inroads on cash
and your half of the bed.

Emily Dickinson, help me.
Stevie, look up from your Aunt.
Some people can stand excitement,
some people can't.

CONNIE BENSLEY

Addiction to an Old Mattress

No, this is not my life, thank God...
...worn out like this, and crippled by brain-fag;
Obsessed first by one person, and then
(Almost at once) most horribly besotted by another;
These Februaries, full of draughts and cracks,
They belong to the people in the streets, the others
Out there – haberdashers, writers of menus.

Salt breezes! Bolsters from Istanbul!
Barometers, full of contempt, controlling moody isobars.
Sumptuous tittle-tattle from a summer crowd
That's fed on lemonades and matinées. And seas
That float themselves about from place to place, and then
Spend *hours* – just moving some clear sleets across glass stones.
Yalta: deck-chairs in Asia's gold cake; thrones.

Meanwhile...I live on...powerful, disobedient,
Inside their draughty haberdasher's climate,
With these people...who are going to obsess me,
Potatoes, dentists, people I hardly know, it's unforgivable
For this is not my life
But theirs, that I am living.
And I wolf, bolt, gulp it down, day after day.

ROSEMARY TONKS

Things

There are worse things than having behaved foolishly in public.
There are worse things than these miniature betrayals,
committed or endured or suspected; there are worse things
than not being able to sleep for thinking about them.
It is 5 a.m. All the worse things come stalking in
and stand icily about the bed looking worse and worse and worse.

FLEUR ADCOCK

Thoughts After Ruskin

Women reminded him of lilies and roses.
Me they remind rather of blood and soap,
Armed with a warm rag, assaulting noses,
Ears, neck, mouth and all the secret places:

Armed with a sharp knife, cutting up liver,
Holding hearts to bleed under a running tap,
Gutting and stuffing, pickling and preserving,
Scalding, blanching, broiling, pulverising,
– All the terrible chemistry of their kitchens.

Their distant husbands lean across mahogany
And delicately manipulate the market,
While safe at home, the tender and the gentle
Are killing tiny mice, dead snap by the neck,
Asphyxiating flies, evicting spiders,
Scrubbing, scouring aloud, disturbing cupboards,
Committing things to dustbins, twisting, wringing,
Wrists red and knuckles white and fingers puckered,
Pulpy, tepid. Steering screaming cleaners
Around the snags of furniture, they straighten
And haul out sheets from under the incontinent
And heavy old, stoop to importunate young,
Tugging, folding, tucking, zipping, buttoning,
Spooning in food, encouraging excretion,
Mopping up vomit, stabbing cloth with needles,
Contorting wool around their knitting needles,
Creating snug and comfy on their needles.

Their huge hands! their everywhere eyes! their voices
Raised to convey across the hullabaloo,
Their massive thighs and breasts dispensing comfort,
Their bloody passages and hairy crannies,
Their wombs that pocket a man upside down!

And when all's over, off with overalls,
Quickly consulting clocks, they go upstairs,
Sit and sigh a little, brushing hair,
And somehow find, in mirrors, colours, odours,
Their essences of lilies and of roses.

ELMA MITCHELL

Themes for women

There is love to begin with, early love,
painful and unskilled, late love for matrons
who eye the beautiful buttocks and thick hair
of young men who do not even notice them.

Parturition, it figures, comes after, cataclysmic
at first, then dissolving into endless care
and rules and baths and orthodontic treatment,
Speech days, Open days, shut days, exams.

There are landscapes and inscapes too, sometimes tracts
of unknown counties, most often the one great hill
in low cloud, the waterfall, the empty sands, the few
snowdrops at the back door, the small birds flying.

Politics crop up at election time and ecology
any old time, no ocelot coats, no South African
oranges, a knowledge of the Screngeti
greater than the positioning of rubbish dumps
here in this off-shore island in hard times.

Seasons never go out of fashion, never will,
the coming of Spring, the dying fall
of Autumn into Winter, fine brash summers,
the red sun going down like a beach ball
into the sea. These do not escape the eyes
of women whose bodies obey the tides
and the cheese-paring sterile moon.

As you might expect, death hangs around a lot.
First ageing mothers, senile fathers; providing
the ham and sherry when the show is over,
examining stretched breasts to catch the process
of decay in time. In farmhouse kitchens they make
pigeon pies, weeping unexpectedly over
curved breasts among the floating feathers.
The men tread mud in after docking lambs' tails,
and smell of blood.

ELIZABETH BARTLETT

What Every Woman Should Carry

My mother gave me the prayer to Saint Theresa.
I added a used tube ticket, kleenex,
several Polo mints (furry), a tampon, pesetas,
a florin. Not wishing to be presumptuous,
not trusting you either, a pack of 3.
I have a pen. There is space for my guardian
angel, she has to fold her wings. Passport.
A key. Anguish, at what I said/didn't say
when once you needed/didn't need me. Anadin.
A credit card. His face the last time,
my impatience, my useless youth.
That empty sack, my heart. A box of matches.

MAURA DOOLEY

Handbag

My mother's old leather handbag,
crowded with letters she carried
all through the war. The smell
of my mother's handbag: mints
and lipstick and Coty powder.
The look of those letters, softened
and worn at the edges, opened,
read, and refolded so often.
Letters from my father. Odour
of leather and powder, which ever
since then has meant womanliness,
and love, and anguish, and war.

RUTH FAINLIGHT

Warning

When I am an old woman I shall wear purple
With a red hat which doesn't go, and doesn't suit me.
And I shall spend my pension on brandy and summer gloves
And satin sandals, and say we've no money for butter.
I shall sit down on the pavement when I'm tired
And gobble up samples in shops and press alarm bells
And run my stick along the public railings
And make up for the sobriety of my youth.
I shall go out in my slippers in the rain
And pick the flowers in other people's gardens
And learn to spit.

You can wear terrible shirts and grow more fat
And eat three pounds of sausages at a go
Or only bread and pickle for a week
And hoard pens and pencils and beermats and things in boxes.

But now we must have clothes that keep us dry
And pay our rent and not swear in the street
And set a good example for the children.
We must have friends to dinner and read the papers.

But maybe I ought to practise a little now?
So people who know me are not too shocked and surprised
When suddenly I am old, and start to wear purple.

JENNY JOSEPH

Dolor

I have known the inexorable sadness of pencils,
Neat in their boxes, dolor of pad and paper-weight,
All the misery of manilla folders and mucilage,
Desolation in immaculate public places,
Lonely reception room, lavatory, switchboard,
The unalterable pathos of basin and pitcher,

Ritual of multigraph, paper-clip, comma,
Endless duplication of lives and objects.
And I have seen dust from the walls of institutions,
Finer than flour, alive, more dangerous than silica,
Sift, almost invisible, through long afternoons of tedium,
Dropping a fine film on nails and delicate eyebrows,
Glazing the pale hair, the duplicate grey standard faces.

THEODORE ROETHKE

One Art

The art of losing isn't hard to master;
so many things seem filled with the intent
to be lost that their loss is no disaster.

Lose something every day. Accept the fluster
of lost door keys, the hour badly spent.
The art of losing isn't hard to master.

Then practice losing farther, losing faster:
places, and names, and where it was you meant
to travel. None of these will bring disaster.

I lost my mother's watch. And look! my last, or
next-to-last, of three loved houses went.
The art of losing isn't hard to master.

I lost two cities, lovely ones. And, vaster,
some realms I owned, two rivers, a continent.
I miss them, but it wasn't a disaster.

– Even losing you (the joking voice, a gesture
I love) I shan't have lied. It's evident
the art of losing's not too hard to master
though it may look like (*Write* it!) like disaster.

ELIZABETH BISHOP

Lamium

This is how you live when you have a cold heart.
As I do: in shadows, trailing over cool rock,
under the great maple trees.

The sun hardly touches me.
Sometimes I see it in early spring, rising very far away.
Then leaves grow over it, completely hiding it. I feel it
glinting through the leaves, erratic,
like someone hitting the side of a glass with a metal spoon.

Living things don't all require
light in the same degree. Some of us
make our own light: a silver leaf
like a path no one can use, a shallow
lake of silver in the darkness under the great maples.

But you know this already.
You and the others who think
you live for truth and, by extension, love
all that is cold.

LOUISE GLÜCK

A Glass of Water

Here is a glass of water from my well.
It tastes of rock and root and earth and rain;
It is the best I have, my only spell,
And it is cold, and better than champagne.
Perhaps someone will pass this house one day
To drink, and be restored, and go his way,
Someone in dark confusion as I was
When I drank down cold water in a glass,
Drank a transparent health to keep me sane,
After the bitter mood had gone again.

MAY SARTON

Sadness

It was everywhere, in the streets and houses,
    on farms and now in the air itself.
It had come from history and we were history
    so it had come from us.
I told my artist friends who courted it
    not to suffer
on purpose, not to fall in love
    with sadness
because it would be naturally theirs
    without assistance,
I had sad stories of my own,
    but they made me quiet
the way my parents' failures once did,
    nobody's business
but our own, and, besides, what was left to say
    these days
when the unspeakable was out there being spoken,
    exhausting all sympathy?
Yet, feeling it, how difficult to keep
    the face's curtains
closed – she left, he left, they died –
    the heart rising
into the mouth and eyes, everything so basic,
    so unhistorical
at such times. And then, too, the woes
    of others would get in,
but mostly I was inured and out
    to make a decent buck
or in pursuit of some slippery pleasure
    that was sadness disguised.
I found it, it found me, oh
    my artist friends
give it up, just mix your paints,
    stroke,
the strokes unmistakably will be yours.

STEPHEN DUNN

Sweetness

Just when it has seemed I couldn't bear
    one more friend
waking with a tumor, one more maniac

with a perfect reason, often a sweetness
    has come
and changed nothing in the world

except the way I stumbled through it,
    for a while lost
in the ignorance of loving

someone or something, the world shrunk
    to mouth-size,
hand-size, and never seeming small.

I acknowledge there is no sweetness
    that doesn't leave a stain,
no sweetness that's ever sufficiently sweet...

Tonight a friend called to say his lover
    was killed in a car
he was driving. His voice was low

and guttural, he repeated what he needed
    to repeat, and I repeated
the one or two words we have for such grief

until we were speaking only in tones.
    Often a sweetness comes
as if on loan, stays just long enough

to make sense of what it means to be alive,
    then returns to its dark
source. As for me, I don't care

where it's been, or what bitter road
    it's traveled
to come so far, to taste so good.

STEPHEN DUNN

121

The Execution

On the night of the execution
a man at the door
mistook me for the coroner.
'Press,' I said.

But he didn't understand. He led me
into the wrong room
where the sheriff greeted me:
'You're late, Padre.'

'You're wrong,' I told him. 'I'm Press,'
'Yes, of course, Reverend Press.'
We went down a stairway.

'Ah, Mr Ellis,' said the Deputy.
'Press!' I shouted. But he shoved me
through a black curtain.
The lights were so bright
I couldn't see the faces
of the men sitting
opposite. But, thank God, I thought
they can see me!

'Look!' I cried. 'Look at my face!
Doesn't anybody know me?'

Then a hood covered my head.
'Don't make it harder for us,' the hangman whispered.

ALDEN NOWLAN

122

A Note Left in Jimmy Leonard's Shack

Near the dry river's water-mark we found
    Your brother Minnegan,
Flopped like a fish against the muddy ground.
Beany, the kid whose yellow hair turns green,
Told me to find you, even in the rain,
    And tell you he was drowned.

I hid behind the chassis on the bank,
    The wreck of someone's Ford:
I was afraid to come and wake you drunk:
You told me once the waking up was hard,
The daylight beating at you like a board.
    Blood in my stomach sank.

Beside, you told him never to go out
    Along the river-side
Drinking and singing, clattering about.
You might have thrown a rock at me and cried
I was to blame, I let him fall in the road
    And pitch down on his side.

Well, I'll get hell enough when I get home
    For coming up this far,
Leaving the note, and running as I came.
I'll go and tell my father where you are.
You'd better go find Minnegan before
    Policemen hear and come.

Beany went home, and I got sick and ran,
    You old son of a bitch.
You better hurry down to Minnegan;
He's drunk or dying now, I don't know which,
Rolled in the roots and garbage like a fish,
    The poor old man.

JAMES WRIGHT

Epistle on suicide

Killing oneself
Is a slight affair.
You can chat about it with your washerwoman.
Elucidate the pros and cons with a friend.
A certain sense of tragedy, however attractive
Is to be avoided.
Though there is no need to make a dogma of that.
But there is more to be said, I think
For the usual slight deception:
You're fed up with changing your linen or, better still
Your wife has been unfaithful
(This is a draw with people who get surprised by such things
And is not too high-flown.)
Anyway
It should not seem
As if one had put
Too high a value on oneself.

BERTOLT BRECHT
translated from the German by John Willett

Harold's Leap

Harold, are you asleep?
Harold, I remember your leap,
It may have killed you
But it was a brave thing to do.
Two promontories ran high into the sky,
He leapt from one rock to the other
And fell to the sea's smother.
Harold was always afraid to climb high,
But something urged him on,
He felt he should try.
I would not say that he was wrong,
Although he succeeded in doing nothing but die.

Would you?
Ever after that steep
Place was called Harold's Leap.
It was a brave thing to do.

STEVIE SMITH

Her Kind

I have gone out, a possessed witch,
haunting the black air, braver at night;
dreaming evil, I have done my hitch
over the plain houses, light by light:
lonely thing, twelve-fingered, out of mind.
A woman like that is not a woman, quite.
I have been her kind.

I have found the warm caves in the woods,
filled them with skillets, carvings, shelves,
closets, silks, innumerable goods;
fixed the suppers for the worms and the elves:
whining, rearranging the disaligned.
A woman like that is misunderstood.
I have been her kind.

I have ridden in your cart, driver,
waved my nude arms at villages going by,
learning the last bright routes, survivor
where your flames still bite my thigh
and my ribs crack where your wheels wind.
A woman like that is not ashamed to die.
I have been her kind.

ANNE SEXTON

Anne Sexton's Last Letter to God

This is the last letter I will write
sitting at my kitchen table
with the blue coffee mug
at my elbow and the pot
roasting each bean to perfection:
faraway continents
in my cluttered suburban kitchen.
The sun is sharp through the blinds,
crisscrossing the kitchen's
clean tiles with yellow and white.
I walk a knife-edge of light.
This is the last letter I will write.

I have been a witch, clothed in rags
and shrieking. I have borrowed
the wings of angels and given them back:
a poor fit, and yes, like Icarus
I had no sense and I didn't much like
falling back to earth. I have had lovers
by the dozen, some poets and others
and a faithful husband that I left
in the end. I have written painfully evocative
letters from Europe and many poems,
but this is the last letter I will write.

God is in your typewriter, the old priest said
and I wanted a father so badly, that for months
I believed him, transfixed by small miracles
and clutching my golden crucifix
on my knees by the empty bed. Lately

I have given a few well-received readings
in my high heels and my favourite red dress,
the posters that displayed me in defiant pose.
I was always dramatic with my husky voice,
my fingers curled around a cigarette
and the ending always upbeat.

I have just lunched with an old friend
saying goodbye and something
'she couldn't quite catch'.

Now I have locked the front door behind me,
squinting a little as autumn spills down
from the skies and the trees. Here
is a small miracle and I am walking away.
I wrap my mother's fur coat
tightly around me, although I have
no need of its warmth today. The sun
is a cat stroking my neck, winding itself
contentedly around my long, slender legs.
I pause by the garage door to admire
the autumn leaves in their *sourball* colours.

A drink is in order. A double.
A toast to old friends, to those
on the other end of the phone and to those
who for one reason or another
have abandoned me. I pull the car door
closed and turn the key.
This, God, is *my* journey.
I have cut the lines
between us: no more tantrums.
No more poems. I am not
your daughter, your mother, your lover.
No more letters then, from me to you, God
and it amuses me to think of your
impotent displeasure as I settle myself
comfortably into the driver's seat.

TRACEY HERD

My November Guest

My Sorrow, when she's here with me,
    Thinks these dark days of autumn rain
Are beautiful as days can be;
She loves the bare, the withered tree;
    She walks the sodden pasture lane.

Her pleasure will not let me stay.
    She talks and I am fain to list:
She's glad the birds are gone away,
She's glad her simple worsted gray
    Is silver now with clinging mist.

The desolate, deserted trees,
    The faded earth, the heavy sky,
The beauties she so truly sees,
She thinks I have no eyes for these,
    And vexes me for reason why.

Not yesterday I learned to know
    The love of bare November days
Before the coming of the snow,
But it were vain to tell her so,
    And they are better for her praise.

ROBERT FROST

She Dotes

She dotes on what the wild birds say
Or hint or mock at, night and day, –
Thrush, blackbird, all that sing in May,
        And songless plover,
Hawk, heron, owl, and woodpecker.
They never say a word to her
        About her lover.

She laughs at them for childishness,
She cries at them for carelessness
Who see her going loverless
    Yet sing and chatter
Just as when he was not a ghost,
Nor ever ask her what she has lost
    Or what is the matter.

Yet she has fancied blackbirds hide
A secret, and that thrushes chide
Because she thinks death can divide
    Her from her lover:
And she has slept, trying to translate
The word the cuckoo cries to his mate
    Over and over.

EDWARD THOMAS

The Cry

Don't think it was all hate
That grew there; love grew there, too,
Climbing by small tendrils where
The warmth fell from the eyes' blue

Flame. Don't think even the dirt
And the brute ugliness reigned
Unchallenged. Among the fields
Sometimes the spirit, enchained

So long by the gross flesh, raised
Suddenly there its wild note of praise.

R.S. THOMAS

The Leaden-Eyed

Let not young souls be smothered out before
They do quaint deeds and fully flaunt their pride.
It is the world's one crime its babes grow dull,
Its poor are ox-like, limp and leaden-eyed.

Not that they starve, but starve so dreamlessly,
Not that they sow, but that they seldom reap,
Not that they serve, but have no gods to serve,
Not that they die, but that they die like sheep.

VACHEL LINDSAY

And the Days Are Not Full Enough

And the days are not full enough
And the nights are not full enough
And life slips by like a field mouse
    Not shaking the grass.

EZRA POUND

A Removal from Terry Street

On a squeaking cart, they push the usual stuff,
A mattress, bed ends, cups, carpets, chairs,
Four paperback westerns. Two whistling youths
In surplus US Army battle-jackets
Remove their sister's goods. Her husband
Follows, carrying on his shoulders the son
Whose mischief we are glad to see removed,
And pushing, of all things, a lawnmower.
There is no grass in Terry Street. The worms
Come up cracks in concrete yards in moonlight.
That man, I wish him well. I wish him grass.

DOUGLAS DUNN

4

Bittersweet

Poetry can tell us what human beings are.
It can tell us why we stumble and fall and how,
miraculously, we can stand up.

MAYA ANGELOU

BITTERSWEET begins with poems from the harsh side of life, but shows the power of poetry to transform. These include poems by Matthew Sweeney (133), Peter Reading (133), Ken Smith (135), Polish Nobel prizewinner Wislawa Szymborska (135) and Bosnian writer Izet Sarajlic (137) which turn news headlines into personal stories. Most people caught up in such events are taken by surprise: anyone could be hurt by fire or flood, bomb or bullet. Illness is even more likely to affect us or our loved ones at some time in our lives, and often a poet will discover that a single poem is totally inadequate as a response, and that a whole series of poems is needed to dramatise a fuller range of the human implications. It's not possible to include such sequences in full here, but there are extracts from Philip Gross's *The Wasting Game* (140-43), about his daughter's anorexia, and from Carole Satyamurti's *Changing the Subject* (145-49), which is set in a cancer ward.

There are poems here by Ken Smith (144) and Basil Bunting (156) about growing old and becoming painfully aware of mortality, but others which discover new hope in later life or after disappointment, such as Fleur Adcock's 'Kissing' (155). Written at the age of 65, Bunting's poem is a free translation or "version" giving new life to a Latin ode by the Roman poet Horace, expressing his disgust with ageing yet also his hope for compassionate sexual love.

Seamus Heaney believes that 'the vision of reality which poetry offers should be transformative, more than just a printout of the given circumstances of its time and place'. Elizabeth Bishop's closely observed poetry mirrors the ambivalence she perceived in the world, 'the always-more-successful surrealism of everyday life'. Other poets have transformed vision through stories of metamorphosis, change and re-emerging, sometimes through the medium of what Matthew Sweeney calls 'alternate realism' (see introduction, 25), as in the poems here by Jo Shapcott (160) and Peter Didsbury (161). When Adrienne Rich goes beneath the surface in 'Diving into the Wreck' (151) her underwater exploration is a metaphorical journey back through the mind which turns into a feminist argument with the poetic tradition she has emerged from.

The mushrooms in Derek Mahon's 'A Disused Shed in Co. Wexford' (166) have been waiting in the dark 'since civil war days'. Their presence is symbolic, standing for all the marginalised people and mute victims of history. Charged with meaning and remembrance by the poem, this forgotten shed behind the rhododendrons is an imagined lost world ('one of those places where a thought might grow') remembered from *Troubles* (1970), a novel set just after the First World War in the decaying Majestic Hotel in rural Ireland by J.G. Farrell, to whom the poem is dedicated (Mahon's friend was a polio victim, and died in Ireland in a drowning accident not long after the poem was written). The political significance claimed by many critics affirms this foremost as a poem about humanity, as Seamus Deane points out: 'It is a poem that heartbreakingly dwells on and gives voice to all those peoples and civilisations that have been lost and/or destroyed. Since it is set in Ireland, with all the characteristics of an Irish "Big House" ruin, it speaks with a special sharpness to the present moment and the fear, rampant in Northern Ireland, of communities that fear they too might perish and be lost, with none to speak for them.'

Mahon's poem achieves its remarkable effects through sound, beginning with a mellifluous evocation through consonance and assonance of fading sounds in the first stanza, through which the first sentence unspools to the metre like a rollcall, with a breath-jump across the stanza gap at the end of line 10, not meeting the first full-stop until the end of the 13th line of the poem, at the light-giving keyhole. Edna Longley's close reading of this poem shows how from this point 'rhythms expressive of the mushrooms crowding to the poem's keyhole, of growth and accumulation, answer those of diminuendo', and also how complementary rhythms trace the 'posture' of 'expectancy' and 'desire' asserted in the narrative. The ten-line stanzas which Mahon handles with such delicacy and consummate skill are "big houses" of his own building indebted to past models, to his formal masters W.B. Yeats and Louis MacNeice.

Peter Reading is one of Britain's most original and controversial poets: angry, uncompromising, gruesomely ironic, hilarious and heartbreaking. I would say he is the most skilful and technically inventive poet writing today, mixing the matter and speech of the gutter with highly sophisticated metrical and syllabic patterns to produce scathing and grotesque accounts of lives blighted by greed, meanness, ignorance, political ineptness and cultural improverishment. He often revives long forgotten verse forms because they are right for his subject, signalling their use and presence through the layout of his lines and stanzas, as in the section from his book-length poem *Evagatory* (311-14). Technique as complex and subtle as Reading's is effective not because the reader is immediately conscious that metrical fireworks are shooting off behind the lines but because the particular metre chosen for each particular poem makes the poem effective in a way that no other alternative would have achieved, especially when read aloud. It is only afterwards, going back over the poem, that you realise just how the poem's effects have been managed, and having analysed and taken in the implications of its structure and prosody, the Reading poem becomes more and more powerful with each subsequent reading. In another book-length poem, *Ukulele Music*, represented here with a short extract (133-34), he uses the elegiac distich (see glossary, 465) to give a disconcerting classical gravitas and elegiac cadence to his evocations of tragic, modern times.

Tube Ride to Martha's

Before the sirens started, he was late –
late for a dinner at his woman's,
but he'd managed to find a good Rioja
and an excellent excuse: his cat
had burned her tail in the toaster
(this was true) and he'd brought her
to the vet and back in a cab.
He thought about a third cab to Martha's
but funds were low, and the tube ride
was four stops, a half hour with the walks.
He had a thriller in his carrier-bag,
a Ross McDonald, long out of print,
which he opened on the escalator, wanting
it finished tonight. When the smoke came
he hardly noticed, till the black guard
tried to hustle everyone upstairs,
and trains rushed by, without stopping,
and people pushed and screamed.
As the smoke got thicker and blacker
with flames growing fast, he realised
it was over almost before it had begun.

MATTHEW SWEENEY

from Ukulele Music

'Life is too black as he paints it' and 'Reading's nastiness sometimes
seems a bit over the top' thinks a review – so does *he*.

Too black and over the top, though, is what the Actual often
happens to be, I'm afraid. He don't *invent* it, you know.

Take, for example, some snippets from last week's dailies before
        they're
screwed up to light the Parkray: Birmingham, March '83,

133

on her allotment in King's Heath, picking daffodils, Dr
Dorris McCutcheon (retired) pauses to look at her veg.

Dr McCutcheon (aged 81) does not know that behind her,
Dennis (aged 36) lurks, clutching an old iron bar.

Unemployed labourer Dennis Bowering sneaks up behind her,
bashes her over the head – jaw, nose and cheek are smashed-in.

Dennis then drags her until he has got her into the tool-shed,
strikes her again and again, there is a sexual assault,

also a watch and some money worth less than ten pounds are stolen.
'Is an appalling offence…' Bowering is told by the Judge.

Amateur frogmen discover a pair of human legs buried
Mafia-style in cement, deep in an Austrian lake.

Smugly, Americans rail over KA 007;
angrily, Moscow retorts. Hokkaido fishermen find

five human bits of meat, one faceless limbless female Caucasian,
shirts, empty briefcases, shoes, fragments of little child's coat,

pieces of movable section of wing of a 747,
one piece of human back flesh (in salmon-fishermen's nets),

one headless human too mangled to ascertain what the sex is.
USA/USSR butcher a Boeing like chess

(probably civil jumbos *are* used for Intelligence business;
pity the poor sods on board don't have the chance to opt out).

Sexual outrage on woman of 88 robbed of her savings.
Finger found stuck on barbed wire. Too black and over the top.

Clearly we no longer hold *H. sapiens* in great reverence
(which situation, alas, no elegiacs can fix).

What do they think they're playing at, then, these Poetry Wallahs?
Grub St. reviewing its own lame valedictory bunk.

PETER READING

AUTHOR'S NOTE: *KA 007:* in September 1983 a Soviet fighter plane shot down a
South Korean airliner when all 269 passengers were killed, causing a brief stir.

Against the grain

Someone must count them, the bodies that come up
one by one out of the fire, up from
the gloomy cradle of the North Sea
that has weighted and washed them, months.

Someone must number them, name each one
by the fingerprints, the rings, by the teeth,
someone must stare at the remnants of the dead
from Zeebrugge, Kings Cross, Piper Alpha:

more oil there than under all Arabia,
I recall long ago, *that we bought and paid for.*
We're dying of neglect. My country
is a free enterprise disaster zone.

And now someone must count them all: one, one.
Someone must zip them into a bag
and bury them, tally the ongoing total,
put up a stone. It goes against the grain.

KEN SMITH

The One Twenty Pub

The bomb is primed to go off at one twenty.
A time-check: one sixteen.
There's still a chance for some to join
the pub's ranks, for others to drop out.

The terrorist watches from across the street.
Distance will shield him
from the impact of what he sees:

A woman, turquoise jacket on her shoulder,
enters; a man with sunglasses departs.
Youths in tee-shirts loiter without intent.

One seventeen and four seconds.
The scrawny motorcyclist, revving up
to leave, won't believe his luck;
but the tall man steps straight in.

One seventeen and forty seconds.
That girl, over there with the walkman
– now the bus has cut her off.
One eighteen exactly.
Was she stupid enough to head inside?
Or wasn't she? We'll know before long,
when the dead are carried out.

It's one nineteen.
Nothing much to report
until a muddled barfly hesitates,
fumbles with his pockets, and, like
a blasted fool, stumbles back
at one nineteen and fifty seconds
to retrieve his goddamn cap.

One twenty
How time drags when...
Any moment now.
Not yet.
Yes.
    Yes,
        there
           it
                goes.

WISLAWA SZYMBORSKA
version from the Polish by Dennis O'Driscoll

Luck in Sarajevo

In Sarajevo
in the spring of 1992,
everything is possible:

you go stand in a bread line
and end up in an emergency room
with your leg amputated.

Afterwards, you still maintain
that you were very lucky.

IZET SARAJLIĆ
translated from the Serbo-Croat by Charles Simic

All of These People

Who was it who suggested that the opposite of war
Is not so much peace as civilisation? He knew
Our assassinated Catholic greengrocer who died
At Christmas in the arms of our Methodist minister,
And our ice-cream man whose continuing requiem
Is the twenty-one flavours children have by heart.
Our cobbler mends shoes for everybody; our butcher
Blends into his best sausages leeks, garlic, honey;
Our cornershop sells everything from bread to kindling.
Who can bring peace to people who are not civilised?
All of these people, alive or dead, are civilised.

MICHAEL LONGLEY

Waking This Morning

Waking this morning,
a violent woman in the violent day
Laughing.
                  Past the line of memory
along the long body of your life
in which move childhood, youth, your lifetime of touch,
eyes, lips, chest, belly, sex, legs, to the waves of the sheet.
I look past the little plant
on the city windowsill
to the tall towers bookshaped, crushed together in greed,
the river flashing flowing corroded,
the intricate harbor and the sea, the wars, the moon, the planets,
        all who people space
in the sun visible invisible.
African violets in the light
breathing, in a breathing universe.   I want strong peace, and delight,
the wild good.
I want to make my touch poems:
to find my morning, to find you entire
alive moving among the anti-touch people.

                  I say across the waves of the air to you:
today once more
I will try to be non-violent
one more day
this morning, waking the world away
in the violent day.

MURIEL RUKEYSER

I Am a Cameraman

They suffer, and I catch only the surface.
The rest is inexpressible, beyond
What can be recorded. You can't be them.
If they'd talk to you, you might guess
What pain is like though they might spit on you.

Film is just a reflection
Of the matchless despair of the century.
There have been twenty centuries since charity began.
Indignation is day-to-day stuff;
It keeps us off the streets, it keeps us watching.

Film has no words of its own.
It is a silent waste of things happening
Without us, when it is too late to help.
What of the dignity of those caught suffering?
It hurts me. I robbed them of privacy.

My young friends think Film will be all of Art.
It will be revolutionary proof
Their films will not guess wrongly and will not lie.
They'll film what is happening behind barbed wire.
They'll always know the truth and be famous.

Politics softens everything.
Truth is known only to its victims.
All else is photographs – a documentary
The starving and the playboys perish in.
Life disguises itself with professionalism.

Life tells the biggest lies of all,
And draws wages from itself.
Truth is a landscape the saintly tribes live on,
And all the lenses of Japan and Germany
Wouldn't know how to focus on it.

Life flickers on the frame like beautiful hummingbirds.
That is the film that always comes out blank.
The painting the artist can't get shapes to fit.
The poem that shrugs off every word you try.
The music no one has ever heard.

DOUGLAS DUNN

from The Wasting Game

1

'I'm fat, look, *fat...*'

Yes and the moon's made of cheese,
that chunk she won't touch in the fridge

dried, creviced, sweating in its cold
like someone with a killing fever.

Half a scrape-of-marmite sandwich,
last night's pushed-aside

potatoes greying like a tramp's teeth,
crusts, crumbs are a danger to her,

so much orbiting space junk
that's weightless for only so long.

Burn it up on re-entry, burn it,
burn it. So she trains

with weights, she jogs, she runs
as if the sky were falling.

3

The eating thing:

the slouching beast
that's come to stay,

to spatter the slops
and foul the manger,

to snap at the hand
that tries to feed it, so

we leave it and we lie
in darkness, trying not to know,

not to hear it gnawing
in the next room, gnawing

itself to the bone.

11

I could hate

those frail maids fading beautifully
in books, wax lilies, pale-succulent

stalks that might snap
at a touch. The bird-dropping of blood

in a lace-bordered handkerchief
like the monstrance on the nuptial sheet.

A consummation most devoutly wished
by death. The maiden turns,

in woodcuts from another age
of plagues, to his knuckleboned touch,

half smiling; the consumptive turns
on her lace-bordered pillow

weakly and away
from any warmth of flesh

as if stung; the anorexic turns
her face towards these stories, stories

which, because I love the girl,
I hate.

12

She left home months ago.
Somehow we never noticed.
She was going solo

as a conjuror:
the egg we found rotting
in the body-folds of the sofa;

caked wads
of tissues in the bin with weetabix
compacted in them like the Mob's

car-crusher sandwiches;
potatoes spirited away
with one pass of the baggy-wristed

sweater she draped
on her bones. (What applause
when she whips it off one day

and she's gone!) Co-ordination
slipping now, caught out –
fraud, fraud! –

she plays the cheapest trick of all.
A toothmug of tap water,
sixty paracetamol.

She tries hissing herself offstage.

13
Drip. Drip.

Those stripped
twigs of her fingers.
Ivy torsions in the wrist.

Two spikes bandaged
to drip in her veins.

Sap sunk
at fifteen, she's been old
for too long, always cold
in her matt blacks, always
in some sort of mourning.

Mulched like leafmould,
mushroom-breathed, shit-smelling,
she's a question: Can
you love this?
Can you sit

and watch the hours dissolving
in the drip
of Parvolax and glucose
clear as rinsings from bare twig tips
when the downpour's gone?

They're trying to wash the river
in her blood. They're on the phone
to the Poisons Unit:
the readings aren't clear.
Nothing's perfect

but it's all there is.
This. Now. The drip
of plain words. Yes.
Love.
This.

PHILIP GROSS

Brinkwomanship

When they come for you no bigger than a piece of fruit,
weighing no more and no less than a water biscuit,
this will be my excuse:
that I hoped you were just testing yourself
as I might subtly and irresistibly
poke at a sensitive tooth. That is, not morbidly,
but out of a curiosity
to locate the exact, minute, sensory transition – between
merely knowing the definition
of pain, and knowing the *meaning*.

LEONTIA FLYNN

Here

I point to where the pain is, the ache
where the blockage is. Here.
The doctor shakes his head at me. Yes
he says, I have that, we all have.

They put the wire in again, on the monitor
I watch the grey map of my heart, the bent
ladder of the spine that outlasts it.
How does it feel? they ask. Here?

I am moving away down the long corridors
of abandoned trolleys, the closed wings
of hospitals, rooms full of yellow bedpans
and screens and walker frames, fading out

into nothing and nothing at all, as we do,
as we all do, as it happens, and no one
can talk of it. Here, where the heart
dies, where all the systems are dying.

KEN SMITH

The Unprofessionals

When the worst thing happens,
That uproots the future,
That you must live for every hour of your future,

They come,
Unorganised, inarticulate, unprofessional;

They come sheepishly, sit with you, holding hands,
From tea to tea, from Anadin to Valium,
Sleeping on put-you-ups, answering the phone,
Coming in shifts, spontaneously,

Talking sometimes,
About wallflowers, and fishing, and why
Dealing with Kleenex and kettles,
Doing the washing up and the shopping,

Like civilians in a shelter, under bombardment,
Holding hands and sitting it out
Through the immortality of all the seconds,
Until the blunting of time.

U.A. FANTHORPE

Visiting Hour

In the pond of our new garden
were five orange stains, under
inches of ice. Weeks since anyone
had been there. Already by far
the most severe winter for years.
You broke the ice with a hammer.
I watched the goldfish appear,
blunt-nosed and delicately clear.

Since then so much has taken place
to distance us from what we were.
That it should come to this.
Unable to hide the horror
in my eyes, I stand helpless
by your bedside and can do no more
than wish it were simply a matter
of smashing the ice and giving you air.

STEWART CONN

from Changing the Subject

2 *Out-Patients*

Women stripped to the waist,
wrapped in blue,
we are a uniform edition
waiting to be read.

These plain covers suit us:
we're inexplicit,
it's not our style to advertise
our fearful narratives.

My turn. He reads my breasts
like braille, finding the lump
I knew was there. This is
the episode I could see coming

— although he's reassuring,
doesn't think it's sinister
but just to be quite clear...
He's taking over,

he'll be the writer now,
the plot-master,
and I must wait
to read my next instalment.

3 *Diagnosis*

He was good at telling,
gentle, but direct;
he stayed with me
while I recovered breath,
started to collect

stumbling questions. He said
cancer with a small c
— the raw stuff of routine —
yet his manner showed
he knew it couldn't be ordinary for me.

Walking down the road
I shivered like a gong
that's just been struck
— mutilation...what have I done...
my child...how long...

– and noticed how
the vast possible array
of individual speech
is whittled by bad news
to what all frightened people say

That night, the freak storm.
I listened to trees fall,
stout fences crack,
felt the house shudder as the wind
howled the truest cliché of them all.

7 *How Are You?*

When he asked me that
what if I'd said,
rather than 'very well',
'dreadful – full of dread'?

Since I have known this,
language has cracked,
meanings have re-arranged;
dream, risk and fact

changed places. Tenses tip,
word-roots are suddenly
important, some grip
on the slippery.

We're on thin linguistic ice
lifelong, but I see through;
I read the sentence
we are all subject to

in the stopped mouths of those
who once were 'I',
full-fleshed, confident
using the verb 'to die'

of plants and pets and parents
until the immense
contingency of things
deleted sense.

They are his future
as well as mine,
but I won't make him look.
I say, 'I'm fine'.

9 *Knowing Our Place*

Class is irrelevant in here.
We're part of a new scale
– mobility is all one way
and the least respected
are envied most.

First, the benigns,
in for a night or two,
nervous, but unappalled;
foolishly glad their bodies
don't behave like *that*.

Then the exploratories;
can't wait to know, but have to.
Greedy for signs, they swing
from misery to confidence,
or just endure.

The primaries are in
for surgery – what kind? What then?
Shocked, tearful perhaps;
things happening too fast.
Still can't believe it, really.

The reconstructions are survivors,
experienced, detached.
They're bent on being almost normal;
don't want to think
of other possibilities.

Secondaries (treatment)
are often angry – with doctors, fate…
– or blame themselves.
They want to tell their stories,
not to feel so alone.

Secondaries (palliative)
are admitted swathed in pain.
They become gentle, grateful,
they've learned to live
one day at a time.

Terminals are royalty,
beyond the rest of us.
They lie in side-rooms
flanked by exhausted relatives,
sans everything.

We learn the social map
fast. Beneath the ordinary chat,
jokes, kindnesses, we're scavengers,
gnawing at each other's histories
for scraps of hope.

13 *I Shall Paint My Nails Red*

because a bit of colour is a public service.

because I am proud of my hands.

because it will remind me I'm a woman.

because I will look like a survivor.

because I can admire them in traffic jams.

because my daughter will say ugh.

because my lover will be surprised.

because it is quicker than dyeing my hair.

because it is a ten-minute moratorium.

because it is reversible.

CAROLE SATYAMURTI

The Cure

Not the laying-on of hands, healing bones and hearts.
Not flowers, protease inhibitors, pills for the pain.
Not a prayer for the dying, for you, for us, not crying, not yet.

Tonight only the clock, each concentrated second one tiny grain
in a thousand thousand parts
of rain.

NICK DRAKE

Past-Lives Therapy

They explained to me the bloody bandages
On the floor in the maternity ward in Rochester, NY,
Cured the backache I acquired bowing to my old master,
Made me stop putting thumbtacks around my bed.

They showed me, instead, an officer on horseback,
Waving a sabre next to a burning house,
And a barefoot woman wearing only her slip,
Hissing after him and calling him Lucifer.

Then, I was a straw-headed boy in patched overalls.
Come dark, a chicken would roost in my hair.
Some even laid eggs while I strummed my banjo,
While my mother and father crossed themselves.

Next, I saw myself inside an abandoned gas station
Constructing a machine made up of a dentist's chair,
A store dummy, an electric hair-dryer, steak knives...
When a lady fainted seeing me in my underwear.

Some nights, however, they opened a hundred doors,
Always to a different room, and could not find me.
There was only a short squeak now and then,
As if bird had been trapped out there in the dark.

CHARLES SIMIC

Diving into the Wreck

First having read the book of myths,
and loaded the camera,
and checked the edge of the knife-blade,
I put on
the body-armor of black rubber
the absurd flippers
the grave and awkward mask.
I am having to do this
not like Cousteau with his
assiduous team
aboard the sun-flooded schooner
but here alone.

There is a ladder.
The ladder is always there
hanging innocently
close to the side of the schooner.
We know what it is for,
we who have used it.
Otherwise
it's a piece of maritime floss
some sundry equipment.

I go down.
Rung after rung and still
the oxygen immerses me
the blue light
the clear atoms
of our human air.
I go down.
My flippers cripple me,
I crawl like an insect down the ladder
and there is no one
to tell me when the ocean
will begin.

First the air is blue and then
it is bluer and then green and then
black I am blacking out and yet
my mask is powerful

it pumps my blood with power
the sea is another story
the sea is not a question of power
I have to learn alone
to turn my body without force
in the deep element.

And now: it is easy to forget
what I came for
among so many who have always
lived here
swaying their crenellated fans
between the reefs
and besides
you breathe differently down here.

I came to explore the wreck.
The words are purposes.
The words are maps.
I came to see the damage that was done
and the treasures that prevail.
I stroke the beam of my lamp
slowly along the flank
of something more permanent
than fish or weed

the thing I came for:
the wreck and not the story of the wreck
the thing itself and not the myth
the drowned face always staring
toward the sun
the evidence of damage
worn by salt and sway into this threadbare beauty
the ribs of the disaster
curving their assertion
among the tentative haunters.

This is the place.
And I am here, the mermaid whose dark hair
streams black, the merman in his armored body.
We circle silently
about the wreck
we dive into the hold.
I am she: I am he

whose drowned face sleeps with open eyes
whose breasts still bear the stress
whose silver, copper, vermeil cargo lies
obscurely inside barrels
half-wedged and left to rot
we are the half-destroyed instruments
that once held to a course
the water-eaten log
the fouled compass

We are, I am, you are
by cowardice or courage
the one who find our way
back to this scene
carrying a knife, a camera
a book of myths
in which
our names do not appear.

ADRIENNE RICH

April 5, 1974

The air was soft, the ground still cold.
In the dull pasture where I strolled
Was something I could not believe.
Dead grass appeared to slide and heave,
Though still too frozen-flat to stir,
And rocks to twitch, and all to blur.
What was this rippling of the land?
Was matter getting out of hand
And making free with natural law,
I stopped and blinked, and then I saw
A fact as eerie as a dream.
There was a subtle flood of steam
Moving upon the face of things.
It came from standing pools and springs
And what of snow was still around;

It came of winter's giving ground
So that the freeze was coming out,
As when a set mind, blessed by doubt,
Relaxes into mother-wit.
Flowers, I said, will come of it.

RICHARD WILBUR

At Poll Salach
Easter Sunday 1998

While I was looking for Easter snow on the hills
You showed me, like a concentration of violets
Or a fragment from some future unimagined sky,
A single spring gentian shivering at our feet.

MICHAEL LONGLEY

Thaw

Over the land freckled with snow half-thawed
The speculating rooks at their nests cawed
And saw from elm-tops, delicate as flower of grass,
What we below could not see, Winter pass.

EDWARD THOMAS

Thaw

Snow curls into the coalhouse, flecks the coal.
We burn the snow as well in bad weather
As though to spring-clean that darkening hole.
The thaw's a blackbird with one feather.

MICHAEL LONGLEY

Kissing

The young are walking on the riverbank,
arms around each other's waists and shoulders,
pretending to be looking at the waterlilies
and what might be a nest of some kind, over
there, which two who are clamped together
mouth to mouth have forgotten about.
The others, making courteous detours
around them, talk, stop talking, kiss.
They can see no one older than themselves.
It's their river. They've got all day.

Seeing's not everything. At this very
moment the middle-aged are kissing
in the backs of taxis, on the way
to airports and stations. Their mouths and tongues
are soft and powerful and as moist as ever.
Their hands are not inside each other's clothes
(because of the driver) but locked so tightly
together that it hurts: it may leave marks
on their not of course youthful skin, which they won't
notice. They too may have futures.

FLEUR ADCOCK

How my true love and I lay without touching

How my true love and I lay without touching
How my hand journeyed to the drumlin of his hip
my pelvis aching
Just like two saints or priests or nuns
my true love and I lay without touching.

How I would long for the brush of a kiss
to travel my cheek or the cheek of my groin
my heart aching
But just like two saints or priests or nuns
my true love and I lay without touching.

Last night in my dreams I spoke with his wife
his true love who had left him surely as they lay without touching
my heart for her was aching
For like two saints or priests or nuns
the two loves once lay without touching

But the dream of her faded before concentrating
each to each in our innocent mutual hating
her hand aching
to blind me with bullets to prevent herself from pining
for a once love she longed for and lay without touching.

Now my true love lies in the mutton of madness
'I was always troubled by sex,' he says, with great sadness
his wife and I aching
in our cold single beds with many seas dividing
as we think of the years that we spent without touching.

LELAND BARDWELL

'You idiot!...'
(*Second Book of Odes*, 4)

You idiot! What makes you think decay will
never stink from your skin? Your warts sicken
typists, girls in the tube avoid you. Must they
also stop their ears to your tomcat
wailing, a promise your body cannot keep?

A lame stag, limping after the hinds, with tines
shivered by impact and scarred neck – but
look! Spittle fills his mouth, overflows,
snuffing their sweet scent. His feet lift lightly
with mere memory of gentler seasons. Lungs
full of the drug, antlers rake back, he
halts the herd, his voice filled with
custom of combat and unslaked lust.

Did the girl shrink from David? Did she hug his
ribs, death shaking them, and milk dry
the slack teat from which Judah had sucked life?

BASIL BUNTING

90 North

At home, in my flannel gown, like a bear to its floe,
I clambered to bed; up the globe's impossible sides
I sailed all right – till at last, with my black beard,
My furs and my dogs, I stood at the northern pole.

There in the childish night my companions lay frozen,
The stiff furs knocked at my starveling throat,
And I gave my great sigh: the flakes came huddling,
Were they really my end? In the darkness I turned to my rest.

   Here, the flag snaps in the glare and silence
Of the unbroken ice. I stand here,
The dogs bark, my beard is black, and I stare
At the North Pole...
                    And now what? Why, go back.

Turn as I please, my step is to the south.
The world – my world spins on this final point
Of cold and wretchedness: all lines, all winds
End in this whirlpool I at last discover.

And it is meaningless. In the child's bed
After the night's voyage, in that warm world
Where people work and suffer for the end
That crowns the pain – in that Cloud-Cuckoo-Land

I reached my North and it had meaning.
Here at the actual pole of my existence,
Where all that I have done is meaningless,
Where I die or live by accident alone –

Where, living or dying, I am still alone;
Here where North, the night, the berg of death
Crowd me out of the ignorant darkness,
I see at last that all the knowledge

I wrung from the darkness – that the darkness flung me –
Is worthless as ignorance: nothing comes from nothing,
The darkness from the darkness. Pain comes from the darkness
And we call it wisdom. It is pain.

RANDALL JARRELL

Listening to Collared Doves

I am homesick now for middle age, as then
For youth. For youth is our home-land: we were born
And lived there long, though afterwards moved on
From state to state, too slowly acclimatising
Perhaps and never fluent, through the surprising
Countries, in any languages but one.

This mourning now for middle age, no more
For youth, confirms me old as not before.
Age rounds the world, they say, to childhood's far
Archaic shores; it may be so at last,
But what now (strength apart) I miss the most
Is time unseen like air, since everywhere.

And yet, when in the months and in the skies
That were the cuckoos', and in the nearer trees
That were the deep-voiced wood-pigeons', it is
Instead now the collared doves that call and call
(Their three flat notes growing traditional),
I think we live long enough, listening to these.

I draw my line out from their simple curve
And say, our natural span may be enough;
And think of one I knew and her long life;
And how the climate changed and how the sign-
Posts changed, defaced, from her Victorian
Childhood and youth, through our century of grief,

And how she adapted as she could, not one
By nature adaptable, bred puritan
(Though quick to be pleased and having still her own
Lightness of heart). She died twenty years ago,
Aged, of life – it seems, all she could do
Having done, all the change that she could know having known.

E.J. SCOVELL

Watching for Dolphins

In the summer months on every crossing to Piraeus
One noticed that certain passengers soon rose
From seats in the packed saloon and with serious
Looks and no acknowledgement of a common purpose
Passed forward through the small door into the bows
To watch for dolphins. One saw them lose

Every other wish. Even the lovers
Turned their desires on the sea, and a fat man
Hung with equipment to photograph the occasion
Stared like a saint, through sad bi-focals; others,
Hopeless themselves, looked to the children for they
Would see dolphins if anyone would. Day after day

Or on their last opportunity all gazed
Undecided whether a flat calm were favourable
Or a sea the sun and the wind between them raised
To a likeness of dolphins. Were gulls a sign, that fell
Screeching from the sky or over an unremarkable place
Sat in a silent school? Every face

After its character implored the sea.
All, unaccustomed, wanted epiphany,
Praying the sky would clang and the abused Aegean
Reverberate with cymbal, gong and drum.
We could not imagine more prayer, and had they then
On the waves, on the climax of our longing come

Smiling, snub-nosed, domed like satyrs, oh
We should have laughed and lifted the children up
Stranger to stranger, pointing how with a leap
They left their element, three or four times, centred
On grace, and heavily and warm re-entered,
Looping the keel. We should have felt them go

Further and further into the deep parts. But soon
We were among the great tankers, under their chains
In black water. We had not seen the dolphins
But woke, blinking. Eyes cast down
With no admission of disappointment the company
Dispersed and prepared to land in the city.

DAVID CONSTANTINE

Goat

Dusk, deserted road, and suddenly
I was a goat. To be truthful it took
two minutes, though it seemed sudden,
for the horns to pop out of my skull,
for the spine to revolutionise and go
horizontal, for the fingers to glue
together and for the nails to become
important enough to upgrade to hoof.
The road was not deserted any more, but full
of goats, and I liked that, even though I hate
the rush hour on the tube, the press of bodies.
Now I loved snuffling behind his or her ear,
licking a flank or two, licking and snuffling here,
there, wherever I liked. I lived for the push
of goat muscle and goat bone, the smell of goat fur,
goat breath and goat sex. I ended up on the edge
of the crowd where the road met the high
hedgerow with the scent of earth, a thousand
kinds of grass, leaves and twigs, flower-heads
and the intoxicating tang of the odd ring-pull
or rubber to spice the mixture. I wanted
to eat everything. I could have eaten the world
and closed my eyes to nibble at the high
sweet leaves against the sunset. I tasted
that old sun and the few dark clouds
and some tall buildings far away in the next town.
I think I must have swallowed an office block
because this grinding enormous digestion tells me
it's stuck on an empty corridor which has
at the far end, I know, a tiny human figure.

JO SHAPCOTT

The Drainage

When he got out of bed the world had changed.
It was very cold. His breath whitened the room.
Chill December clanked at the panes.
There was freezing fog.
He stepped outside.
Not into his street but a flat wet landscape.
Sluices. Ditches. Drains. Frozen mud and leafcake. Dykes.
He found he knew the names of them all.
Barber's Cut. Cold Track. Lament. Meridian Stream.
He found himself walking.
It was broad cold day but the sky was black.
Instead of the sun it was Orion there.
Seeming to pulse his meaning down.
He was naked. He had to clothe himself.
The heifers stood like statues in the fields.
They didn't moan when he sliced the hides from them.
He looked at the penknife in his hand.
The needle, the thread, the clammy strips.
Now his face mooned out through a white hole.
The cape dripped. He knew he had
the bounds of a large parish to go.
His feet refused to falter.
Birds sat still in the trees.
Fast with cold glue. Passing their clumps
he watched them rise in their species.
The individuals. Sparrow. Starling. Wren.
He brought them down with his finger
Knife needle and thread again.
It happened with the streams.
Pike barbel roach minnow gudgeon.
Perch dace eel. Grayling lamprey bream.
His feet cracked puddles and were cut on mud. They bled.
There was movement. He pointed. He stitched.
His coat hung reeking on him.
He made cut after cut in the cold.
Coldness and the colours of blood.
Red blue and green. He glistened.
He stitched through white fat.
Weight of pelts and heads. Nodding at the hem.

Feathers. Scales. Beaks and strips of skin.
He had the bounds of a large parish to go.
Oh Christ, he moaned. Sweet Christ.
The Hunter hung stretched in the Sky.
He looked at the creatures of the bankside.
He glistened. He pointed. He stitched.

PETER DIDSBURY

Three Ways of Recovering a Body

By chance I was alone in my bed the morning
I woke to find my body had gone.
It had been coming. I'd cut off my hair in sections
so each of you would have something to remember,
then my nails worked loose from their beds
of oystery flesh. Who was it got them?
One night I slipped out of my skin. It lolloped
hooked to my heels, hurting. I had to spray on
more scent so you could find me in the dark,
I was going so fast. One of you begged for my ears
because you could hear the sea in them.

First I planned to steal myself back. I was a mist
on thighs, belly and hips. I'd slept with so many men.
I was with you in the ash-haunted stations of Poland,
I was with you on that grey plaza in Berlin
while you wolfed three doughnuts without stopping,
thinking yourself alone. Soon I recovered my lips
by waiting behind the mirror while you shaved.
You pouted. I peeled away kisses like wax
no longer warm to the touch. Then I flew off.

Next I decided to become a virgin. Without a body
it was easy to make up a new story. In seven years
every invisible cell would be renewed
and none of them would have touched any of you.
I went to a cold lake, to a grey-lichened island,
I was gold in the wallet of the water.

I was known to the inhabitants, who were in love
with the coveted whisper of my virginity:
all too soon they were bringing me coffee and perfume,
cash under stones. I could really do something for them.

Thirdly I tried marriage to a good husband
who knew my past but forgave it. I believed in the power
of his penis to smoke out all those men
so that bit by bit my body service would resume,
although for a while I'd be the one woman in the world
who was only present in the smile of her vagina.
He stroked the air where I might have been.
I turned to the mirror and saw mist gather
as if someone lived in the glass. Recovering
I breathed to myself, '*Hold on! I'm coming.*'

HELEN DUNMORE

Bride and Groom Lie Hidden for Three Days

She gives him his eyes, she found them
Among some rubble, among some beetles

He gives her her skin
He just seemed to pull it down out of the air and lay it over her
She weeps with fearfulness and astonishment

She has found his hands for him, and fitted them freshly at the
wrists
They are amazed at themselves, they go feeling all over her

He has assembled her spine, he cleaned each piece carefully
And sets them in perfect order
A superhuman puzzle but he is inspired
She leans back twisting this way and that,
using it and laughing, incredulous

Now she has brought his feet, she is connecting them
So that his whole body lights up

And he has fashioned her new hips
With all fittings complete and with newly wound coils, all
                                                    shiningly oiled
He is polishing every part, he himself can hardly believe it

They keep taking each other to the sun, they find they can easily
To test each new thing at each new step

And now she smooths over him the plates of his skull
So that the joints are invisible
And now he connects her throat
                        her breasts and the pit of her stomach
With a single wire

She gives him his teeth, tying their roots
                                    to the centrepin of his body

He sets the little circlets on her fingertips

She stitches his body here and there with steely purple silk

He oils the delicate cogs of her mouth

She inlays with deep-cut scrolls the nape of his neck

He sinks into place the inside of her thighs

So, gasping with joy, with cries of wonderment
Like two gods of mud
Sprawling in the dirt, but with infinite care

They bring each other to perfection.

TED HUGHES

Mushrooms

Overnight, very
Whitely, discreetly,
Very quietly

Our toes, our noses
Take hold on the loam,
Acquire the air.

Nobody sees us,
Stops us, betrays us;
The small grains make room.

Soft fists insist on
Heaving the needles,
The leafy bedding,

Even the paving.
Our hammers, our rams,
Earless and eyeless,

Perfectly voiceless,
Widen the crannies,
Shoulder through holes. We

Diet on water,
On crumbs of shadow,
Bland-mannered, asking

Little or nothing.
So many of us!
So many of us!

We are shelves, we are
Tables, we are meek,
We are edible,

Nudgers and shovers
In spite of ourselves.
Our kind multiplies:

We shall by morning
Inherit the earth.
Our foot's in the door.

SYLVIA PLATH

A Disused Shed in Co. Wexford

Let them not forget us, the weak souls among the asphodels.
SEFERIS, Mythistorema

(for J.G. Farrell)

Even now there are places where a thought might grow –
Peruvian mines, worked out and abandoned
To a slow clock of condensation,
An echo trapped for ever, and a flutter
Of wild flowers in the lift-shaft,
Indian compounds where the wind dances
And a door bangs with diminished confidence,
Lime crevices behind rippling rain-barrels,
Dog corners for bone burials;
And in a disused shed in Co. Wexford,

Deep in the grounds of a burnt-out hotel,
Among the bathtubs and the washbasins
A thousand mushrooms crowd to a keyhole.
This is the one star in their firmament
Or frames a star within a star.
What should they do there but desire?
So many days beyond the rhododendrons
With the world waltzing in its bowl of cloud,
They have learnt patience and silence
Listening to the rooks querulous in the high wood.

They have been waiting for us in a foetor
Of vegetable sweat since civil war days,
Since the gravel-crunching, interminable departure
Of the expropriated mycologist.
He never came back, and light since then
Is a keyhole rusting gently after rain.
Spiders have spun, flies dusted to mildew
And once a day, perhaps, they have heard something –
A trickle of masonry, a shout from the blue
Or a lorry changing gear at the end of the lane.

There have been deaths, the pale flesh flaking
Into the earth that nourished it;
And nightmares, born of these and the grim
Dominion of stale air and rank moisture.

Those nearest the door grow strong –
'Elbow room! Elbow room!'
The rest, dim in a twilight of crumbling
Utensils and broken pitchers, groaning
For their deliverance, have been so long
Expectant that there is left only the posture.

A half century, without visitors, in the dark –
Poor preparation for the cracking lock
And creak of hinges; magi, moonmen,
Powdery prisoners of the old regime,
Web-throated, stalked like triffids, racked by drought
And insomnia, only the ghost of a scream
At the flash-bulb firing-squad we wake them with
Shows there is life yet in their feverish forms.
Grown beyond nature now, soft food for worms,
They lift frail heads in gravity and good faith.

They are begging us, you see, in their wordless way,
To do something, to speak on their behalf
Or at least not to close the door again.
Lost people of Treblinka and Pompeii!
'Save us, save us,' they seem to say,
'Let the god not abandon us
Who have come so far in darkness and in pain.
We too had our lives to live.
You with your light meter and relaxed itinerary,
Let not our naive labours have been in vain!'

DEREK MAHON

Unwittingly

I've visited the place
where thought begins:
pear trees suspended in sunlight, narrow shops,
alleys to nothing

but nettles
and broken wars;
and though it might look different
to you:

a seaside town, with steep roofs
the colour of oysters,
the corner of some junkyard with its glint
of coming rain,

though someone else again would recognise
the warm barn, the smell of milk,
the wintered cattle
shifting in the dark,

it's always the same lit space,
the one good measure:
Sometimes you'll wake in a chair
as the light is fading,

or stop on the way to work
as a current of starlings
turns on itself
and settles above the green,

and because what we learn in the dark
remains all our lives,
a noise like the sea, displacing the day's
pale knowledge,

you'll come to yourself
in a glimmer of rainfall or frost,
the burnt smell of autumn,
a meeting of parallel lines,

and know you were someone else
for the longest time,
pretending you knew where you were, like a diffident tourist,
lost on the one main square, and afraid to enquire.

JOHN BURNSIDE

5

Growing up

Poetry helps us understand common things better...
Poetry will not teach us how to live well,
but it will incite in us the wish to.

DAVID CONSTANTINE

Poetry is the voice of spirit and imagination and all
that is potential, as well as of the healing benevolence
that used to be the privilege of the gods.

TED HUGHES

THE EMBLEMATIC PHRASE chosen by Christabel Bielenberg for her auto-
biography, *The Past Is Myself*, would be equally apt for many books of poetry,
especially those concerned with growing up.

'I can foretell the past' was one of Michael Hartnett's many provocative
pronouncements. He took impish delight in imaginative reversals and duality,
and his poems in English (381) and Irish are both heartbreaking in their honesty
and despair as well as heartwarming in their childlike wonder and questioning.
As a poet, he was unafraid to be both child and man, almost as if he were
daring himself and those who read and judged him to be as naked in the world
as we had entered it; almost inevitably, that same openness extended to drink
and good company, and Hartnett became an alcoholic. Wordsworth was far
more cautious in his self-examination, yet Hartnett's playful paradox isn't so
far from Wordsworth's perspective in 'The Child is the father of the Man'.

The poems in this section are about childhood, memory and how we see
the past. Many poets have written about growing up, about their own child-
hood and their own children. They relive their pasts in poems exploring
early relationships with parents and other influential relatives, trying to make
connections which have meaning and resonance for them now. They also write
about themselves as adults and about the lives of their children, sometimes in
response to difficult times.

Ken Smith grew up in the North Riding of Yorkshire, the son of an itin-
erant farm labourer, and his poem 'Being the third song of Urias' (171) is
written from both these perspectives, evoking the boy back in the raw land-
scape of his childhood as well as the grown-up man looking back at his life,

examining his feelings of separation from the inarticulate, unloving father he has sought to understand in this and other poems. This section includes a number of poems in which writers attempt to come to terms with what is lost and gained in the formative years of childhood, and about how we are formed by our parents, as in Philip Larkin's much quoted 'This Be the Verse' (205) and Caitríona O'Reilly's 'Possession' (205).

The poems about pregnancy and childbirth (172-83) include some about the difficulties involved. Kona Macphee's 'IVF' (178) is a sestina (see Glossary, 469), a form in which strictly ordered rhyme words emphasise key elements in a poem's argument, in this case a woman's lack of control over her situation. The poem's unchangeable structure enacts the tyranny of infertility.

In her two poems (181-82), Sharon Olds evokes the miracle of birth as well as the vulnerability of the newborn child, while Gavin Ewart (184) and Ellen Bryant Voigt (185) write sharply contrasting poems about a son and a daughter who nearly die, each of these very short poems taking the reader through the heart-stopping drama of threat and survival. In Anne Stevenson's 'Poem for a Daughter', the baby is the 'heart's needle', the same phrase taken by W.D. Snodgrass for his sequence *Heart's Needle* (186), about the separation of a divorced father from a much loved daughter.

Julia Copus's 'The Back Seat of My Mother's Car' (202) is a *specular* poem, a form invented by her 'where the second half unfolds mirror-like from the first, using the same lines but in reverse order. The result of this discipline should be no more mechanical than a good sonnet or fugue.' She wrote of this and another specular poem about familial love that the form 'echoes the way my mind remembered these two traumas at the time of writing, replaying events until the precise sequence of them became obscured'.

The interplay of thought and feeling may be set off through a formal structure, but the poet's chosen difficulty – an integral part of the poem's conception – may be to make the diction so apparently casual that at first the reader fails to notice that the poem is intricately structured, often using unexpected half-rhymes, as in Paul Muldoon's 'Quoof' (213), which does not proclaim itself as a sonnet, and yet works as one (chiming 'breast' with 'beast', 'City' with 'yeti'). Similarly, it is not immediately apparent that Randall Jarrell's 'A Night with Lions' uses the chain-rhyme scheme of terza rima (see Glossary, 467), though not the tercet stanza arrangement which would make the form more obvious. The poem is from *The Lost World*, a sequence recalling his childhood, the second of three poems using the terza rima rhyme scheme, a form helpful for extended narrative which gives the series a strong sense of continuity. Dante used it for *The Divine Comedy* and Shelley in his 'Ode to the West Wind'.

Many of Jarrell's poems return to his Lost World of childhood, exploring the nature of memory and the past. These are triggered by the bitter smell of the herb Lad's-love in Edward Thomas's poem 'Old Man' (209), just as Proust's famous madeleine prompts his own remembrance of times past. Names are part of the act of remembering. In Thomas's poem, and those by Billy Collins (214) and W.S. Merwin (215), loss of memory is linked to loss of name and loss of identity.

Being the third song of Urias

Lives ago, years past generations
perhaps nowhere I dreamed it:
the foggy ploughland of wind
and hoofprints, my father
off in the mist topping beets.

Where I was eight, I knew nothing,
the world a cold winter light
on half a dozen fields, then
all the winking blether of stars.

Before like a fool I began
explaining the key in its lost locked box
adding words to the words to the sum
that never works out.

         Where I was
distracted again by the lapwing,
the damp morning air of my father's
gregarious plainchant cursing
all that his masters deserved
and had paid for.
        Sure I was
then for the world's mere being
in the white rime on weeds
among the wet hawthorn berries
at the field's edge darkened by frost,
and none of these damned words to say it.

I began trailing out there in voices,
friends, women, my children,
my father's tetherless anger, some
like him who are dead who are
part of the rain now.

KEN SMITH

White Asparagus

Who speaks of the strong currents
streaming through the legs, the breasts
of a pregnant woman
in her fourth month?

She's young, this is her first time,
she's slim and the nausea has gone.
Her belly's just starting to get rounder
her breasts itch all day,

and she's surprised that what she wants
is *him*
   inside her again.
Oh come like a horse, she wants to say,
move like a dog, a wolf,
        become a suckling lion-cub –

Come here, and here, and here –
but swim fast and don't stop.

Who speaks of the green coconut uterus
the muscles sliding, a deeper undertow
and the green coconut milk that seals
her well, yet flows so she is wet
from his softest touch?

Who understands the logic
behind this desire?
Who speaks of the rushing tide
      that awakens
her slowly increasing blood – ?
And the hunger
     raw obsessions beginning
with the shape of asparagus:
sun-deprived white and purple-shadow-veined,
she buys three kilos
of the fat ones, thicker than anyone's fingers,
she strokes the silky heads,
some are so jauntily capped...
     even the smell pulls her in –

SUJATA BHATT

It's Good To Be Here

I'm in trouble, she said
to him. That was the first
time in history that anyone
had ever spoken of me.

It was 1932 when she
was just fourteen years old
and men like him
worked all day for
one stinking dollar.

There's quinine, she said.
That's bullshit, he told her.

Then she cried and then
for a long time neither of them
said anything at all and then
their voices kept rising until
they were screaming at each other
and then there was another long silence and then
they began to talk very quietly and at last he said
well, I guess we'll just have to make the best of it.

While I lay curled up,
my heart beating,
in the darkness inside her.

ALDEN NOWLAN

Ultrasound
(for Duncan)

I *Ultrasound*

Oh whistle and I'll come to ye,
my lad, my wee shilpit ghost
summonsed from tomorrow.

Second sight,
a seer's mothy flicker,
an inner sprite:

this is what I see
with eyes closed;
a keek-aboot among secrets.

If Pandora
could have scanned
her dark box,

and kept it locked –
this ghoul's skull, punched eyes
is tiny Hope's,

hauled silver-quick
in a net of sound,
then, for pity's sake, lowered.

II *Solstice*

To whom do I talk, an unborn thou,
sleeping in a bone creel.

Look what awaits you:
stars, milk-bottles, frost
on a broken outhouse roof

Let's close the door,
and rearrange
the dark red curtain.

Can you tell the days are opening,
admit a touch more light,
just a touch more?

III *Thaw*

When we brought you home in a taxi
through the steel-grey thaw
after the coldest week in memory
– even the river sealed itself –
it was I, hardly breathing,
who came through the passage to our yard
welcoming our simplest things:
a chopping block, the frost-
split lintels; and though it meant a journey
through darkening snow,
arms laden with you in a blanket,
I had to walk to the top of the garden,
to touch, in a complicit
homage of equals, the spiral
trunks of our plum trees, the moss,
the robin's roost in the holly.
Leaning back on the railway wall,
I tried to remember;
but even my footprints were being erased
and the rising stars of Orion
denied what I knew: that as we were
hurled on a trolley through swing doors to theatre
they'd been there, aligned on the ceiling,
      ablaze with concern
for that difficult giving,
before we were two, from my one.

IV *February*

To the heap of nappies
carried from the automatic
in a red plastic basket

to the hanging out, my mouth
crowded with pegs;
to the notched prop

hoisting the wash,
a rare flight of swans,
hills still courying snow;

to spring's hint sailing
the westerly, snowdrops
sheltered by rowans –

to the day of St Bride, the first
sweet-wild weeks of your life
I willingly surrender.

v *Bairnsang*

Wee toshie man,
          gean tree and rowan
gif ye could staun
yer feet wad lichtsome tread
granite an saun,
but ye cannae yet staun
sae maun courie tae ma airm
an greetna, girna, Gretna Green

Peedie wee lad
          saumon, siller haddie
gin ye could rin
ye'd rin richt easy-strang
ower causey an carse,
but ye cannae yet rin
sae maun jist courie in
and fashna, fashna, Macrahanish Sand

Bonny wee boy
          peeswheep an whaup
gin ye could sing, yer sang
wad be caller
as a lauchin mountain burn
but ye cannae yet sing
sae maun courie tae ma hert
an grieve nat at aa, Ainster an Crail

My ain tottie bairn
      sternie an lift
gin ye could daunce, yer daunce
wad be that o life itsel,
but ye cannae yet daunce
sae maun courie in my erms
and sleep, saftly sleep, Unst and Yell

VI *Sea Urchin*

Between my breast
and cupped hand,
        your head

rests as tenderly
as once I may
        have freighted

water, or drawn
treasure, whole
        from a rockpool

with no premonition
of when next I find one
cast up
        broken.

VII *Prayer*

Our baby's heart, on the sixteen-week scan
was a fluttering bird, held in cupped hands.

I thought of St Kevin, hands opened in prayer
and a bird of the hedgerow nesting there,

and how he'd borne it, until the young had flown
– and I prayed: this new heart must outlive my own.

KATHLEEN JAMIE

177

Safe period

Your dry voice from the centre of the bed
asks 'Is it safe?'

and I answer for the days as if I owned them.
Practised at counting, I rock
the two halves of the month like a cradle.

The days slip over their stile
and expect nothing. They are just days,

and we're at it again, thwarting
souls from the bodies they crave.

They'd love to get into this room
under the yellow counterpane
we've torn to make a child's cuddly,

they'd love to slide into the sheets
between soft, much-washed
flannelette fleece,

they'd love to be here in the moulded spaces
between us, where there is no room,

but we don't let them. They fly about gustily,
noisy as our own children.

HELEN DUNMORE

IVF

I come home early, feel the pale house close
around me as the pressure of my blood
knocks at my temples, feel it clench me in
its cramping grasp, the fierceness of its quiet
sanctioning the small and listless hope
that I might find it mercifully empty.

Dazed, I turn the taps to fill the empty
tub, and draw the bathroom door to close
behind me. I lie unmoving, feel all hope
leaching from between my legs as blood
tinges the water, staining it the quiet
shade of a winter evening drifting in

on sunset. Again, no shoot of life sprouts in
this crumbling womb that wrings itself to empty
out the painfully-planted seeds. The quiet
doctors, tomorrow, will check their notes and close
the file, wait for the hormones in my blood
to augur further chances, more false hope.

My husband holds to patience, I to hope,
and yet our clockworks are unwinding. In
the stillness of the house, we hear our blood
pumped by hearts that gall themselves, grow empty:
once, this silence, shared, could draw us close
that now forebodes us with a desperate quiet.

I hear him at the door, but I lay quiet,
as if, by saying nothing, I may hope
that somehow his unknowingness may close
a door on all the darkness we've let in:
the nursery that's seven years too empty;
the old, unyielding stains of menstrual blood.

Perhaps I wish the petitioning of my blood
for motherhood might falter and fall quiet,
perhaps I wish that we might choose to empty
our lives of disappointment, and of hope,
but wishes founder – we go on living in
the shadow of the cliffs now looming close:

the blood that's thick with traitorous clots of hope;
the quiet knack we've lost, of giving in;
the empty room whose door we cannot close.

KONA MACPHEE

Miscarriage

The womb refused,
backed up,
its particles of silk
wasted, perish.
Breathless –
the cloudy silo,
the yolk sea.

In the ceremony
of lifting
and enclosing
the womb refused.
The ceremony of no-child
followed.

On either side
its ostrich neck
its camel neck
wavered,
swallowed the high
midnight.

The womb held back.
It had an eye
for sand,
spread its cool
oranges and reds
on dry land,

and bright
and fierce
as a lair,
the womb bear-hugged
its dead,
and let go.

JANE DURAN

Freight

I am the ship in which you sail,
little dancing bones,
your passage between the dream
and the waking dream,
your sieve, your pea-green boat.
I'll pay whatever toll your ferry needs.
And you, whose history's already charted
in a rope of cells, be tender to
those other unnamed vessels
who will surprise you one day,
tug-tugging, irresistible,
and float you out beyond your depth,
where you'll look down, puzzled, amazed.

MAURA DOOLEY

First Birth

I had thought so little, really, of *her*,
inside me, all that time, not breathing –
intelligent, maybe curious,
her eyes closed. When the vagina opened,
slowly, from within, from the top, my eyes
rounded in shock and awe, it was like being
entered for the first time, but entered
from the inside, the child coming in
from the other world. Enormous, stately,
she was pressed through the channel, she turned, and rose,
they held her up by a very small ankle,
she dangled indigo and scarlet, and spread
her arms out in this world. Each thing
I did, then, I did for the first
time, touched the flesh of our flesh,
brought the tiny mouth to my breast,

she drew the avalanche of milk
down off the mountain, I felt as if
I was nothing, no one, I was everything to her, I was hers.

SHARON OLDS

Her First Week

She was so small I would scan the crib a half-second
to find her, face-down in a corner, limp
as something gently flung down, or fallen
from some sky an inch above the mattress. I would
tuck her arm along her side
and slowly turn her over. She would tumble
over part by part, like a load
of damp laundry in the dryer, I'd slip
a hand in, under her neck,
slide the other under her back,
and evenly lift her up. Her little bottom
sat in my palm, her chest contained
the puckered, moire sacs, and her neck –
I was afraid of her neck, once I almost
thought I heard it quietly snap,
I looked at her and she swivelled her slate
eyes and looked at me. It was in
my care, the creature of her spine, like the first
chordate, as if, history
of the vertebrate had been placed in my hands.
Every time I checked, she was still
with us – someday, there would be a human
race. I could not see it in her eyes,
but when I fed her, gathered her
like a loose bouquet to my side and offered
the breast, greyish-white, and struck with
minuscule scars like creeks in sunlight, I
felt she was serious, I believed she was willing to stay.

SHARON OLDS

The Spirit is too Blunt an Instrument

The spirit is too blunt an instrument
to have made this baby.
Nothing so unskilful as human passions
could have managed the intricate
exacting particulars: the tiny
blind bones with their manipulating tendons,
the knee and the knucklebones, the resilient
fine meshings of ganglia and vertebrae
in the chain of the difficult spine.

Observe the distinct cyclashes and sharp crescent
fingernails, the shell-like complexity
of the ear with its firm involutions
concentric in miniature to the minute
ossicles. Imagine the
infinitesimal capillaries, the flawless connections
of the lungs, the invisible neural filaments
through which the completed body
already answers to the brain.

Then name any passion or sentiment
possessed of the simplest accuracy.
No. No desire or affection could have done
with practice what habit
has done perfectly, indifferently,
through the body's ignorant precision.
It is left to the vagaries of the mind to invent
love and despair and anxiety
and their pain.

ANNE STEVENSON

Sonnet: How Life Too Is Sentimental

When our son was a few weeks old he had bronchial trouble
and picked up a cross-infection in the hospital
(salmonella typhimurium) through sluttish feeding –
but a hospital never admits it's responsible –
and was rushed away behind glass in an isolation ward,
at the point, it might be, of death. Our daughter,
eighteen months old, was just tall enough
to look into his empty cot and say: 'Baby gone!'

A situation, an action and a speech
so tear-jerking that Dickens might have thought of them –
and indeed, in life, when we say 'It couldn't happen!'
almost at once it happens. And the word "sentimental"
has come to mean exaggerated feeling.
It would have been hard to exaggerate *our* feelings then.

GAVIN EWART

Poem for a Daughter

'I think I'm going to have it,'
I said, joking between pains.
The midwife rolled competent
sleeves over corpulent milky arms.
'Dear, you never have it,
we deliver it.'
A judgement years proved true.
Certainly I've never had you

as you still have me, Caroline.
Why does a mother need a daughter?
Heart's needle, hostage to fortune,
freedom's end. Yet nothing's more perfect
than that bleating, razor-shaped cry
that delivers a mother to her baby.
The bloodcord snaps that held
their sphere together. The child,
tiny and alone, creates the mother.

A woman's life is her own
until it is taken away
by a first particular cry.
Then she is not alone
but part of the premises
of everything there is:
a time, a tribe, a war.
When we belong to the world
we become what we are.

ANNE STEVENSON

Daughter

There is one grief worse than any other.

When your small feverish throat clogged, and quit,
I knelt beside the chair on the green rug
and shook you and shook you,
but the only sound was mine shouting you back,
the delicate curls at your temples,
the blue wool blanket,
your face blue,
your jaw clamped against remedy –

how could I put a knife to that white neck?
With you in my lap,
my hands fluttering like flags,
I bend instead over your dead weight
to administer a kiss so urgent, so ruthless,
pumping breath into your stilled body,
counting out the rhythm for how long until
the second birth, the second cry
oh Jesus that sudden noisy musical inhalation
that leaves me stunned
by your survival.

ELLEN BRYANT VOIGT

Beattie Is Three

At the top of the stairs
I ask for her hand. O.K.
She gives it to me.
How her fist fits my palm,
A bunch of consolation.
We take our time
Down the steep carpetway
As I wish silently
That the stairs were endless.

ADRIAN MITCHELL

from Heart's Needle
(for Cynthia)

Child of my winter, born
When the new fallen soldiers froze
In Asia's steep ravines and fouled the snows,
When I was torn

By love I could not still,
By fear that silenced my cramped mind
To that cold war where, lost, I could not find
My peace in my will,

All those days we could keep
Your mind a landscape of new snow
Where the chilled tenant-farmer finds, below,
His fields asleep

In their smooth covering, white
As quilts to warm the resting bed
Of birth or pain, spotless as paper spread
For me to write,

And thinks: Here lies my land
Unmarked by agony, the lean foot
Of the weasel tracking, the thick trapper's boot;
And I have planned

My chances to restrain
The torments of demented summer or
Increase the deepening harvest here before
It snows again.
[...]

Love's wishbone, child, although I've gone
As men must and let you be drawn
   Off to appease another,
It may help that a Chinese play
Or Solomon himself might say
   I am your real mother.

*

   No one can tell you why
the season will not wait;
   the night I told you I
must leave, you wept a fearful rate
     to stay up late.

   Now that it's turning Fall,
we go to take our walk
   among municipal
flowers, to steal one off its stalk,
     to try and talk.
[...]

Winter again and it is snowing;
Although you are still three,
You are already growing
Strange to me.

You chatter about new playmates, sing
Strange songs; you do not know
Hey ding-a-ding-a-ding
Or where I go

Or when I sang for bedtime, *Fox*
Went out on a chilly night,
Before I went for walks
And did not write;

187

You never mind the squalls and storms
That are renewed long since;
Outside the thick snow swarms
Into my prints

And swirls out by warehouses, sealed,
Dark cowbarns, huddled, still,
Beyond to the blank field,
The fox's hill

Where he backtracks and sees the paw,
Gnawed off, he cannot feel;
Conceded to the jaw
Of toothed, blue steel.
[...]

    You raise into my head
  Fall night that I came once more
      to sit on your bed;
  sweat beads stood out on your arms and fore-
      head and you wheezed for breath,
  for help, like some child caught beneath
its comfortable woolly blankets, drowning there.
  Your lungs caught and would not take the air.

    Of all things, only we
  have power to choose that we should die;
    nothing else is free
  in this world to refuse it. Yet I,
    who say this, could not raise
  myself from bed how many days
to the thieving world. Child, I have another wife,
  another child. We try to choose our life.

*

Here in the scuffled dust
  is our ground of play.
I lift you on your swing and must
  shove you away,
see you return again,
  drive you off again, then

stand quiet till you come.
   You, though you climb
higher, farther from me, longer,
   will fall back to me stronger.
Bad penny, pendulum,
   you keep my constant time

to bob in blue July
   where fat goldfinches fly
over the glittering, fecund
   reach of our growing lands.
Once more now, this second,
   I hold you in my hands.
[...]

   I get numb and go in
though the dry ground will not hold
   the few dry swirls of snow
and it must not be very cold.
A friend asks how you've been
      and I don't know

   or see much right to ask.
Or what use it could be to know.
   In three months since you came
the leaves have fallen and the snow;
your pictures pinned above my desk
      seem much the same.
[...]

   The window's turning white.
The world moves like a diseased heart
   packed with ice and snow.
Three months now we have been apart
less than a mile. I cannot fight
      or let you go.

*

The vicious winter finally yields
   the green winter wheat;
the farmer, tired in the tired fields
   he dare not leave, will eat.

Once more the runs come fresh; prevailing
      piglets, stout as jugs,
harry their old sow to the railing
      to ease her swollen dugs

and game colts trail the herded mares
      that circle the pasture courses;
our seasons bring us back once more
      like merry-go-round horses.

With crocus mouths, perennial hungers,
      into the park Spring comes;
we roast hot dogs on old coat hangers
      and feed the swan bread crumbs,

pay our respects to the peacocks, rabbits,
      and leathery Canada goose
who took, last Fall, our tame white habits
      and now will not turn loose.

In full regalia, the pheasant cocks
      march past their dubious hens;
the porcupine and the lean, red fox
      trot around bachelor pens

and the miniature painted train
      wails on its oval track:
you said, I'm going to Pennsylvania!
      and waved. And you've come back.

If I loved you, they said I'd leave
      and find my own affairs.
Well, once again this April, we've
      come around to the bears;

punished and cared for, behind bars,
      the coons on bread and water
stretch thin black fingers after ours.
      And you are still my daughter.

W.D. SNODGRASS

Supernatural Love

My father at the dictionary-stand
Touches the page to fully understand
The lamplit answer, tilting in his hand

His slowly scanning magnifying lens,
A blurry, glistening circle he suspends
Above the word 'Carnation'. Then he bends

So near his eyes are magnified and blurred,
One finger on the miniature word,
As if he touched a single key and heard

A distant, plucked, infinitesimal string,
'The obligation due to every thing
That's smaller than the universe.' I bring

My sewing needle close enough that I
Can watch my father through the needle's eye,
As through a lens ground for a butterfly

Who peers down flower-hallways toward a room
Shadowed and fathomed as this study's gloom
Where, as a scholar bends above a tomb

To read what's buried there, he bends to pore
Over the Latin blossom. I am four,
I spill my pins and needles on the floor

Trying to stitch 'Beloved' X by X.
My dangerous, bright needle's point connects
Myself illiterate to this perfect text

I cannot read. My father puzzles why
It is my habit to identify
Carnations as 'Christ's flowers', knowing I

Can give no explanation but 'Because'.
Word-roots blossom in speechless messages
The way the thread behind my sampler does

Where following each X I awkward move
My needle through the word whose root is love.
He reads, 'A pink variety of Clove,

Carnatio, the Latin, meaning flesh.'
As if the bud's essential oils brush
Christ's fragrance through the room, the iron-fresh

Odor carnations have floats up to me,
A drifted, secret, bitter ecstasy,
The stems squeak in my scissors, *Child, it's me*,

He turns the page to 'Clove' and reads aloud:
'The clove, a spice, dried from a flower-bud.'
Then twice, as if he hasn't understood,

He reads, 'From French, for *clou*, meaning a nail.'
He gazes, motionless. 'Meaning a nail.'
The incarnation blossoms, flesh and nail,

I twist my threads like stems into a knot
And smooth 'Beloved', but my needle caught
Within the threads, *Thy blood so dearly bought*,

The needle strikes my finger to the bone.
I lift my hand, it is myself I've sewn,
The flesh laid bare, the threads of blood my own,

I lift my hand in startled agony
And call upon his name, 'Daddy Daddy' –
My father's hand touches the injury

As lightly as he touched the page before,
Where incarnation bloomed from roots that bore
The flowers I called Christ's when I was four.

GJERTRUD SCHNACKENBERG

Poem from a Three Year Old

And will the flowers die?

And will the people die?

And every day do you grow old, do I
grow old, no I'm not old, do
flowers grow old?

Old things – do you throw them out?

Do you throw old people out?

And how you know a flower that's old?

The petals fall, the petals fall from flowers,
and do the petals fall from people too,
every day more petals fall until the
floor where I would like to play I
want to play is covered with old
flowers and people all the same
together lying there with petals fallen
on the dirty floor I want to play
the floor you come and sweep
with the huge broom.

The dirt you sweep, what happens that,
what happens all the dirt you sweep
from flowers and people, what
happens all the dirt? Is all the
dirt what's left of flowers and
people, all the dirt there in a
heap under the huge broom that
sweeps everything away?

Why you work so hard, why brush
and sweep to make a heap of dirt?
And who will bring new flowers?
And who will bring new people? Who will
bring new flowers to put in water
where no petals fall on to the

floor where I would like to
play? Who will bring new flowers
that will not hang their heads
like tired old people wanting sleep?
Who will bring new flowers that
do not split and shrivel every
day? And if we have new flowers,
will we have new people too to
keep the flowers alive and give
them water?

And will the new young flowers die?

And will the new young people die?

And why?

BRENDAN KENNELLY

Cinders

After the pantomime, carrying you back to the car
On the coldest night of the year
My coat, black leather, cracking in the wind.

Through the darkness we are guided by a star.
It is the one the Good Fairy gave you
You clutch it tightly, your magic wand.

And I clutch you tightly for fear you blow away
For fear you grow up too soon and – suddenly,
I almost slip, so take it steady down the hill.

Hunched against the wind and hobbling
I could be mistaken for your grandfather
And sensing this, I hold you tighter still.

Knowing that I will never see you dressed for the Ball
Be on hand to warn you against Prince Charmings
And the happy ever afters of pantomime.

On reaching the car I put you into the baby seat
And fumble with straps I have yet to master
Thinking, if only there were more time. More time.

You are crying now. Where is your wand?
Oh no. I can't face going back for it,
Let some kid find it in tomorrow's snow.

Waiting in the wings, the witching hour,
Already the car is changing. Smells sweet
Of ripening seed. We must go. Must go.

ROGER McGOUGH

A Sword in a Cloud of Light

Your hand in mine, we walk out
To watch the Christmas Eve crowds
On Fillmore Street, the Negro
District. The night is thick with
Frost. The people hurry, wreathed
In their smoky breaths. Before
The shop windows the children
Jump up and down with spangled
Eyes. Santa Clauses ring bells.
Cars stall and honk. Street cars clang.
Loud speakers on the lampposts
Sing carols, on juke boxes
In the bars Louis Armstrong
Plays *White Christmas*. In the joints
The girls strip and grind and bump
To *Jingle Bells*. Overhead
The neon signs scribble and
Erase and scribble again
Messages of avarice,
Joy, fear, hygiene, and the proud
Names of the middle classes.
The moon beams like a pudding.
We stop at the main corner

And look up, diagonally
Across, at the rising moon,
And the solemn, orderly
Vast winter constellations.
You say, 'There's Orion!'
The most beautiful object
Either of us will ever
Know in the world or in life
Stands in the moonlit empty
Heavens, over the swarming
Men, women, and children, black
And white, joyous and greedy,
Evil and good, buyer and
Seller, master and victim,
Like some immense theorem,
Which, if once solved would forever
Solve the mystery and pain
Under the bells and spangles.
There he is, the man of the
Night before Christmas, spread out
On the sky like a true god
In whom it would only be
Necessary to believe
A little. I am fifty
And you are five. It would do
No good to say this and it
May do no good to write it.
Believe in Orion. Believe
In the night, the moon, the crowded
Earth. Believe in Christmas and
Birthdays and Easter rabbits.
Believe in all those fugitive
Compounds of nature, all doomed
To waste away and go out.
Always be true to these things.
They are all there is. Never
Give up this savage religion
For the blood-drenched civilised
Abstractions of the rascals
Who live by killing you and me.

KENNETH REXROTH

On the Back of a Photograph

Hunched I make my way, uncertainly.
The other hand is only three years old.
An eighty-year-old hand and a three-year-old.
We hold each other. We hold each other tight.

JÁNOS PILINSZKY
translated from the Hungarian by Peter Jay

The Video

When Laura was born, Ceri watched.
They all gathered around Mum's bed –
Dad and the midwife and Mum's sister
and Ceri. 'Move over a bit,' Dad said –
he was trying to focus the camcorder
on Mum's legs and the baby's head.

After she had a little sister,
and Mum had gone back to being thin,
and was twice as busy, Ceri played
the video again and again.
She watched Laura come out, and then,
in reverse, she made her go back in.

FLEUR ADCOCK

Young Girls

Nothing, not even fear of punishment
can stop the giggle in a girl.
Oh, mothers' trim
shapes on the chesterfield cannot dispel
their lolloping fatness.
Adolescence tumbles about in them
on the cinder schoolyard or behind the expensive gates.

See them in class like porpoises
with smiles and tears
loosed from the same subterranean faucet; some
find individual adventure in
the obtuse angle, some in a phrase
that leaps like a smaller fish from a sea of words.
But most, deep in their daze, dawdle and roll;
their little breasts like wounds beneath their clothes.

A shoal of them in a room makes it a pool.
How can one teacher keep the water out,
or, being adult, find the springs and taps
of their tempers and tortures?
Who, on a field filled with their female cries
can reel them in on a line of words
or land them neatly in a net?
On the dry ground they goggle, flounder, flap.

Too much weeping in them and unfamiliar blood
has set them perilously afloat.
Not divers these – but as if the waters rose in flood –
making them partially amphibious
and always drowning a little and hearing bells;
until the day the shoreline wavers less,
and caught and swung on the bright hooks of their sex,
earth becomes home – their natural element.

P.K. PAGE

A Puppy Called Puberty

It was like keeping a puppy in your underpants
A secret puppy you weren't allowed to show to anyone
Not even your best friend or your worst enemy

You wanted to pat him stroke him cuddle him
All the time but you weren't supposed to touch him

He only slept for five minutes at a time
Then he'd suddenly perk up his head

In the middle of school medical inspection
And always on bus rides

So you had to climb down from the upper deck
All bent double to smuggle the puppy off the bus
Without the buxom conductress spotting
Your wicked and ticketless stowaway.

Jumping up, wet-nosed, eagerly wagging –
He only stopped being a nuisance
When you were alone together
Pretending to be doing your homework
But really gazing at each other
Through hot and hazy daydreams

Of those beautiful schoolgirls on the bus
With kittens bouncing in their sweaters.

ADRIAN MITCHELL

A Dog Called Elderly

And now I have a dog called Elderly
And all he ever wants to do
Is now and then be let out for a piss
But spend the rest of his lifetime
Sleeping on my lap in front of the fire.

ADRIAN MITCHELL

Cuba

My eldest sister arrived home that morning
In her white muslin evening dress.
'Who the hell do you think you are,
Running out to dances in next to nothing?
As though we hadn't enough bother
With the world at war, if not at an end.'
My father was pounding the breakfast-table.

'Those Yankees were touch and go as it was –
If you'd heard Patton in Armagh –
But this Kennedy's nearly an Irishman
So he's not much better than ourselves.
And him with only to say the word.
If you've got anything on your mind
Maybe you should make your peace with God.'

I could hear May from beyond the curtain.
'Bless me, Father, for I have sinned.
I told a lie once, I was disobedient once.
And, Father, a boy touched me once.'
'Tell me, child. Was this touch immodest?
Did he touch your breast, for example?'
'He brushed against me, Father. Very gently.'

PAUL MULDOON

My Flu

I'd swear blind it's June, 1962.
Oswald's back from Minsk. U2s glide over Cuba.
My cousin's in Saigon. My father's in bed
with my mother. I'm eight and in bed with my flu.
I'd *swear*, but I can't be recalling this sharp reek of Vicks,
the bedroom's fevered wallpaper, the neighbour's TV,
the rain, the tyres' hiss through rain, the rain smell.
This would never stand up in court – I'm asleep.

I'm curled up, shivering, fighting to wake,
but I can't turn my face from the pit in the woods
– snow filling the broken suitcases, a boy curled up,
like me, as if asleep, except he has no eyes.
One of my father's stories from the war
has got behind my face and filmed itself:
the village written off the map, its only witnesses
marched to the trees. Now all the birds fly up at once.

And who filmed *this* for us, a boy asleep in 1962,
his long-forgotten room, his flu, this endless rain,
the skewed fan rattling, the shouts next door?
My fever reaches 104. But suddenly he's here,
I'd swear, all round me, his hand beneath my head
until one world rings truer than the other.

MICHAEL DONAGHY

'We were so poor...'

We were so poor I had to take the place of the bait in the mousetrap.
All alone in the cellar, I could hear them pacing upstairs, tossing
and turning in their beds. 'These are dark and evil days,' the mouse
told me as he nibbled my ear. Years passed. My mother wore a
cat-fur collar which she stroked until its sparks lit up the cellar.

CHARLES SIMIC

Those Winter Sundays

Sundays too my father got up early
and put his clothes on in the blueblack cold,
then with cracked hands that ached
from labor in the weekday weather made
banked fires blaze. No one ever thanked him.

I'd wake and hear the cold splintering, breaking.
When the rooms were warm, he'd call,
and slowly I would rise and dress,
fearing the chronic angers of that house,

Speaking indifferently to him,
who had driven out the cold
and polished my good shoes as well.
What did I know, what did I know
of love's austere and lonely offices?

ROBERT HAYDEN

The Back Seat of My Mother's Car

We left before I had time
to comfort you, to tell you that we nearly touched
hands in that vacuous half-dark. I wanted
to stem the burning waters running over me like tiny
rivers down my face and legs, but at the same time I was reaching out
for the slit in the window where the sky streamed in,
cold as ether, and I could see your fat mole-fingers grasping
the dusty August air. I pressed my face to the glass;
I was calling to you – *Daddy!* – as we screeched away into
the distance, my own hand tingling like an amputation.
You were mouthing something I still remember, the noiseless words
piercing me like that catgut shriek that flew up, furious as a sunset
pouring itself out against the sky. The ensuing silence
was the one clear thing I could decipher –
the roar of the engine drowning your voice,
with the cool slick glass between us.

With the cool slick glass between us,
the roar of the engine drowning, your voice
was the one clear thing I could decipher –
pouring itself out against the sky, the ensuing silence
piercing me like that catgut shriek that flew up, furious as a sunset.
You were mouthing something: I still remember the noiseless words,
the distance, my own hand tingling like an amputation.
I was calling to you, Daddy, as we screeched away into
the dusty August air. I pressed my face to the glass,
cold as ether, and I could see your fat mole-fingers grasping
for the slit in the window where the sky streamed in
rivers down my face and legs, but at the same time I was reaching out
to stem the burning waters running over me like tiny
hands in that vacuous half-dark. I wanted
to comfort you, to tell you that we nearly touched.
We left before I had time.

JULIA COPUS

Mirror Image

Tonight I saw myself in the dark window as
the image of my father, whose life
was spent like this,
thinking of death, to the exclusion
of other sensual matters, so in the end that life
was easy to give up, since
it contained nothing: even
my mother's voice couldn't make him
change or turn back
as he believed
that once you can't love another human being
you have no place in the world.

LOUISE GLÜCK

Mirror

I am silver and exact. I have no preconceptions.
Whatever I see I swallow immediately
Just as it is, unmisted by love or dislike.
I am not cruel, only truthful –
The eye of a little god, four-cornered.
Most of the time I meditate on the opposite wall.
It is pink, with speckles. I have looked at it so long
I think it is a part of my heart. But it flickers.
Faces and darkness separate us over and over.

Now I am a lake. A woman bends over me,
Searching my reaches for what she really is.
Then she turns to those liars, the candles or the moon.
I see her back, and reflect it faithfully.
She rewards me with tears and an agitation of hands.
I am important to her. She comes and goes.
Each morning it is her face that replaces the darkness.
In me she has drowned a young girl, and in me an old woman
Rises toward her day after day, like a terrible fish.

SYLVIA PLATH

Father's Old Blue Cardigan

Now it hangs on the back of the kitchen chair
where I always sit, as it did
on the back of the kitchen chair where he always sat.

I put it on whenever I come in,
as he did, stamping
the snow from his boots.

I put it on and sit in the dark.
He would not have done this.
Coldness comes paring down from the moonbone in the sky.

His laws were a secret.
But I remember the moment at which I knew
he was going mad inside his laws.

He was standing at the turn of the driveway when I arrived.
He had on the blue cardigan with the buttons done up all the way
        to the top.
Not only because it was a hot July afternoon

but the look on his face –
as a small child who has been dressed by some aunt early in the
        morning
for a long trip

on cold trains and windy platforms
will sit very straight at the edge of his seat
while the shadows like long fingers

over the haystacks that sweep past
keep shocking him
because he is riding backwards.

ANNE CARSON

This Be the Verse

They fuck you up, your mum and dad.
    They may not mean to, but they do.
They fill you with the faults they had
    And add some extra, just for you.

But they were fucked up in their turn
    By fools in old-style hats and coats,
Who half the time were soppy-stern
    And half at one another's throats.

Man hands on misery to man.
    It deepens like a coastal shelf.
Get out as early as you can,
    And don't have any kids yourself.

PHILIP LARKIN

Possession

That anxious way you have of closing doors
(like the brown of your eyes and hair)
was never really yours.
My arms and elongated nose were owned before –
fragments of jigsaw
in the rough art of assemblage whose end we are.

Sometimes I don't know where we live
or whose voice I still
hear and remember
inside my head at night. In darkness and in love
we are dismembered,
so that the fact of our coming to at all

becomes a morning miracle. Let's number
our fingers and toes again.
Do I love you piecemeal
when I see in your closing hand a valve-flower
like a sea-anemone,
or is it our future I remember, as the White Queen

remembered her pinpricked finger? All of you
that's to be known
resides in that small gesture.
And though our days consist of letting go –
since neither one can own
the other – what still deepens pulls us back together.

CAITRÍONA O'REILLY

A Night with Lions

When I was twelve we'd visit my aunt's friend
Who owned a lion, the Metro-Goldwyn-Mayer
Lion. I'd play with him, and he'd pretend
To play with me. I was the real player
But he'd trot back and forth inside his cage
Till he got bored. I put Tawny in the prayer
I didn't believe in, not at my age,
But said still; just as I did everything in fours
And gave to Something, on the average,
One cookie out of three. And by my quartz, my ores,
My wood with the bark on it, from the Petrified
Forest, I put his dewclaw...
                              Now the lion roars
His slow comfortable roars; I lie beside
My young, tall, brown aunt, out there in the past
Or future, and I sleepily confide
My dream-discovery: my breath comes fast
Whenever I see someone with your skin,
Hear someone with your voice. The lion's steadfast
Roar goes on in the darkness. I have been
Asleep a while when I remember: you
Are – you, and Tawny was the lion in –
In *Tarzan*. In *Tarzan!* Just as we used to,
I talk to you, you talk to me or pretend
To talk to me as grown-up people do,
Of *Jurgen* and Rupert Hughes, till in the end
I think as a child thinks: 'You're my real friend.'

RANDALL JARRELL

from **A Part of Speech**

I was born and grew up in the Baltic marshland
by zinc-gray breakers that always marched on
in twos. Hence all rhymes, hence that wan flat voice
that ripples between them like hair still moist,
if it ripples at all. Propped on a pallid elbow,
the helix picks out of them no sea rumble
but a clap of canvas, of shutters, of hands, a kettle
on the burner, boiling – lastly, the seagull's metal
cry. What keeps hearts from falseness in this flat region
is that there is nowhere to hide and plenty of room for vision.
Only sound needs echo and dreads its lack.
A glance is accustomed to no glance back.

[...]

You've forgotten that village lost in the rows and rows
of swamp in a pine-wooded territory where no scarecrows
ever stand in orchards: the crops aren't worth it,
and the roads are also just ditches and brushwood surface.
Old Nastasya is dead, I take it, and Pesterev, too, for sure,
and if not, he's sitting drunk in the cellar or
is making something out of the headboard of our bed:
a wicket gate, say, or some kind of shed.
And in winter they're chopping wood, and turnips is all they live on,
and a star blinks from all the smoke in the frosty heaven,
and no bride in chintz at the window, but dust's gray craft,
plus the emptiness where once we loved.

*

In the little town out of which death sprawled over the classroom map
the cobblestones shine like scales them coat a carp,
on the secular chestnut tree melting candles hung,
and a cast-iron lion pines for a good harangue.
Through the much laundered, pale window gauze
woundlike carnations and *kirchen* needles ooze;
a tram rattles far off, as in days of yore,
but no one gets off at the stadium any more.

207

The real end of the war is a sweet blonde's frock
across a Viennese armchair's fragile back
while the humming winged silver bullets fly,
taking lives southward, in mid-July.

Munich

*

As for the stars, they are always on.
That is, one appears, then others adorn the inklike
sphere. That's the best way from there to look upon
here: well after hours, blinking.
The sky looks better when they are off.
Though, with them, the conquest of space is quicker.
Provided you haven't got to move
from the bare veranda and squeaking-rocker.
As one spacecraft pilot has said, his face
half sunk in the shadow, it seems there is
no life anywhere, and a thoughtful gaze
can be rested on none of these.

[...]

If anything's to be praised, it's most likely how
the west wind becomes the east wind, when a frozen bough
sways leftward, voicing its creaking protests,
and your cough flies across the Great Plains to Dakota's forests.
At noon, shouldering a shotgun, fire at what may well
be a rabbit in snowfields, so that a shell
widens the breach between the pen that puts up these limping
awkward lines and the creature leaving
real tracks in the white. On occasion the head combines
its existence with that of a hand, not to fetch more lines
but to cup an ear under the pouring slur
of their common voice. Like a new centaur.

[...]

...and when 'the future' is uttered, swarms of mice
rush out of the Russian language and gnaw a piece
of ripened memory which is twice
as hole-ridden as real cheese.

After all these years it hardly matters who
or what stands in the corner, hidden by heavy drapes,
and your mind resounds not with a seraphic "doh,"
only their rustle. Life, that no one dares
to appraise, like that gift horse's mouth,
bares its teeth in a grin at each
encounter. What gets left of a man amounts
to a part. To his spoken part. To a part of speech.

*

Not that I am losing my grip: I am just tired of summer.
You reach for a shirt in a drawer and the day is wasted.
If only winter were here for snow to smother
all these streets, these humans; but first, the blasted
green. I would sleep in my clothes or just pluck a borrowed
book, while what's left of the year's slack rhythm,
like a dog abandoning its blind owner,
crosses the road at the usual zebra. Freedom
is when you forget the spelling of the tyrant's name
and your mouth's saliva is sweeter than Persian pie,
and though your brain is wrung tight as the horn of a ram
nothing drops from your pale-blue eye.

[1975-76]

JOSEPH BRODSKY
translated from the Russian by the author

Old Man

Old Man, or Lad's-love, – in the name there's nothing
To one that knows not Lad's-love, or Old Man,
The hoar-green feathery herb, almost a tree,
Growing with rosemary and lavender.
Even to one that knows it well, the names
Half decorate, half perplex, the thing it is:
At least, what that is clings not to the names
In spite of time. And yet I like the names.

The herb itself I like not, but for certain
I love it, as some day the child will love it
Who plucks a feather from the door-side bush
Whenever she goes in or out of the house.
Often she waits there, snipping the tips and shrivelling
The shreds at last on to the path, perhaps
Thinking, perhaps of nothing, till she sniffs
Her fingers and runs off. The bush is still
But half as tall as she, though it is as old;
So well she clips it. Not a word she says;
And I can only wonder how much hereafter
She will remember, with that bitter scent,
Of garden rows, and ancient damson-trees
Topping a hedge, a bent path to a door,
A low thick bush beside the door, and me
Forbidding her to pick.

                    As for myself,
Where first I met the bitter scent is lost.
I, too, often shrivel the grey shreds,
Sniff them and think and sniff again and try
Once more to think what it is I am remembering,
Always in vain. I cannot like the scent,
Yet I would rather give up others more sweet,
With no meaning, than this bitter one.

I have mislaid the key. I sniff the spray
And think of nothing; I see and I hear nothing;
Yet seem, too, to be listening, lying in wait
For what I should, yet never can, remember:
No garden appears, no path, no hoar-green bush
Of Lad's-love, or Old Man, no child beside,
Neither father nor mother, nor any playmate;
Only an avenue, dark, nameless, without end.

EDWARD THOMAS

Thinking of the Lost World

This spoonful of chocolate tapioca
Tastes like – like peanut butter, like the vanilla
Extract Mama told me not to drink.
Swallowing the spoonful, I have already traveled
Through time to my childhood. It puzzles me
That age is like it.
                    Come back to that calm country
Through which the stream of my life first meandered,
My wife, our cat, and I sit here and see
Squirrels quarrcling in the feeder, a mockingbird
Copying our chipmunk, as our end copies
Its beginning.
                    Back in Los Angeles, we missed
Los Angeles. The sunshine of the Land
Of Sunshine is a gray mist now, the atmosphere
Of some factory planet: when you stand and look
You see a block or two, and your eyes water.
The orange groves are all cut down... My bow
Is lost, all my arrows are lost or broken,
My knife is sunk in the eucalyptus tree
Too far for even Pop to get it out,
And the tree's sawed down. It and the stair-sticks
And the planks of the tree house are all firewood
Burned long ago; its gray smoke smells of Vicks.

Twenty Years After, thirty-five years after,
Is as good as ever – better than ever,
Now that D'Artagnan is no longer old –
Except that it is unbelievable.

I say to my old self: 'I believe. Help thou
Mine unbelief.'
                    I believe the dinosaur
Or pterodactyl's married the pink sphinx
And lives with those Indians in the undiscovered
Country between California and Arizona
That the mad girl told me she was princess of –
Looking at me with the eyes of a lion,
Big, golden, without human understanding,

211

As she threw paper-wads from the back seat
Of the car in which I drove her with her mother
From the jail in Waycross to the hospital
In Daytona. If I took my eyes from the road
And looked back into her eyes, the car would – I'd be –

Or if only I could find a crystal set
Sometimes, surely, I could still hear their chief
Reading to them from Dumas or *Amazing Stories*;
If I could find in some Museum of Cars
Mama's dark blue Buick, Lucky's electric,
Couldn't I be driven there? Hold out to them,
The paraffin half picked out, Tawny's dewclaw –
And have walk to me from among their wigwams
My tall brown aunt, to whisper to me: 'Dead?
They told you I was dead?'
                                      As if you could die!
If I never saw you, never again
Wrote to you, even, after a few years,
How often you've visited me, having put on,
As a mermaid puts on her sealskin, another face
And voice, that don't fool me for a minute –
That are yours for good... All of them are gone
Except for me; and for me nothing is gone –
The chicken's body is still going round
And round in widening circles, a satellite
From which, as the sun sets, the scientist bends
A look of evil on the unsuspecting earth.

Mama and Pop and Dandeen are still there
In the Gay Twenties.
                                The Gay Twenties! You say
The Gay Nineties... But it's all right: they *were* gay,
O so gay! A certain number of years after,
Any time is Gay, to the new ones who ask:
'Was that the first World War or the second?'
Moving between the first world and the second,
I hear a boy call, now that my beard's gray:
'Santa Claus! Hi, Santa Claus!' It *is* miraculous
To have the children call you Santa Claus.
I wave back. When my hand drops to the wheel,
It is brown and spotted, and its nails are ridged

Like Mama's. Where's my own hand? My smooth
White bitten-fingernailed one? I seem to see
A shape in tennis shoes and khaki riding-pants
Standing there empty-handed; I reach out to it
Empty-handed, my hand comes back empty,
And yet my emptiness is traded for its emptiness,
I have found that Lost World in the Lost and Found
Columns whose gray illegible advertisements
My soul has memorised world after world:
LOST – NOTHING. STRAYED FROM NOWHERE. NO REWARD.
I hold in my own hands, in happiness,
Nothing: the nothing for which there's no reward.

RANDALL JARRELL

Quoof

How often have I carried our family word
for the hot water bottle
to a strange bed,
as my father would juggle a red-hot half-brick
in an old sock
to his childhood settle.
I have taken it into so many lovely heads
or laid it between us like a sword.

An hotel room in New York City
with a girl who spoke hardly any English,
my hand on her breast
like the smouldering one-off spoor of the yeti
or some other shy beast
that has yet to enter the language.

PAUL MULDOON

Forgetfulness

Forgetfulness is like a song
That, freed from beat and measure, wanders.
Forgetfulness is like a bird whose wings are reconciled,
Outspread and motionless, –
A bird that coasts the wind unwearyingly.

Forgetfulness is rain at night,
Or an old house in a forest, – or a child.
Forgetfulness is white, – white as a blasted tree,
And it may stun the sybil into prophecy,
Or bury the Gods.

I can remember much forgetfuless.

HART CRANE

Forgetfulness

The name of the author is the first to go
followed obediently by the title, the plot,
the heartbreaking conclusion, the entire novel
which suddenly becomes one you have never read, never even
          heard of.

It is as if, one by one, the memories you used to harbor
decided to retire to the southern hemisphere of the brain,
to a little fishing village where there are no phones.

Long ago you kissed the names of the nine Muses goodbye
and watched the quadratic equation pack its bag,
and even now as you memorise the order of the planets,

something else is slipping away, a state flower perhaps,
the address of an uncle, the capital of Paraguay.

Whatever it is you are struggling to remember
it is not poised on the tip of your tongue,
not even lurking in some obscure corner of your spleen.

It has floated away down a dark mythological river
whose name begins with an *L* as far as you can recall,
well on your own way to oblivion where you will join those
who have even forgotten how to swim and how to ride a bicycle.

No wonder you rise in the middle of the night
to look up the date of a famous battle in a book on war.
No wonder the moon in the window seems to have drifted
out of a love poem that you used to know by heart.

BILLY COLLINS

Unknown Forebear

Somebody who knew him
ninety years ago
called him by a name
he answered to
come out now they said to him
onto the porch and stand
right there

it was summer and the nine windows
that they could see
were open all the way
so was the front door
and the curtains faded as aprons hung
limp past the sills while he stood
there alone in his dark suit
and white beard in the sunshine

he appeared to know where he was
whose porch that was and whose
house behind him
younger than he was
and who had opened the windows

and who had left the ladder
propped in the branches up the lane
and the names of his children and their children

and the name of the place
with the pine tree out front
and the mullein a foot high growing
on the green bank
beyond the stones of the walk

as he stood still looking out
through the opening in the painted
picket fence
one tall picket one short picket
all the way along

and no gate in the opening

W.S. MERWIN

Groundsmen

The pile of cuttings puts on dreadful weight,
swelters in the season, and leaks treacle.
Beside it, the tractor and the cutters drip oil
into the earth floor, in a shed where cobwebs
link the roof to the wired window and the oil drums.
The twisted blades and the spiked roller
rest from the nibbling and pricking of the pitch;
and in the corner a white liner, clogged white
round the wheels, darkens towards the handles.
The quiet men whose stuff this is
have the next shed along. Their door shuts
neatly to, unlike the tractor shed
where the door drags and billows against the bricks.
It was a secret kingdom for a boy.
I envied them their work; lending out bats,
lowering the posts, the twirl of the cutter
at the end of a straight run; and their shed
at the edge of the known world.

DAVID SCOTT

6

Man and beast

Poetry is a zoo in which you keep demons and angels.

LES MURRAY

Poetry is a brilliant vibrating interface
between the human and the non-human.

EDWIN MORGAN

ANIMAL POEMS can say as much about people as the beast described, but they can do both things without being anthropomorphic. The poems in this section are not only about animals but also about our relationships with them, and how the way we view animals often says much about our treatment of each other. As Paul Muldoon has said, the question 'What am I?' is 'central not only to animal poetry but to all forms of poetry'. Since the relationship with animals involves the act of eating, I've included poems about various kinds of food.

The only poem here which needs any kind of gloss is probably 'Salmon' (241) by Jorie Graham, a difficult but rewarding American poet influenced by Wallace Stevens's poetry of ideas. This isn't a poem of close observation but an evocation of procreation by imaginative association. The salmon is seen not in the flesh but on television, swimming into the eye and mind of the poet in the separate world of a motel room, the poem's imaginative leaps following the movement of the salmon. Where these shift through abstractions, Graham is drawing on her reading of Heidegger, whose philosophy connects the idea of justice to birth and death, as Justin Quinn notes in his short essay on this poem: 'Our life is a debt the account of which we settle by dying; that is, a kind of "justification", or righting of life.' Caitríona O'Reilly says that 'to read Jorie Graham is to enter the illusion (and it is always an illusion) of a mind at work, seismographically mapping its sense data'. I don't try to unpick this complex poem like a puzzle whose meanings must be teased out, but I feel that my "understanding" is deepened each time I've tried to enter and experience the poem with an open mind.

Readers interested in animal poems should seek out *The Oxford Book of Creatures* (ed. Fleur Adcock & Jacqueline Simms) and Paul Muldoon's *Faber Book of Beasts*. There is not much overlap between this selection and theirs.

Pigs

Us all on sore cement was we.
Not warmed then with glares. Not glutting mush
under that pole the lightning's tied to.
No farrow-shit in milk to make us randy.
Us back in cool god-shit. We ate crisp.
We nosed up good rank in the tunnelled bush.
Us all fuckers then. And Big, huh? Tusked
the balls-biting dog and gutsed him wet.
Us shoved down the soft cement of rivers.
Us snored the earth hollow, filled farrow, grunted.
Never stopped growing. We sloughed, we soughed
and balked no weird till the high ridgebacks was us
with weight-buried hooves. Or bristly, with milk.
Us never knowed like slitting nor hose-biff then.
Not the terrible sheet-cutting screams up ahead.
The burnt water kicking. This gone-already feeling
here in no place with our heads on upside down.

LES MURRAY

Experimental Animals
(after Miroslav Holub)

It's much cushier when it's raining rabbits
than cats and dogs. The animals for experiment
should not betray too much intelligence.
It grows unnerving to watch their actions mimic yours;
terror and horror you can empathise with.

But, for real heartbreak, take a newborn pig.
Fantastically ugly; possessing nothing
and desiring nothing except its swig of milk;
legs warping under all that weight
of uselessness, stupidity and snout.

When I must kill a piglet, I hesitate a while.
For about five or six seconds.
In the name of all the beauty of the world.
In the name of all the sadness of the world.
'What's keeping you?', someone bursts in then.

Or I burst in on myself.

DENNIS O'DRISCOLL

Weakness

Old mare whose eyes
are like cracked marbles,
drools blood in her mash,
shivers in her jute blanket.

My father hates weakness worse than hail;
in the morning
    without haste
he will shoot her in the ear, once,
shovel her under in the north pasture.

Tonight
    leaving the stables
he stands his lantern on an overturned water pail,
turns,
    cursing her for a bad bargain,
and spreads his coat
carefully over her sick shoulders.

ALDEN NOWLAN

Spiritual Chickens

A man eats a chicken every day for lunch,
and each day the ghost of another chicken
joins the crowd in the dining room. If he could
only see them! Hundreds and hundreds of spiritual
chickens, sitting on chairs, tables, covering
the floor, jammed shoulder to shoulder. At last
there is no more space and one of the chickens
is popped back across the spiritual plain to the earthly.
The man is in the process of picking his teeth.
Suddenly there's a chicken at the end of the table,
strutting back and forth, not looking at the man
but knowing he is there, as is the way with chickens.
The man makes a grab for the chicken but his hand
passes right through her. He tries to hit the chicken
with a chair and the chair passes through her.
He calls in his wife but she can see nothing.
This is his own private chicken, even if he
fails to recognise her. How is he to know
this is a chicken he ate seven years ago
on a hot and steamy Wednesday in July,
with a little tarragon, a little sour cream?
The man grows afraid. He runs out of his house
flapping his arms and making peculiar hops
until the authorities take him away for a cure.
Faced with the choice between something odd
in the world or something broken in his head,
he opts for the broken head. Certainly,
this is safer than putting his opinions
in jeopardy. Much better to think he had
imagined it, that he had made it happen.
Meanwhile, the chicken struts back and forth
at the end of the table. Here she was, jammed in
with the ghosts of six thousand dead hens, when
suddenly she has the whole place to herself.
Even the nervous man has disappeared. If she
had a brain, she would think she had caused it.
She would grow vain, egotistical, she would
look for someone to fight, but being a chicken
she can just enjoy it and make little squawks,
silent to all except the man who ate her,

who is far off banging his head against a wall
like someone trying to repair a leaky vessel,
making certain that nothing unpleasant gets in
or nothing of value falls out. How happy
he would have been to be born a chicken,
to be of good use to his fellow creatures
and rich in companionship after death.
As it is he is constantly being squeezed
between the world and his idea of the world.
Better to have a broken head – why surrender
his corner on truth? – better just to go crazy.

STEPHEN DOBYNS

The Heaven of Animals

Here they are. The soft eyes open.
If they have lived in a wood
It is a wood.
If they have lived on plains
It is grass rolling
Under their feet forever.

Having no souls, they have come,
Anyway, beyond their knowing.
Their instincts wholly bloom
And they rise.
The soft eyes open.

To match them, the landscape flowers,
Outdoing, desperately
Outdoing what is required:
The richest wood,
The deepest field.

For some of these,
It could not be the place
It is, without blood.
These hunt, as they have done,
But with claws and teeth grown perfect,

221

More deadly than they can believe.
They stalk more silently,
And crouch on the limbs of trees,
And their descent
Upon the bright backs of their prey

May take years
In a sovereign floating of joy.
And those that are hunted
Know this as their life,
Their reward: to walk

Under such trees in full knowledge
Of what is in glory above them,
And to feel no fear,
But acceptance, compliance.
Fulfilling themselves without pain

At the cycle's center,
They tremble, they walk
Under the tree,
They fall, they are torn,
They rise, they walk again.

JAMES DICKEY

Sacrilege

I ate the tongue of the stag,
the thick stag-tongue that used
to lick the foliage, the brook;
on it I munched, amused.

I ate the flesh of the stag,
the virile flesh at his throat.
I consumed his heart, and then
on his antlers hung my raincoat.

While the hooves, the nostrils, and the skin –
all unpalatable –
lay scattered all around,

still bleeding on the ground.

NINA CASSIAN
translated from the Romanian by Petre Solomon & William Jay Smith

Remembrance of Strange Hospitality

Once I had a taste
Of a girlfriend's milk,
My sister's milk –
Not to quench my thirst
But satisfy my soul.
Into a cup she squeezed
Milk from her left breast
And in that simple vessel
It gently frothed, rejoiced.
There was something birdlike in its odour,
Whiffs of sheep and wolf, and something older
Than the Milky Way, it was
Somehow warm and dense.
A daughter in the wilderness,
Once let her aged father drink
From her breasts and thus became
His mother. By this act of grace
Her whiteness drove away the dark,
A cradle substituted for a tomb.
From the duct next to your heart
You offered me a drink –
I'm not a vampire, am I? – Horror.
It frothed and tinkled, warm
And sweet, soft, everlasting,
Crowding time back in a corner.

ELENA SHVARTS
translated from the Russian by Michael Molnar

Federal Case

Wow, I said I'd love a Big Mac
with piles of mush spurting out the sides.
So what? Is it such a Federal Case?
Maybe it's a mortal sin cuz
I've got a yen for some junk food.
You'd have thought I'd cursed his mother
or told him I hated his guts
the way he looked at me
like I was a gun-lobby supporter.
Holy cow, it isn't the end of the world
if some processed, bleached, portion-controlled,
regulated bun and a little cereal-filled meat,
cheese and slop goes plonk into my stomach!
I've gone out with this guy
only five times and already he's getting
like a Nazi over what I want to eat.

JULIE O'CALLAGHAN

Animals

Have you forgotten what we were like then
when we were still first rate
and the day came fat with an apple in its mouth

it's no use worrying about Time
but we did have a few tricks up our sleeves
and turned some sharp corners

the whole pasture looked like our meal
we didn't need speedometers
we could manage cocktails out of ice and water

I wouldn't want to be faster
or greener than now if you were with me O you
were the best of all my days

FRANK O'HARA

'The city had fallen...'

The city had fallen. We came to the window of a house drawn by a madman. The setting sun shone on a few abandoned machines of futility. 'I remember,' someone said, 'how in ancient times one could turn a wolf into a human and then lecture it to one's heart's content.'

CHARLES SIMIC

The stone curlew

I am writing this inside the head
of a bush stone curlew,
we have been travelling for days

moving over the earth
flying when necessary.
I am not the bird itself, only its passenger

looking through its eyes.
The world rocks slightly as we move
over the stubble grass of the dunes,

at night shooting stars draw lines
across the velvet dark
as I hang in a sling of light

between the bird's nocturnal eyes.
The heavens make sense, seeing this way
makes me want to believe

words have meanings,
that Australia is no longer a wound
in the side of the earth.

I think of the white settlers
who compared the curlew's song
to the cries of women being strangled,

and remember the poets who wrote
anthropomorphically as I sing softly
from the jelly of the stone curlew's brain.

ROBERT ADAMSON

My Life with Horses

Before I knew there were men
I galloped a pony bareback;
it was a hard winter, but
how sure-footed we were, resolute
in frozen emptiness, stamping
the ice with our names.

Years later I lay like a foal in the grass,
wanting to touch your hair;
we clutched like shadows,
I twined the past through my fingers, kissing
great gulps of father, of mother,
galloping, with nothing to stop me.

Now in the evening I put on my dress
like a secret; will you see
how my elbow pokes like a hock,
the way I have carefully cut my mane,
the way my eyes roll from fear of you?
I'm trying to hide the animal I am;

and you give me a necklace,
bright as a bit, and you're
stamping your name
into the earth, and my arm
is around you, weak as a halter,
and nothing can stop me, no mother or father.

POLLY CLARK

Switch

'Come here,' said Turnbull, 'till you see the sadness
    In the horse's eyes,
If you had such big hooves under you there'd be sadness
    In your eyes too.'

It was clear that he understood so well the sadness
    In the horse's eyes,
And had pondered it so long that in the end he'd plunged
    Into the horse's mind.

I looked at the horse to see the sadness
    Obvious in its eyes,
And saw Turnbull's eyes looking in my direction
    From the horse's head.

I looked at Turnbull one last time
    And saw on his face
Outsize eyes that were dumb with sadness –
    The horse's eyes.

SEÁN Ó RIORDÁIN
translated from the Irish by Patrick Crotty

A Blessing

Just off the highway to Rochester, Minnesota,
Twilight bounds softly forth on the grass.
And the eyes of those two Indian ponies
Darken with kindness.
They have come gladly out of the willows
To welcome my friend and me.
We step over the barbed wire into the pasture
Where they have been grazing all day, alone.
They ripple tensely, they can hardly contain their happiness
That we have come.

They bow shyly as wet swans. They love each other.
There is no loneliness like theirs.
At home once more,
They begin munching the young tufts of spring in the darkness.
I would like to hold the slenderer one in my arms,
For she has walked over to me
And nuzzled my left hand.
She is black and white,
Her mane falls wild on her forehead,
And the light breeze moves me to caress her long ear
That is delicate as the skin over a girl's wrist.
Suddenly I realise
That if I stepped out of my body I would break
Into blossom.

JAMES WRIGHT

The Horses

For all of the horses butchered on the battlefield,
Shell-shocked, tripping over their own intestines,
Drowning in the mud, the best war memorial
Is in Homer: two horses that refuse to budge
Despite threats and sweet-talk and the whistling whip,
Immovable as a tombstone, their heads drooping
In front of the streamlined motionless chariot,
Hot tears spilling from their eyelids onto the ground
Because they are still in mourning for Patroclus
Their charioteer, their shiny manes bedraggled
Under the yoke pads on either side of the yoke.

MICHAEL LONGLEY

The Skunk

Up, black, striped and damasked like the chasuble
At a funeral Mass, the skunk's tail
Paraded the skunk. Night after night
I expected her like a visitor.

The refrigerator whinnied into silence.
My desk light softened beyond the verandah.
Small oranges loomed in the orange tree.
I began to be tense as a voyeur.

After eleven years I was composing
Love-letters again, broaching the word 'wife'
Like a stored cask, as if its slender vowel
Had mutated into the night earth and air

Of California. The beautiful, useless
Tang of eucalyptus spelt your absence.
The aftermath of a mouthful of wine
Was like inhaling you off a cold pillow.

And there she was, the intent and glamorous,
Ordinary, mysterious skunk,
Mythologised, demythologised,
Snuffing the boards five feet beyond me.

It all came back to me last night, stirred
By the sootfall of your things at bedtime,
Your head-down, tail-up hunt in a bottom drawer
For the black plunge-line nightdress.

SEAMUS HEANEY

Considering the Snail

The snail pushes through a green
night, for the grass is heavy
with water and meets over

the bright path he makes, where rain
has darkened the earth's dark. He
moves in a wood of desire,

pale antlers barely stirring
as he hunts. I cannot tell
what power is at work, drenched there
with purpose, knowing nothing.
What is a snail's fury? All
I think is that if later
I parted the blades above
the tunnel and saw the thin
trail of broken white across
litter, I would never have
imagined the slow passion
to that deliberate progress.

THOM GUNN

For a Five-Year-Old

A snail is climbing up the window-sill
into your room, after a night of rain.
You call me in to see, and I explain
that it would be unkind to leave it there:
it might crawl to the floor; we must take care
that no one squashes it. You understand,
and carry it outside, with careful hand,
to eat a daffodil.

I see, then, that a kind of faith prevails:
your gentleness is moulded still by words
from me, who have trapped mice and shot wild birds,
from me, who drowned your kittens, who betrayed
your closest relatives, and who purveyed
the harshest kind of truth to many another.
But that is how things are: I am your mother,
and we are kind to snails.

FLEUR ADCOCK

Full Moon and Little Frieda

A cool small evening shrunk to a dog bark and the clank of a
      bucket –

And you listening.
A spider's web, tense for the dew's touch.
A pail lifted, still and brimming – mirror
To tempt a first star to a tremor.

Cows are going home in the lane there, looping the hedges with
      their warm wreaths of breath –
A dark river of blood, many boulders,
Balancing unspilled milk.

'Moon!' you cry suddenly, 'Moon! Moon!'

The moon has stepped back like an artist gazing amazed at a work

That points at him amazed.

TED HUGHES

Birds

The poet as a penguin
Sat in his snow-cold, nursing
The egg his wife had left him.

There it was, born of them both,
Like it or not. Rounded in words,
And cracking open its shell for a voice.

In the blizzard,
Beaten up from the arctic flats
Were the audience.
From the glass extensions
Of their eyes, they watched
The skuas rise on the updraft,

Every snap of their beaks
Like the tick of a knitting needle,
Hitching a stitch in the wait

For a rolling head.

FRIEDA HUGHES

The Trout

Flat on the bank I parted
Rushes to ease my hands
In the water without a ripple
And tilt them slowly downstream
To where he lay, tendril-light,
In his fluid sensual dream.

Bodiless lord of creation,
I hung briefly above him
Savouring my own absence,
Senses expanding in the slow
Motion, the photographic calm
That grows before action.

As the curve of my hands
Swung under his body
He surged, with visible pleasure.
I was so preternaturally close
I could count every stipple
But still cast no shadow, until

The two palms crossed in a cage
Under the lightly pulsing gills.
Then (entering my own enlarged
Shape, which rode on the water)
I gripped. To this day I can
Taste his terror on my hands.

JOHN MONTAGUE

Night Toad

You can hardly see him –
his outline, his cold skin
almost a dead leaf,
blotched brown, dull green,
khaki. He sits so quietly
pumping his quick breath
just at the edge of water
between ruts in the path.

And suddenly he is the centre
of a cone of light
falling from the night sky –
ruts running with liquid fire,
cobwebs imprinted on black,
each grass-blade clear
and separate – until the hiss
of human life removes itself,
the air no longer creaks,
the shaking stops
and he can crawl back
to where he came from.

But what *was* this,
if it was not death?

SUSAN WICKS

A Bird

Unexplained
In the salt meadow
Lay the dead bird.
The wind
Was fluttering its wings.

SHEILA WINGFIELD

233

Emu Hunt

They'd drive them down this stretch of track
At breakneck speed, and then two guys
Hiding behind those thick-set wandoo trees
Would snap the rope tight at breast height
And toss them arse-up, leave them sprawling
Bulbous-eyed, with claws grasping at thin air,
Necks twitching like headless snakes
Waiting for the calm of sunset, tarantismic
Feathers fanning the ground like chopper blades
Skewed off-centre, the staccato of bullets
Sprayed from rapid-fire semi-automatics,
Reverberating through the forest canopy,
Meat ants driving hastily towards the corpses.

JOHN KINSELLA

Night Parrot

The feathers were taken from the front wheel of a juggernaut.
All the colours of a winter morning, hinged with pink and bone.
The driver sensed that here was something he had stolen
and had to hide in a box at the back of an empty cupboard
in the attic of an almost empty house. The night parrot.
He had heard some story, a reason not to enter the forest after dark.
And it came true, this curse he couldn't quite remember,
for whatever he now held left him empty-handed,
and he could not sleep for the weight of what it felt like,
the air filled with the impossibility of its cries.

LAVINIA GREENLAW

The Thought-Fox

I imagine this midnight moment's forest:
Something else is alive
Beside the clock's loneliness
And this blank page where my fingers move.

Through the window I see no star:
Something more near
Though deeper within darkness
Is entering the loneliness:

Cold, delicately as the dark snow
A fox's nose touches twig, leaf;
Two eyes serve a movement, that now
And again now, and now, and now

Sets neat prints into the snow
Between trees, and warily a lame
Shadow lags by stump and in hollow
Of a body that is bold to come

Across clearings, an eye,
A widening deepening greenness,
Brilliantly, concentratedly,
Coming about its own business

Till, with a sudden sharp hot stink of fox
It enters the dark hole of the head.
The window is starless still; the clock ticks,
The page is printed.

TED HUGHES

Swans Mating

Even now I wish that you had been there
Sitting beside me on the riverbank:
The cob and his pen sailing in rhythm
Until their small heads met and the final
Heraldic moment dissolved in ripples.

This was a marriage and a baptism,
A holding of breath, nearly a drowning,
Wings spread wide for balance where he trod,
Her feathers full of water and her neck
Under the water like a bar of light.

MICHAEL LONGLEY

The Strange Case

My dog's assumed my alter ego.
Has taken over – walks the house
phallus hanging wealthy and raw
in front of guests, nuzzling head up skirts
while I direct my mandarin mood.

Last week driving the babysitter home.
She, unaware dog sat in the dark back seat,
talked on about the kids' behaviour.
On Huron Street the dog leaned forward
and licked her ear.
The car going 40 miles an hour
she seemed more amazed at my driving ability
than my indiscretion.

It was only the dog I said.
Oh she said.
Me interpreting her reply all the way home.

MICHAEL ONDAATJE

Cow

I want to be a cow
and not my mother's daughter.
I want to be a cow
and not in love with you.
I want to feel free to feel calm.
I want to be a cow who never knows
the kind of love you 'fall in love with' with;
a queenly cow, with hips as big and sound
as a department store,
a cow the farmer milks on bended knee,
who when she dies will feel dawn
bending over her like lawn to wet her lips.

I want to be a cow,
nothing fancy –
a cargo of grass,
a hammock of soupy milk
whose floating and rocking and dribbling's undisturbed
by the echo of hooves to the city;
of crunching boots;
of suspicious-looking trailers parked on verges;
of unscrupulous restaurant-owners
who stumble, pink-eyed, from stale beds
into a world of lobsters and warm telephones;
of streamlined Japanese freighters
ironing the night,
heavy with sweet desire like bowls of jam.

The Tibetans have 85 words for states of consciousness.
This dozy cow I want to be has none.
She doesn't speak.
She doesn't do housework or worry about her appearance.
She doesn't roam.
Safe in her fleet
of shorn-white-bowl-like friends,
she needs, and loves, and's loved by,
only this –
the farm I want to be a cow on too.

Don't come looking for me.
Don't come walking out into the bright sunlight
looking for me,
black in your gloves and stockings and sleeves
and large hat.
Don't call the tractorman.
Don't call the neighbours.
Don't make a special fruit-cake for when I come home:
I'm not coming home.
I'm going to be a cowman's counted cow.
I'm going to be a cow
and you won't know me.

SELIMA HILL

Seven Silences
(FROM *An Ill Wind*)

These are the seven silences of a black season:
First, all movement frozen. Shut down
The invisible machinery of the countryside – the hunt, the patter,
The auctioneer's song.

Next comes the silence you wait for the telephone to shatter.
You can't sleep. Can't eat. The silence of fear
Crackles like electricity down the wires; and the silence of paper
Drifts like snow through the door.

Such a queer thing to tell in sheep: a lamb a bit 'hangy'
Or a ewe that will not come to the trough.
Ice-sharp, the silence after the vet has given his verdict.
This is the silence of disbelief.

The next silence is the worst silence. This is the silence
Of the steaming kitchen at three a.m.
When half the cattle lie stiff in the yard and half are still waiting.
This is a silence with no name.

The sixth silence is the silence of grass growing,
Oceans of grass that hush, hush in the wind.
It is hard to get used to this silence: grass growing, and questions
Swelling like streams underground.

And what will you do with all the questions? When a whisper,
        a rush, a torrent
Bursts from the farmyard into Whitehall, what will you get?
Nothing but frozen faces, and the last silence:
A barred gate.

KATRINA PORTEOUS

Lies

In reality, sheep are brave, enlightened
and sassy. They are walking clouds
and like clouds have forgotten
how to jump. As lambs they knew.
Lambs jump because in their innocence
they still find grass exciting.
Some turf is better for tiptoeing
say the lambs. Springy meadows
have curves which invite fits
of bouncing and heel-kicking
to turn flocks of lambs
into demented white spuds boiling in the pot.
Then there is a French style of being a lamb
which involves show and a special touch
at angling the bucking legs. Watch carefully
next time: Lambs love to demonstrate –
you won't have to inveigle.
Eventually, of course, lambs grow trousers
and a blast of wool
which keeps them anchored to the sward.
Then grass is first and foremost
savoury, not palpable.

I prefer the grown sheep: even when damp
she is brave, enlightened and sassy,
her eye a kaleidoscope of hail and farewell,
her tail her most eloquent organ of gesture.
When she speaks, it is to tell me
that she is under a spell, polluted.
Her footwear has been stolen
and the earth rots her feet.
In reality she walks across the sky
upside down in special pumps.

JO SHAPCOTT

Glow Worm

Talking about the chemical changes
that make a body in love shine,
or even, for months, immune to illness,
you pick a grub from the lawn
and let it lie on your palm – glowing
like the emerald-burning butt
of a cigarette. (We still haven't touched,
only lain side by side
the half stories of our half lives.)
You call them lightning bugs
from the way the males gather in clouds
and simultaneously flash.
This is the female, fat from a diet
of liquefied snails, at the stage in her cycle
when she hardly eats; when all her energy's
directed to drawing water and oxygen
to a layer of luciferin.
Wingless, wordless,
in a flagrant and luminous bid
to resist the narrative's pull to death,
she lifts her shining green abdomen
to signal *yes yes yes*.

VICKI FEAVER

Salmon

I watched them once, at dusk, on television, run,
in our motel room half-way through
Nebraska, quick, glittering, past beauty, past
the importance of beauty,
archaic,
not even hungry, not even endangered, driving deeper and deeper
into less. They leapt up falls, ladders,
and rock, tearing and leaping, a gold river
and a blue river traveling
in opposite directions.
They would not stop, resolution of will
and helplessness, as the eye
is helpless
when the image forms itself, upside-down, backward,
driving up into
the mind, and the world
unfastens itself
from the deep ocean of the given....Justice, aspen
leaves, mother attempting
suicide, the white night-flying moth
the ants dismantled bit by bit and carried in
right through the crack
in my wall....How helpless
the still pool is,
upstream,
awaiting the gold blade
of their hurry. Once, indoors, a child,
I watched, at noon, through slatted wooden blinds,
a man and woman, naked, eyes closed,
climb onto each other,
on the terrace floor,
and ride – two gold currents
wrapping round and round each other, fastening,
unfastening. I hardly knew
what I saw. Whatever shadow there was in that world
it was the one each cast
onto the other,
the thin black seam
they seemed to be trying to work away
between them. I held my breath.

As far as I could tell, the work they did
with sweat and light
was good. I'd say
they traveled far in opposite
directions. What is the light
at the end of the day, deep, reddish-gold, bathing the walls,
the corridors, light that is no longer light, no longer clarifies,
illuminates, antique, freed from the body of
the air that carries it. What is it
for the space of time
where it is useless, merely
beautiful? When they were done, they made a distance
one from the other
and slept, outstretched,
on the warm tile
of the terrace floor,
smiling, faces pressed against the stone.

JORIE GRAHAM

Seals at High Island

The calamity of seals begins with jaws.
Born in caverns that reverberate
With endless malice of the sea's tongue
Clacking on shingle, they learn to bark back
In fear and sadness and celebration.
The ocean's mouth opens forty feet wide
And closes on a morsel of their rock.

Swayed by the thrust and backfall of the tide,
A dappled grey bull and a brindled cow
Copulate in the green water of a cove.
I watch from a cliff-top, trying not to move.
Sometimes they sink and merge into black shoals;
Then rise for air, his muzzle on her neck,
Their winged feet intertwined as a fishtail.

She opens her fierce mouth like a scarlet flower
Full of white seeds; she holds it open long
At the sunburst in the music of their loving;
And cries a little. But I must remember
How far their feelings are from mine marooned.
If there are tears at this holy ceremony
Theirs are caused by brine and mine by breeze.

When the great bull withdraws his rod, it glows
Like a carnelian candle set in jade.
The cow ripples ashore to feed her calf;
While an old rival, eyeing the deed with hate,
Swims to attack the tired triumphant god.
They rear their heads above the boiling surf,
Their terrible jaws open, jetting blood.

At nightfall they haul out, and mourn the drowned,
Playing to the sea sadly their last quartet,
An improvised requiem that ravishes
Reason, while ripping scale up like a net:
Brings pity trembling down the rocky spine
Of headlands, till the bitter ocean's tongue
Swells in their cove, and smothers their sweet song.

RICHARD MURPHY

Of Love, Death and the Sea-Squirt

Hoping publicly to humiliate her husband,
she filmed herself swallowing whiskey and pills.

That night, watching in snowy low-grade colour
his wife's self-slaughter reproduced,

he fast-forwarded through all the abuse,
but stopped when she spoke of the sea-squirt,

listening with a sympathetic taste of acid on his tongue
to details of the creature's life-long

search for a rock to make its home;
then the hideous consummation

as it set about eating its own brain.
That was the only part he watched again.

CHRIS GREENHALGH

Octopus

Mariners call them devil fish,
noting the eerie symmetry
of those nervy serpentine arms.
They resemble nothing so much
as a man's cowled head and shoulders.
Mostly they are sessile, and shy
as monsters, waiting in rock-clefts
or coral for a swimming meal.

They have long since abandoned their
skulls to the depths, and go naked
in this soft element, made of
a brain-sac and elephant eye.
The tenderness of their huge heads
makes them tremble at the shameful
intimacy of the killing
those ropes of sticky muscle do.

Females festoon their cavern roofs
with garlands of ripening eggs
and stay to tickle them and die.
Their reproductive holocaust
leaves them pallid and empty. Shoals
of shad and krill, like sheet lightning,
and the ravenous angelfish
consume their flesh before they die.

CAITRÍONA O'REILLY

Fable of the mermaid and the drunks

All these fellows were there inside
when she entered, utterly naked.
They had been drinking, and began to spit at her.
Recently come from the river, she understood nothing.
She was a mermaid who had lost her way.
The taunts flowed over her glistening flesh.
Obscenities drenched her golden breasts.
A stranger to tears, she did not weep.
A stranger to clothes, she did not dress.
They pocked her with cigarette ends and with burnt corks,
and rolled on the tavern floor in raucous laughter.
She did not speak, since speech was unknown to her.
Her eyes were the colour of faraway love,
her arms were matching topazes.
Her lips moved soundlessly in coral light,
and ultimately, she left by that door.
Hardly had she entered the river than she was cleansed,
gleaming once more like a white stone in the rain;
and without a backward look, she swam once more,
swam towards nothingness, swam to her dying.

PABLO NERUDA
translated from the Spanish by Alastair Reid

The Mermaid Tank

Beneath my weight, the duckboards bow.
    Two buckets, slopping water, weigh me down.
A cold wind howls around the cages now,
    While rain sweeps in – across the town –
Again; and while our rheumy-eyed,
    Arthritic monsters fall asleep
        Or vegetate
            I kneel beside
The Songstress Of The Deep
    And wait.

All afternoon, the punters pass
   Her tank in single file; because it's dark
Inside, they press their faces to the glass.
   I breathe, at night, on every mark.
Behind my cloth, the water churns
    And curls around our fat dugong
      And when it clears
        (Like smoke) she turns
Away, and any song
   I hear

Is 'just the wind' or 'my mistake'...
   Outside, discarded handbills catch their wings
On tents or in the mud while, in their wake,
   Paper cups, ticket stubs and things
The rain dismantles every night
    Turn cartwheels in the foreign air
      Before they throng
        The sky, too light
To settle anywhere
   For long.

STEPHEN KNIGHT

The Loch Ness Monster's Song

Sssnnnwhufffffll?
Hnwhuffl hhnnwfl hnfl hfl?
Gdroblboblhobngbl gbl gl g g g g gIbgl.
Drublhaflablhaflubhafgabhaflhafl fl fl –
gm grawwwww grf grawf awfgm graw gm.
Hovoplodok-doplodovok-plovodokot-doplodokosh?
Splgraw fok fok splgrafhatchgabrlgabrl fok splfok!
Zgra kra gka fok!
Grof grawff gabf?
Gombl mbl b! –
blm plm,
blm plm,
blm plm,
blp.

EDWIN MORGAN

The Death of the Loch Ness Monster

Consider that the thing has died before we proved it ever lived
    and that it died of loneliness, dark lord of the loch,
fathomless Worm, great Orm, this last of our mysteries –
    haifend ane meikill fin on ilk syde
    with ane taill and ane terribill heid –
and that it had no tales to tell us, only that it lived there,
    lake-locked, lost in its own coils,
waiting to be found; in the black light of midnight
    surfacing, its whole elastic length unwound,
and the sound it made as it broke the water
    was the single plucked string of a harp –
this newt or salamander, graceful as a swan,
    this water-snake, this water-horse, this water-dancer.

Consider him tired of pondering the possible existence of man
    whom he thinks he has sighted sometimes on the shore,
and rearing up from the purple churning water,
    weird little worm head swaying from side to side,
he denies the vision before his eyes;
    his long neck, swan of Hell, a silhouette against the moon,
his green heart beating its last,
    his noble, sordid soul in ruins.

Now the mist is a blanket of doom, and we pluck from the depths
    a prize of primordial slime –
the beast who was born from some terrible ancient kiss,
    lovechild of unspeakable histories,
this ugly slug half blind no doubt, and very cold,
    his head which is horror to behold
no bigger than our own;
    whom we loathe, for his kind ruled the earth before us,
who died of loneliness in a small lake in Scotland,
    and in his mind's dark land,
where he dreamed up his luminous myths, the last of which was man.

GWENDOLYN MacEWEN

Oysters

Our shells clacked on the plates.
My tongue was a filling estuary,
My palate hung with starlight:
As I tasted the salty Pleaides
Orion dipped his foot in the water.

Alive and violated
They lay on their beds of ice:
Bivalves: the split bulb
And philandering sigh of ocean.
Millions of them ripped and shucked and scattered.

We had driven to that coast
Through flowers and limestone
And there we were, toasting friendship,
Laying down a perfect memory
In the cool of thatch and crockery.

Over the Alps, packed deep in hay and snow,
The Romans hauled their oysters south to Rome:
I saw damp panniers disgorge
The frond-lipped, brine-stung
Glut of privilege

And was angry that my trust could not repose
In the clear light, like poetry or freedom
Leaning in from sea. I ate the day
Deliberately, that its tang
Might quicken me all into verb, pure verb.

SEAMUS HEANEY

7

In and out of love

The best love poems confirm something
we secretly felt but never said.

TESS GALLAGHER

Every new poem is like finding a new bride.
Words are so erotic, they never tire of their coupling.

STANLEY KUNITZ

BOOKS OF LOVE POEMS can be too earnest. They don't always give a real and
truly heart-felt sense of the joyful side of love. As in a marriage, the passion can
get lost as the editor makes the usual compromises. I've tried to avoid that by
making a very personal selection. Many of the writers I've chosen don't always
take themselves seriously. Their poems are fired up with self-abandonment, with
the sheer wild joy of new love. Thus the American C.K. Williams writes of
'the old, sore heart, the battered, foundered, faithful heart, snorting again,
stamping in its stall' (254). The heart is all those things, especially when love
comes creeping back unexpectedly after many years of desertion. The poets here
also write of love as a strongly physical experience, about its sensory and sensual
delights as well as that animal 'stamping in its stall', and the lover as 'a new
creature, prowling behind bars' in Linda France's poem (264). The muse of
Jo Shapcott's poems (265, 266) is often an animal, or an animal part of herself.

But with love comes heartbreak too: expectation and disappointment, lust
and loss, adultery and betrayal. All these are treated powerfully here. After a
delightful immersion in the headiness of what Sharon Olds titles 'True Love'
(and then goes on to evoke in lines of great passion and tenderness), this selec-
tion takes you in and out of love. It includes some of the finest love poems in
the English language, notably those by W.H. Auden (259, 292) and W.B. Yeats,
whose 'When You Are Old' (290) was one of many poems of unrequited love
written for his beloved Maud Gonne. The Yeats poem – itself a variation on
a famous love sonnet by Pierre de Ronsard – is the literary ghost behind Kate
Clanchy's 'Spell' (291), a love poem about love poetry.

Other marvellous poems here include a love poem by the Australian Judith
Wright (268) from a woman to a man which acknowledges, with wonder and
amazement, a third presence, that of their future child, while another Australian
writer, Kevin Hart (274), writes of the powerful absence felt from a vacant
room, which could equally be a locked room in his heart.

249

My Belovèd Compares Herself to a Pint of Stout

When in the heat of the first night of summer
I observe with a whistle of envy
That Jackson has driven out the road for a pint of stout,
She puts her arm around my waist and scolds me:
Am I not your pint of stout? Drink me.
There is nothing except, of course, self-pity
To stop you also having your pint of stout.

Putting self-pity on a leash in the back of the car,
I drive out the road, do a U-turn,
Drive in the hall door, up the spiral staircase,
Into her bedroom. I park at the foot of her bed,
Nonchalantly step out leaving the car unlocked,
Stroll over to the chest of drawers, lean on it,
Circumspectly inspect the backs of my hands,
Modestly request from her a pint of stout.
She turns her back, undresses, pours herself into bed,
Adjusts the pillows, slaps her hand on the coverlet:
Here I am – at the very least
Look at my new cotton nightdress before you shred it
And do not complain that I have not got a head on me.

I look around to see her foaming out of the bedclothes
Not laughing but gazing at me out of four-leggèd eyes.
She says: Close your eyes, put your hands around me.
I am the blackest, coldest pint you will ever drink
So sip me slowly, let me linger on your lips,
Ooze through your teeth, dawdle down your throat,
Before swooping down into your guts.

While you drink me I will deposit my scum
On your rim and when you get to the bottom of me,
No matter how hard you try to drink my dregs –
And being a man, you will, no harm in that –
I will keep bubbling up back at you.
For there is no escaping my aftermath.
Tonight – being the first night of summer –
You may drink as many pints of me as you like.
There are barrels of me in the tap room.

In thin daylight at nightfall,
You will fall asleep drunk on love.
When you wake early in the early morning
You will have a hangover,
All chaste, astringent, aflame with affirmation,
Straining at the bit to get to first mass
And holy communion and work – the good life.

PAUL DURCAN

Finney's Bar

Ah, you rare old devil, you fine fellow Finney,
Ravishing your fiddle so the tendons won't sing
Of virginity's meaning, Finney, you dog
With your dead-born tunes,
Elbows to the big bugger moon, in Dublin,
Your backside afire as you saw at the throat,
And Irishman's Fancy is spilled.

Finney, you swore on your fathers, you'd kissed
The hem of her sky-blue dress,
Emulsion-skinned holy mother whose waters
Are breaking with sin and piss; and she unbandaged
Her bleeding heart, she reeled
As you cut your fiddle,
And the boys in the backroom reeled with her.

Finney, I'll never forget you, a bless and a curse
On your head and the murder you did,
To music, the black and amber we passed together,
Your white confessional walls,
They fell like snow on my head, Finney, you rogue,
I've looked up your trouser leg.
I'd die to drink with you again.

DEBORAH RANDALL

Bite

Dark corsage I can't
unpin, I'm stuck with it,
drawing wry comment
for days, however I hide
this stamp that approves
the boundary, proves that you
stop short of blood, all jokes
aside. But note
how readily my veins
leap up: a little harder and
the whole heart would follow,
I'd turn inside out, bleak pocket
for your rummaging,
magician's hat. And yet
I don't; I let you pass
like this small stormcloud on
my white, impassive throat.

TRACY RYAN

Desire's a Desire

It taunts me
like the muzzle of a gun;
it sinks into my soul like chilled honey
packed into the depths of treacherous wounds;
it wraps me up in cold green sheets
like Indian squaws
who wrap their babies in the soft green sheathes of irises
that smell of starch;
it tattooes my shins;
it itches my thighs
like rampant vaginal flora;
it tickles my cheeks
like silkworms munching mulberry leaves
on silk farms;
it nuzzles my plucked armpits like fat dogs;
it plays me

like a piano being played
by regimented fingers
through pressed sheets;
it walks across my back
like geese at dawn,
or the gentle manners
of my only nurse,
who handles me like glass, or Bethlehem.

My skin is white.
I neither eat nor sleep.
My only desire's a desire
to be free from desire.

SELIMA HILL

Raisin Pumpernickel

You shine, my love, like a sugar maple in October,
a golden-orange overarching blaze of leaves,
each painted its own tint of flames
tossed on the ground bright as silk scarves.
So are you happy.

My curly one, my stubborn fierce butter,
down with the head and charge all horns
and the blattering thunk of bone head on bone,
the smoke and hot rubber stench of overheated temper.
So are you angry.

The tomcat is a ready lover. He can do it at dawn
when the birds are still yawning, he can do it
while the houseguest walks up the drive, do it after
four parties and an all-night dance, on a convenient floor.
So are you able.

Your love comes down rich as the warm spring rain.
Now it charges like a tawny dark maned lion.
Now it envelopes me in wraiths of silken mist.
Now it is a thick hot soup that sustains me.
So are you loving.

You're an endless sink of love, a gaping maw
into which I shovel attention like soft coal
into an old furnace; you're a limitless love source,
a great underground spring surging out of rock
to feed a river.

You cry your needs, bold as a six-week kitten.
You're devious as a corporate takeover and direct
as an avalanche. What ten years into this conversation
commands my interest? You're still the best novel
I've ever read.

Secretly we both think we were bred for each other
as part of an experiment in getting dreams made
flesh and then having to feed on the daily bread
of passion. So we die and die with loving
and go on living.

MARGE PIERCY

Love: Beginnings

They're at that stage where so much desire streams between them,
  so much frank need and want,
so much absorption in the other and the self and the self-admiring
  entity and unity they make –
her mouth so full, breast so lifted, head thrown back *so* far in her
  laughter at his laughter,
he so solid, planted, oaky, firm, so resonantly factual in the headiness
  of being craved so,
she almost wreathed upon him as they intertwine again, touch again,
  cheek, lip, shoulder, brow,
every glance moving toward the sexual, every glance away soaring
  back in flame into the sexual –
that just to watch them is to feel again that hitching in the groin, that
  filling of the heart,
the old, sore heart, the battered, foundered, faithful heart, snorting
  again, stamping in its stall.

C.K. WILLIAMS

The Honeycomb

They had made love early in the high bed,
Not knowing the honeycomb stretched
Between lath and plaster of the outer wall.

For a century
The bees had wintered there,
Prisoning sugar in the virgin wax.

At times of transition,
Spring and autumn,
Their vibration swelled the room.

Laying his hand against the plaster
In the May sunrise,
He felt the faint frequency of their arousal,

Nor winters later, burning the beeswax candle,
Could he forget his tremulous first loving
Into the humming dawn.

PAULINE STAINER

The Linen Industry

Pulling up flax after the blue flowers have fallen
And laying our handfuls in the peaty water
To rot those grasses to the bone, or building stooks
That recall the skirts of an invisible dancer,

We become a part of the linen industry
And follow its processes to the grubby town
Where fields are compacted into window-boxes
And there is little room among the big machines.

But even in our attic under the skylight
We make love on a bleach green, the whole meadow
Draped with material turning white in the sun
As though snow reluctant to melt were our attire.

What's passion but a battering of stubborn stalks,
Then a gentle combing out of fibres like hair
And a weaving of these into christening robes,
Into garments for a marriage or funeral?

Since it's like a bereavement once the labour's done
To find ourselves last workers in a dying trade,
Let flax be our matchmaker, our undertaker,
The provider of sheets for whatever the bed –

And be shy of your breasts in the presence of death,
Say that you look more beautiful in linen
Wearing white petticoats, the bow on your bodice
A butterfly attending the embroidered flowers.

MICHAEL LONGLEY

Last Night

The next day, I am almost afraid.
Love? It was more like dragonflies
in the sun, 100 degrees at noon,
the ends of their abdomens stuck together, I
close my eyes when I remember. I hardly
knew myself, like something twisting and
twisting out of a chrysalis,
enormous, without language, all
head, all shut eyes, and the humming
like madness, the way they writhe away,
and do not leave, back, back,
away, back. Did I know you? No kiss,
no tenderness – more like killing, death-grip
holding to life, genitals
like violent hands clasped tight
barely moving, more like being closed
in a great jaw and eaten, and the screaming
I groan to remember it, and when we started
to die, then I refuse to remember,
the way a drunkard forgets. After,

you held my hands extremely hard as my
body moved in shudders like the ferry when its
axle is loosed past engagement, you kept me
sealed exactly against you, our hairlines
wet as the arc of a gateway after
a cloudburst, you secured me in your arms till I slept –
that was love, and we woke in the morning
clasped, fragrant, buoyant, that was
the morning after love.

SHARON OLDS

Definition of Your Attraction

On a fully broken-in animal's back
a fully broken-in animal rides.

JÁNOS PILINSZKY
translated from the Hungarian by Peter Jay

The Cinnamon Peeler

If I were a cinnamon peeler
I would ride your bed
and leave the yellow bark dust
on your pillow.

Your breast and shoulders would reek
you could never walk through markets
without the profession of my fingers
floating over you. The blind would
stumble certain of whom they approached
though you might bathe
under rain gutters, monsoon.

Here on the upper thigh
at this smooth pasture
neighbour to your hair
or the crease
that cuts your back. This ankle.
You will be known among strangers
as the cinnamon peeler's wife.

I could hardly glance at you
before marriage
never touch you
– your keen-nosed mother, your rough brothers.
I buried my hands
in saffron, disguised them
over smoking tar,
helped the honey gatherers...

When we swam once
I touched you in water
and our bodies remained free,
you could hold me and be blind of smell.
You climbed the bank and said

        this is how you touch other women
the grass cutter's wife, the lime burner's daughter.
And you searched your arms
for the missing perfume

        and knew

        what good is it
to be the lime burner's daughter
left with no trace
as if not spoken to in the act of love
as if wounded without the pleasure of a scar.

You touched
your belly to my hands
in the dry air and said
I am the cinnamon
peeler's wife. Smell me.

MICHAEL ONDAATJE

True Love

In the middle of the night, when we get up
after making love, we look at each other in
complete friendship, we know so fully
what the other has been doing. Bound to each other
like mountaineers coming down from a mountain,
bound with the tie of the delivery-room,
we wander down the hall to the bathroom, I can
hardly walk, I wobble through the granular
shadowless air, I know where you are
with my eyes closed, we are bound to each other
with huge invisible threads, our sexes
muted, exhausted, crushed, the whole
body a sex – surely this
is the most blessed time of my life,
our children asleep in their beds, each fate
like a vein of abiding mineral
not discovered yet. I sit
on the toilet in the night, you are somewhere in the room,
I open the window and snow has fallen in a
steep drift, against the pane, I
look up, into it,
a wall of cold crystals, silent
and glistening, I quietly call to you
and you come and hold my hand and I say
I cannot see beyond it, I cannot see beyond it.

SHARON OLDS

Lullaby

Lay your sleeping head, my love,
Human on my faithless arm;
Time and fevers burn away
Individual beauty from
Thoughtful children, and the grave

Proves the child ephemeral:
But in my arms till break of day
Let the living creature lie,
Mortal, guilty, but to me
The entirely beautiful.

Soul and body have no bounds:
To lovers as they lie upon
Her tolerant enchanted slope
In their ordinary swoon,
Grave the vision Venus sends
Of supernatural sympathy,
Universal love and hope;
While an abstract insight wakes
Among the glaciers and the rocks
The hermit's sensual ecstasy.

Certainty, fidelity
On the stroke of midnight pass
Like vibrations of a bell,
And fashionable madmen raise
Their pedantic boring cry:
Every farthing of the cost,
All the dreaded cards foretell,
Shall be paid, but from this night
Not a whisper, not a thought,
Not a kiss nor look be lost.

Beauty, midnight, vision dies:
Let the winds of dawn that blow
Softly round your dreaming head
Such a day of sweetness show
Eye and knocking heart may bless,
Find the mortal world enough;
Noons of dryness see you fed
By the involuntary powers,
Nights of insult let you pass
Watched by every human love.

W.H. AUDEN

In Defence of Adultery

We don't fall in love: it rises through us
the way that certain music does –
whether a symphony or ballad –
and it is sepia-coloured,
like tea that stains as it creeps up
the tiny tube-like gaps inside
a cube of sugar lying by a cup.
Yes, love's like that: just when we least
needed or expected it
a part of us dips into it
by chance or mishap and it seeps
through our capillaries, it clings
inside the chambers of the heart
to atriums and ventricles. We're
victims, we say: merely vessels
drinking the vanilla scent
of this one's skin, the lustre
of another's blue eyes skilfully
darkened with bistre. And whatever
damage might result we're not
to blame for it: love is an autocrat
and won't be disobeyed.
Sometimes we almost manage
to convince ourselves of that.

JULIA COPUS

The Did-You-Come-Yets of the Western World

When he says to you:
You look so beautiful
you smell so nice –
how I've missed you –
and did you come yet?

It means nothing,
and he is smaller,
than a mouse's fart.

Don't listen to him...
Go to Annaghdown Pier
with your father's rod.
Don't necessarily hold out
for the biggest one;
oftentimes the biggest ones
are the smallest in the end.

Bring them all home,
but not together.
One by one is the trick;
avoid red herrings and scandal.

Maybe you could take two
on the shortest day of the year.
Time is the cheater here
not you, so don't worry.

Many will bite the usual bait:
They will talk their slippery way
through fine clothes and expensive perfume,
fishing up your independence.

These are,
The did-you-come-yets of the western world,
the feather and fin rufflers.
Pity for them they have no wisdom.

Others will bite at any bait.
Maggot, suspender, or dead worm.
Throw them to the sharks.

In time one will crawl
out from under thigh-land.
Although drowning he will say,

'Woman I am terrified, why is the house shaking?'

And you'll know he's the one.

RITA ANN HIGGINS

The Mistress

After the drink, after dinner, after the half-hour idiot kids' cartoon
　　special on the TV,
after undressing his daughter, mauling at the miniature buttons on
　　the back of her dress,
the games on the bed – 'Look at my pee-pee,' she says, pulling her
　　thighs wide, 'isn't it pretty?' –
after the bath, pajamas, the song and the kiss and the telling his wife
　　it's her turn now,
out now, at last, out of the house to make the call (out to take a stroll,
　　this evening's lie),
he finds the only public phone booth in the neighborhood's been
　　savaged, receiver torn away,
wires thrust back up the coin slot to its innards, and he stands there,
　　what else? what now?
and notices he's panting, he's panting like an animal, he's breathing
　　like a bloody beast.

C.K. WILLIAMS

Ecstasy

As we made love for the third day,
cloudy and dark, as we did not stop
but went into it and into it and
did not hesitate and did not hold back we
rose through the air, until we were up above
timber line. The lake lay
icy and silver, the surface shirred,
reflecting nothing. The black rocks
lifted around it into the grainy
sepia air, the patches of snow
brilliant white, and even though we
did not know where we were, we could not
speak the language, we could hardly see, we
did not stop, rising with the black

263

rocks to the black hills, the black
mountains rising from the hills. Resting
on the crest of the mountains, one huge
cloud with scalloped edges of blazing
evening light, we did not turn back,
we stayed with it, even though we were
far beyond what we knew, we rose
into the grain of the cloud, even though we were
frightened, the air hollow, even though
nothing grew there, even though it is a
place from which no one has ever come back.

SHARON OLDS

Zoology Is Destiny

You won't let me be ostrich, armadillo,
invertebrate. Although for you I'm zoo,
a new creature, prowling behind bars, howling
at the moon, the way you can stroke the hairs
riding the roaring switchback of my spine –
a terrible gesture of tenderness.

If I can't come out, you'll come in – pick
the lock on the door of my cage with your teeth.
We dine on watermelon and figs, milk
and almonds, our tongues cunning as Eden snakes.
Our hands build an ark, two by two, for fur,
feathers flying, hoof, breastbone, muzzle, wing.

This is not a parable wishing itself
would happen, like weather in a fable
by Aesop, a date in *The Fox and Grapes*.
It's simply the vatic utterance
of a white rhinoceros who knows
the difference between rocks and crocodiles.

LINDA FRANCE

Only if Love Should Pierce You

Do not forget that you live in the midst of the animals,
horses, cats, sewer rats
brown as Solomon's woman, terrible
camp with colours flying,
do not forget the dog with harmonies of the unreal
in tongue and tail, nor the green lizard, the blackbird,
the nightingale, viper, drone. Or you are pleased to think
that you live among pure men and virtuous
women who do not touch
the howl of the frog in love, green
as the greenest branch of the blood.
Birds watch you from trees, and the leaves
are aware that the Mind is dead
forever, its remnant savours of burnt
cartilage, rotten plastic; do not forget
to be animal, fit and sinuous,
torrid in violence, wanting everything here
on earth, before the final cry
when the body is cadence of shrivelled memories
and the spirit hastens to the eternal end;
remember that you can be the being of being
only if love should pierce you deep inside.

SALVATORE QUASIMODO
translated from the Italian by Jack Bevan

Muse

When I kiss you in all the folding places
of your body, you make that noise like a dog
dreaming, dreaming of the long runs he makes
in answer to some jolt to his hormones,
running across landfills, running, running
by tips and shorelines from the scent of too much,
but still going with head up and snout
in the air because he loves it all

and has to get away. I have to kiss deeper
and more slowly – your neck, your inner arm,
the neat creases under your toes, the shadow
behind your knee, the white angles of your groin –
until you fall quiet because only then
can I get the damned words to come into my mouth.

JO SHAPCOTT

Life

My life as a bat
is for hearing
the world.

If I pitch it right
I can hear
just where you are.

If I pitch it right
I can hear inside your body:
the state of your health,

and more, I can hear
into your mind.
Bat death is not listening.

My life as a frog
is for touching
other things.

I'm very moist
so I don't get stuck
in the water.

I'm very moist
so I can cling
onto your back

for three days
and nights.
Frog death is separation.

My life as an iguana
is for tasting
everything.

My tongue is very fast
because the flavour
of the air is so subtle.

It's long enough
to surprise
the smallest piece of you

from extremely
far away.
Iguana death is a closed mouth.

JO SHAPCOTT

Distances

Swifts turn in the heights of the air;
higher still turn the invisible stars.
When day withdraws to the ends of the earth
their fires shine on a dark expanse of sand.

We live in a world of motion and distance.
The heart flies from tree to bird,
from bird to distant star,
from star to love; and love grows
in the quiet house, turning and working,
servant of thought, a lamp held in one hand.

PHILIPPE JACCOTTET
translated from the French by Derek Mahon

'As our bloods separate'

As our bloods separate the clock resumes,
I hear the wind again as our hearts quieten.
We were a ring: the clock ticked round us
For that time and the wind was deflected.

The clock pecks everything to the bone.
The wind enters through the broken eyes
Of houses and through their wide mouths
And scatters the ashes from the hearth.

Sleep. Do not let go my hand.

DAVID CONSTANTINE

Woman to Man

The eyeless labourer in the night,
the selfless, shapeless seed I hold,
builds for its resurrection day –
silent and swift and deep from sight
foresees the unimagined light.

This is no child with a child's face;
this has no name to name it by:
yet you and I have known it well.
This is our hunter and our chase,
the third who lay in our embrace.

This is the strength that your arm knows,
the arc of flesh that is my breast,
the precise crystals of our eyes.
This is the blood's wild tree that grows
the intricate and folded rose.

This is the maker and the made;
this is the question and reply;
the blind head butting at the dark,
the blaze of light along the blade.
Oh hold me, for I am afraid.

JUDITH WRIGHT

Snow Melting

Snow melting when I left you, and I took
This fragile bone we'd found in melting snow
Before I left, exposed beside a brook
Where raccoons washed their hands. And this, I know,

Is that raccoon we'd watched for every day.
Though at the time her wild human hand
Had gestured inexplicably, I say
Her meaning now is more than I can stand.

We've reasons, we have reasons, so we say,
For giving love, and for withholding it.
I who would love must marvel at the way
I know aloneness when I'm holding it,

Know near and far as words for live and die,
Know distance, as I'm trying to draw near,
Growing immense, and know, but don't know why,
Things seen up close enlarge, then disappear.

Tonight this small room seems too huge to cross.
And my life is that looming kind of place.
Here, left with this alone, and at a loss
I hold an alien and vacant face

Which shrinks away, and yet is magnified –
More so than I seem able to explain.
Tonight the giant galaxies outside
Are tiny, tiny on my windowpane.

GJERTRUD SCHNACKENBERG

August

Skin-tight with longing, like dangerous girls,
the tomatoes reel, drunk
from the vine.

The corn, its secret ears
studded like microphones, transmits August
across the field: paranoid crickets, the noise of snakes
between stalks, peeling themselves from
themselves.

I am burdened as the sky,
clouds, upset buckets pour
their varnish onto earth.

Last year you asked if I was
faint *because of the blood*. The tomatoes
bristled in their improbable skins,
eavesdropping.

*

This is one way to say it.
The girl gone, you left.

& this another.
Last year in August I hung
my head between my knees, looked up
flirting with atmosphere
but you were here
& the sky had no gravity.

*Now love falls from me,
walls from a besieged city.*
When I move the mountains shrug off
skin, horizon shudders, I wear the moon
a cowbell.

My symptom:
the earth's
constant rotation.

*

On the surface the sea argues.
The tide pulls water like a cloth
from the table, beached boats, dishes
left standing. Without apology
nature abandons us.
Returns, promiscuous, & slides between
sheets, unspooling the length
of our bodies.

Black wild rabbits beside the lighthouse
at Letite. They disappear before
I am certain I've seen them.
Have they learned this from you?

*

I read the journal of the boy who starved
to death on the other side of a river
under trees grown so old he would not feed them
to a signal fire. His last entry:
August 12 Beautiful Blueberries!

Everything I say about desire or
hunger is only lip service
in the face of it.

Still there were days I know
your mouth gave that last taste of blue.

*

When you said you were
leaving
I pictured a tree;
spring, the green
nippled buds

not the fall
when we are banished
from the garden.

*

Another woman fell
in love with the sea,
land kissed by salt, the skin
at the neck a tidal zone, she rowed
against the escaping tide
fighting to stay afloat.

To find the sea she had to turn her back to it,
stroke.

The sea is a wound
& in loving it
she learned to love what goes missing.

*

Once the raspberries grew
into our room, swollen as the
brains of insects, I dreamt a
wedding. We could not find our
way up the twisted ramp, out from under
ground, my hair earth-damp.

I woke. A raspberry bush clung to us
sticky as the toes of frogs.
A warning: you carried betrayal
like a mantis
folded to your chest – legs, wings, tongue
would open, knife
the leaves above us.

*

If I could step into
your skin, my fingers
into your fingers putting on
gloves, my legs, your legs,
a snake zipping
up. If I could look
out of your tired eyeholes
brain of my brain,
I might know
why we failed.
(Once we thought the same
thoughts, felt the same things.)

A heavy cloak, I wear
you, an old black wing
I can't shrug off.

O heart of my heart,
come home. O flesh,
come to me before
the worm, before earth
ate the girl,
before you left without
belongings.

*

You said, *there are women*
I know whose presence
changes the quality of air.

I am not one of those. The leaves
lift & sigh, the river
keeps saying the unsayable things.
I hesitate to prod the corn from the coals
though I have soaked it in Arctic water.
I stop the knife near the tomato
skin, all summer coiled there.
You are not coming back.

One step is closer
to the fire.

September will fall
with twilight's metal,
                              loose change
from a pocket. Quicker than
an oar can fight water,
I will look up from my feet
catch the leaves red-handed
embracing smoke.

Around me, lost things gather
for an instant
in earth-dark air.

ESTA SPALDING

The Room

It is my house, and yet one room is locked.
The dark has taken root on all four walls.
It is a room where knots stare out from wood,
A room that turns its back on the whole house.

At night I hear the crickets list their griefs
And let an ancient peace come into me.
Sleep intercepts my prayer, and in the dark
The house turns slowly round its one closed room.

KEVIN HART

Don't Let's Talk About Being in Love

Don't let's talk about being in love, OK?
– about *me* being in love, in fact, OK?
about your bloated face, like a magnolia;
about marsupials,
whose little blunted pouches
I'd like to crawl inside, lips first;
about the crashing of a million waterfalls
– as if LOVE were a dome of glass beneath a lake
entered through a maze of dripping tunnels
I hoped and prayed I'd never be found inside.

At night I dream that your bedroom's crammed with ducks.
You smell of mashed-up meal and scrambled egg.
Some of the ducks are broody, and won't stand up.
And I dream of the fingers of your various wives
reaching into your private parts like beaks.
And you're lying across the bed like a man shouldn't be.
And I'm startled awake by the sound of creaking glass
as if the whole affair's about to collapse
and water come pouring in with a rush of fishes
going *slurpetty-slurpetty-slurp* with their low-slung mouths.

SELIMA HILL

Yearn On

I want you to feel
the unbearable lack of me.
I want your skin
to yearn for the soft lure of mine;
I want those hints of red
on your canvas
to deepen in passion for me:
carmine, burgundy.
I want you to keep
stubbing your toe
on the memory of me;
I want your head to be dizzy
and your stomach in a spin;
I want you to hear my voice
in your ear, to touch your face
imagining it is my hand.
I want your body to shiver and quiver
at the mere idea of mine.
I want you to feel as though
life after me is dull, and pointless,
and very, very aggravating;
that with me you were lifted
on a current you waited all your life to find,
and had despaired of finding,
as though you were wading
through a soggy swill of inanity and ugliness
every minute we are apart.
I want you to drive yourself crazy
with the fantasy of me,
and how we will meet again, against all odds,
and there will be tears and flowers,
and the vast relief of not I,
but us.
I am haunting your dreams,
conducting these fevers
from a distance,
a distance that leaves me weeping,
and storming,
and bereft.

KATIE DONOVAN

Bitch

Now, when he and I meet, after all these years,
I say to the bitch inside me, don't start growling.
He isn't a trespasser anymore,
just an old acquaintance tipping his hat.
My voice says, 'Nice to see you,'
As the bitch starts to bark hysterically.
He isn't an enemy now,
Where are your manners, I say, as I say,
'How are the children? They must be growing up.'
At a kind word from him, a look like the old days,
The bitch changes her tone: she begins to whimper.
She wants to snuggle up to him, to cringe.
Down, girl! Keep your distance
Or I'll give you a taste of the choke-chain.
'Fine, I'm just fine,' I tell him.
She slobbers and grovels.
After all, I am her mistress. She is basically loyal.
It's just that she remembers how she came running
Each evening, when she heard his step;
How she lay at his feet and looked up adoringly
Though he was absorbed in his paper;
Or, bored with her devotion, ordered her to the kitchen
Until he was ready to play.
But the small careless kindnesses
When he'd had a good day, or a couple of drinks,
Come back to her now, seem more important
Than the casual cruelties, the ultimate dismissal.
'It's nice to see you are doing so well,' I say.
He couldn't have taken you with him;
You were too demonstrative, too clumsy,
Not like the well-groomed pets of his new friends.
'Give my regards to your wife,' I say. You gag
As I drag you off by the scruff,
Saying, 'Goodbye! Goodbye! Nice to have seen you again.'

CAROLYN KIZER

Bitcherel

You ask what I think of your new acquisition;
and since we are now to be 'friends',
I'll strive to the full to cement my position
with honesty. Dear – it depends.

It depends upon taste, which must not be disputed;
for which of us *does* understand
why some like their furnishings pallid and muted,
their cookery wholesome, but bland?

There isn't a *law* that a face should have features,
it's just that they generally *do*;
God couldn't give colour to *all* of his creatures,
and only gave wit to a few;

I'm sure she has qualities, much underrated,
that compensate amply for this,
along with a charm that is so understated
it's easy for people to miss.

And if there are some who choose clothing to flatter
what beauties they think they possess,
when what's underneath has no shape, does it matter
if there is no shape to the dress?

It's not that I think she is *boring*, precisely,
that isn't the word I would choose;
I know there are men who like girls who talk nicely
and always wear sensible shoes.

It's not that I think she is vapid and silly;
it's not that her voice makes me wince;
but – chilli con carne without any chilli
is only a plateful of mince...

ELEANOR BROWN

This Dead Relationship

I carry a dead relationship around everywhere with me.
It's my hobby.
How lucky to have a job that's also my hobby,
To do it all the time.

A few people notice, and ask if they can help carry this thing.
But, like an alcoholic scared they will hear the clink of glass in
            the bag,
I refuse – scared they'll smell rottenness,
Scared of something under their touch
That will cave in, a skin over brown foam on a bad apple.
I cram this thing over the threshold
Into the cold and speechless house,
Lean against the front door for a moment to breathe in the dark,
Then start the slow haul to the kitchen.
Steel knives catch the moonlight on white tiles.

This dead relationship.

Or not yet dead.

Or dead and half-eaten,
One eye and one flank open, like a sheep under a hedge.

Or dead but still farting like the bodies in the trenches,
Exploding with their own gas. Hair and nails still growing.

It has the pins and needles of returning feeling in a deadness.
It is a reptile in my hand, quick and small and cool;
The flip of life in a dry, cold bag of loose skin.
A pressure without warmth of small claws and horn moving on
            my palm.

At night it slips slow but purposeful across the floor towards the bed.
Next thing it's looking out of my eyes in the morning –
And in the mirror, though my eyes are not my own,
My mouth shows surprise that I am still there at all.

Oh, a sickness that can make you so ill,
Yet doesn't have the decency to kill you.
A mad free-fall that never hits the ground,
Never knows even the relief of sudden shock;
Just endless medium-rare shock, half-firm, half-bloody all the time.
A long, slow learning curve.
The overheating that can strip an engine badly,
Strain it far worse than a racing rally.
The fear that you will slow to a stop
Then start a soft, thick, slow-gathering roll backwards.

I want something that is familiar but not
To feel in someone else's pocket for a key
While they lean away, laughing, their arms up,
Hands in the air covered in grease or dough or paint or clay.

I have to carry it around.
A weeping mother brings a baby to hospital,
Late-night emergency.
The tired doctor smooths the hand-made lace back from its face.
He sees it was stillborn weeks ago, has been dead for weeks.
He looks at her, there is no air in the room...

This dead relationship. This dead and sinking ship.
Bulbs lie, unplanted, on a plate of dust.
Dry and puckered pouches, only slightly mouldy;
Embalmed little stomachs but with hairy, twisted fingers,
Waiting for something to happen without needing to know what it is.
When it happens everything else in the universe can start.

This dead relationship.

I am this thing's twin.
One of us is dead
And we don't know which, we are so close.

KATHERINE PIERPOINT

279

Each from Different Heights

That time I thought I was in love
and calmly said so
was not much different from the time
I was truly in love
and slept poorly and spoke out loud
to the wall
and discovered the hidden genius
of my hands.
And the times I felt less in love,
less than someone,
were, to be honest, not so different
either.
Each was ridiculous in its own way
and each was tender, yes,
sometimes even the false is tender.
I am astounded
by the various kisses we're capable of.
Each from different heights
diminished, which is simply the law.
And the big bruise
from the longer fall looked perfectly white
in a few years.
That astounded me most of all.

STEPHEN DUNN

Badly-Chosen Lover

Criminal, you took a great piece of my life,
And you took it under false pretences,
That piece of time
– In the clear muscles of my brain
I have the lens and jug of it!
Books, thoughts, meals, days, and houses,
Half Europe, spent like a coarse banknote,
You took it – leaving mud and cabbage stumps.

And, Criminal, I damn you for it (very softly).
My spirit broke her fast on you. And, Turk,
You fed her with the breath of your neck
– In my brain's clear retina
I have the stolen love-behaviour.
Your heart, greedy and tepid, brothel-meat,
Gulped it, like a flunkey with erotica.
And very softly, Criminal, I *damn* you for it.

ROSEMARY TONKS

After the End of It

You gave and gave,
and now you say you're poor.
I'm in your debt, you say,
and there's no way to repay you
but by my giving more.

Your pound of flesh is what you must have?
Here's what I've saved.

This sip of wine is yours,
this sieve of laughter. Yours,
too, these broken halocs
from my cigarette, these coals
that flicker when the salt wind howls
and the letter box blinks like a loud
eyelid over the empty floor.

I'll send this, too, this gale between rains,
this wild day. Its cold so cold
I want to break it into panes
like new ice on a pond; then pay it
pain by pain to your account.
Let it freeze us both into some numb country!
Giving and taking might be the same there.
A future of measurement and blame
gone in a few bitter minutes.

ANNE STEVENSON

Relationship

What a silence, when you are here. What
a hellish silence.
You sit and I sit.
You lose and I lose.

JÁNOS PILINSZKY
translated from the Hungarian by Peter Jay

Hesitate to Call

Lived to see you throwing
Me aside. That fought
Like netted fish inside me. Saw you throbbing
In my syrups. Saw you sleep. And lived to see
That all that all flushed down
The refuse. Done?
It lives in me.
You live in me. Malignant.
Love, you ever want me, don't.

LOUISE GLÜCK

Lady of Miracles

Since you walked out on me
I'm getting lovelier by the hour.
I glow like a corpse in the dark.
No one sees how round and sharp
my eyes have grown
how my carcass looks like a glass urn,
how I hold up things in the rags of my hands,
the way I can stand though crippled by lust.
No, there's just your cruelty circling
my head like a bright rotting halo.

NINA CASSIAN
translated from the Romanian by Laura Schiff

Advice to a Discarded Lover

Think, now: if you have found a dead bird,
not only dead, not only fallen,
but full of maggots: what do you feel –
more pity or more revulsion?

Pity is for the moment of death,
and the moments after. It changes
when decay comes, with the creeping stench
and the wriggling, munching scavengers.

Returning later, though, you will see
a shape of clean bone, a few feathers,
an inoffensive symbol of what
once lived. Nothing to make you shudder.

It is clear then. But perhaps you find
the analogy I have chosen
for our dead affair rather gruesome –
too unpleasant a comparison.

It is not accidental. In you
I see maggots close to the surface.
You are eaten up by self-pity,
crawling with unlovable pathos.

If I were to touch you I should feel
against my fingers fat, moist worm-skin.
Do not ask me for charity now:
go away until your bones are clean.

FLEUR ADCOCK

The All Purpose Country and Western Self Pity Song

He jumped off the box-car
In Eastbourne, the beast born
In him was too hungry to hide:

His neck in grief's grommet,
He groaned through his vomit
At the churn
And the yearn
At the turn
Of the tide.

He headed him soon
For a sad-lit saloon
In back of the edge of the strand,
Where a man almost ended
Sat down and extended

His speckled,
Blue-knuckled
And cuckolded
Hand.

Cried, The wind broke my marriage in two.
Clean through the bones of it,
Christ how it blew!
I got no tomorrow
And sorrow
Is tough to rescind:
So forgive me if I should break wind, son,
Forgive me
If I should break wind.

At this the bartender
Addressed the agenda,
A dish-cloth kept dabbing his eye.

Said, Pardon intrusion
Upon your effusion
Of loss but none wooed it
Or rued it
As I.

For after the eve of Yvonne,
My God, how it hurts now the woman has gone!
Heart-sick as a dog,
I roll on like a log
Down the roaring black river
Where once sailed
A swan.

Then the dog on the floor,
Who'd not spoken before,
Growled, Ain't it the truth you guys said?
I may be a son-
Of-a-bitch but that bitch

Was my Sun
And she dumped me,
The bitch did,
For dead.

So three lonely guys in the night and a hound
Drank up, and they headed them out to the Sound,
Threw up, then they threw themselves
In and they
Drowned.

> O dee-o-dayee...
> O dee-o-dayee...
> Woe-woe-dalayee...

KIT WRIGHT

Because

My father and my mother never quarrelled.
They were united in a kind of love
As daily as the *Sydney Morning Herald*,
Rather than like the eagle or the dove.

I never saw them casually touch,
Or show a moment's joy in one another.
Why should this matter to me now so much?
I think it bore more hardly on my mother,

Who had more generous feelings to express.
My father had dammed up his Irish blood
Against all drinking praying fecklessness,
And stiffened into stone and creaking wood.

His lips would make a switching sound, as though
Spontaneous impulse must be kept at bay.
That it was mainly weakness I see now,
But then my feelings curled back in dismay.

Small things can pit the memory like a cyst:
Having seen other fathers greet their sons,
I put my childish face up to be kissed
After an absence. The rebuff still stuns

My blood. The poor man's curt embarrassment
At such a delicate proffer of affection
Cut like a saw. But home the lesson went:
My tenderness thenceforth escaped detection.

My mother sang *Because*, and *Annie Laurie*,
White Wings, and other songs; her voice was sweet.
I never gave enough, and I am sorry;
But we were all closed in the same defeat.

People do what they can; they were good people,
They cared for us and loved us. Once they stood
Tall in my childhood as the school, the steeple.
How can I judge without ingratitude?

Judgment is simply trying to reject
A part of what we are because it hurts.
The living cannot call the dead collect:
They won't accept the charge, and it reverts.

It's my own judgment day that I draw near,
Descending in the past, without a clue,
Down to that central deadness: the despair
Older than any hope I ever knew.

JAMES McAULEY

Cross

IIe has leaned for hours against the veranda railing
gazing the darkened garden out of mind
while she with battened hatches rides out the wind
that will blow for a year or a day, there is no telling.

As to why they are cross she barely remembers now.
That they *are* cross, she is certain. They hardly speak.
Feel cold and hurt and stony. For a week
have without understanding behaved so.

And will continue so to behave for neither
can come to that undemanded act of love –
kiss the sleeping princess or sleep with the frog –
and break the spell which holds them each from the other.

Or if one ventures towards it, the other, shy,
dissembles, regrets too late the dissimulation
and sits, hands slack, heart tiny, the hard solution
having again passed by.

Silly the pair of them. Yet they make me weep.
Two on a desert island, back to back
who, while the alien world howls round them black
go their own ways, fall emptily off to sleep.

P.K. PAGE

The Quarrel

Suddenly, after the quarrel, while we waited,
Disheartened, silent, with downcast looks, nor stirred
Eyelid nor finger, hopeless both, yet hoping
Against all hope to unsay the sundering word:

While all the room's stillness deepened, deepened about us
And each of us crept his thought's way to discover
How, with as little sound as the fall of a leaf,
The shadow had fallen, and lover quarreled with lover;

And while, in the quiet, I marveled – alas, alas –
At your deep beauty, your tragic beauty, torn
As the pale flower is torn by the wanton sparrow –
This beauty, pitied and loved, and now forsworn;

It was then, when the instant darkened to its darkest, –
When faith was lost with hope, and the rain conspired
To strike its gray arpeggios against our heartstrings, –
When love no longer dared, and scarcely desired:

It was then that suddenly, in the neighbor's room,
The music started: that brave quartette of strings
Breaking out of the stillness, as out of our stillness,
Like the indomitable heart of life that sings

When all is lost; and startled from our sorrow,
Tranced from our grief by that diviner grief,
We raised remembering eyes, each looked at other,
Blinded with tears of joy; and another leaf

Fell silently as that first; and in the instant
The shadow had gone, our quarrel became absurd;
And we rose, to the angelic voices of the music,
And I touched your hand, and we kissed, without a word.

CONRAD AIKEN

And they were both right

There is so much violence yet to be done.
He falls into her body
blind because desire makes him blind
deaf and limbless for the same reason.

But what is love?
And is this a question or a statement?

He will be
undone by it, she shudders in jubilation,
and pulls him to her night – like a dress
to be undone.

Love will be made and unmade – naturally,
unnaturally. It will be invoked
like a reason, like a form of life.
It will be forgotten.

What if love is no more than
a tangle of muscles
aching to be untied
by knowing fingers?

What if love is made and nothing else –
asked Narcissus, leaning over the green iris of water.

Nothing else,
cried Echo from the green cochlea of the woods.

And they were both right.
And they were both lonely.

KAPKA KASSABOVA

Between

As we fall into step I ask a penny for your thoughts.
'Oh, nothing,' you say, 'well, nothing so easily bought.'

Sliding into the rhythm of your silence, I almost forget
how lonely I'd been until that autumn morning we met.

At bedtime up along my childhood's stairway, tongues
of fire cast shadows. Too earnest, too highstrung.

My desire is endless: others ended when I'd only started.
Then, there was you: so whole-hog, so wholehearted.

Think of the thousands of nights and the shadows fought.
And the mornings of light. I try to read your thought.

In the strange openness of your face, I'm powerless.
Always this love. Always this infinity between us.

MICHEAL O'SIADHAIL

When You Are Old

When you are old and grey and full of sleep,
And nodding by the fire, take down this book,
And slowly read, and dream of the soft look
Your eyes had once, and of their shadows deep;

How many loved your moments of glad grace,
And loved your beauty with love false or true,
But one man loved the pilgrim soul in you,
And loved the sorrows of your changing face;

And bending down beside the glowing bars,
Murmur, a little sadly, how Love fled
And paced upon the mountains overhead
And hid his face amid a crowd of stars.

W.B. YEATS

Spell

If, at your desk, you push aside your work,
take down a book, turn to this verse
and read that I kneel there, pressing
my ear where on your chest the muscles
arch as great books part, in seagull curves,
bridging the seasounds of your heart,

and that your hands run through my hair,
draw the wayward mass to strands
as flat as scarlet silk-thread bookmarks,
and stroke my cheeks as if smoothing
back the tissue leaves from chilly,
plated pages, and pull me near

to read my eyes alone, then you shall see,
silvered and monochrome, yourself,
sitting at your desk, taking down a book,
turning to this verse, and then, my love,
you shall not know which one of us is reading
now, which writing, and which written.

KATE CLANCHY

Conch

In front of the mirror in my parents' bedroom lay a pink conch. I
used to approach it on tiptoes, and with a sudden movement put
it against my ears. I wanted to surprise it one day when it wasn't
longing with a monotonous hum for the sea. Although I was small
I knew that even if we love someone very much, at times it happens
that we forget about it.

ZBIGNIEW HERBERT
translated from the Polish by John & Bogdana Carpenter

'O tell me the truth about love'

Some say that love's a little boy,
    And some say it's a bird,
Some say it makes the world go round,
    And some say that's absurd,
And when I asked the man next-door,
    Who looked as if he knew,
His wife got very cross indeed,
    And said it wouldn't do.

    Does it look like a pair of pyjamas,
      Or the ham in a temperance hotel?
    Does its odour remind one of llamas,
      Or has it a comforting smell?
    Is it prickly to touch as a hedge is,
      Or soft as eiderdown fluff
    Is it sharp or quite smooth at the edges?
      O tell me the truth about love.

Our history books refer to it
    In cryptic little notes,
It's quite a common topic on
    The Transatlantic boats;
I've found the subject mentioned in
    Accounts of suicides,
And even seen it scribbled on
    The backs of railway-guides.

    Does it howl like a hungry Alsatian,
      Or boom like a military band?
    Could one give a first-rate imitation
      On a saw or a Steinway Grand?
    Is its singing at parties a riot?
      Does it only like Classical stuff ?
    Will it stop when one wants to be quiet?
      O tell me the truth about love.

I looked inside the summer-house;
    It wasn't ever there:
I tried the Thames at Maidenhead,
    And Brighton's bracing air.

I don't know what the blackbird sang,
       Or what the tulip said;
But it wasn't in the chicken-run,
       Or underneath the bed.

   Can it pull extraordinary faces?
     Is it usually sick on a swing?
   Does it spend all its time at the races,
     Or fiddling with pieces of string?
   Has it views of its own about money?
     Does it think Patriotism enough?
   Are its stories vulgar but funny?
     O tell me the truth about love.

   When it comes, will it come without warning
     Just as I'm picking my nose?
   Will it knock on my door in the morning,
     Or tread in the bus on my toes?
   Will it come like a change in the weather?
     Will its greeting be courteous or rough?
   Will it alter my life altogether?
     O tell me the truth about love.

W.H. AUDEN

Lightness

It was your lightness that drew me,
the lightness of your talk and your laughter,
the lightness of your cheek in my hands,
your sweet gentle modest lightness;
and it is the lightness of your kiss
that is starving my mouth,
and the lightness of your embrace
that will let me go adrift.

MEG BATEMAN
translated from the Gaelic by the author

In Paris with You

Don't talk to me of love. I've had an earful
And I get tearful when I've downed a drink or two.
I'm one of your talking wounded.
I'm a hostage. I'm maroonded.
But I'm in Paris with you.

Yes I'm angry at the way I've been bamboozled
And resentful at the mess that I've been through.
I admit I'm on the rebound
And I don't care where are *we* bound.
I'm in Paris with you.

> Do you mind if we do *not* go to the Louvre,
> If we say sod off to sodding Notre Dame,
> If we skip the Champs Elysées
> And remain here in this sleazy
> Old hotel room
> Doing this and that
> To what and whom
> Learning who you are,
> Learning what I am.

Don't talk to me of love. Let's talk of Paris,
The little bit of Paris in our view.
There's that crack across the ceiling
And the hotel walls are peeling
And I'm in Paris with you.

Don't talk to me of love. Let's talk of Paris.
I'm in Paris with the slightest thing you do.
I'm in Paris with your eyes, your mouth,
I'm in Paris with... all points south.
Am I embarrassing you?
I'm in Paris with you.

JAMES FENTON

8

My people

There is no use coming to poets, either in Soviet Russia or
Northern Ireland, and expecting or ordering them to deliver
a certain product to fit a certain agenda, for although
they must feel answerable to the world they inhabit, poets,
if they are to do their proper work, must also feel free.

SEAMUS HEANEY

In the deserts of the heart
Let the healing fountain start,
In the prison of his days
Teach the free man how to praise.

W.H. AUDEN
from 'In Memory of W.B. Yeats'

When poets portray their people and explore their countries, they must cross
what Seamus Heaney calls 'the frontier of writing'. This is 'the line that divides
the actual conditions of our daily lives from the imaginative representation of
those conditions in literature, and divides the world of social speech from the
world of poetic language'. The rhetoric of politicians turns individuals into social
types while the news media change people into caricatures, but the language
of poetry transforms the familiar into something rich and strangely revealing.

Because their own backgrounds and perspectives are so diverse, contemp-
orary poets show us many different kinds of people living different kinds of
lives in the same countries, and how there are many different Englands, many
different versions of Scotland, Wales and Ireland. There's a country for the
rich, the lucky and the privileged, a country for the poor, the outcast and the
down-and-out, and another country where most of us live, less defined, some-
where, somehow, inbetween. Peter Reading's England is 'an island farctate with
feculence' in *Evagatory* (311), an unreal yet recognisable place which he trans-
forms like a visiting explorer using a disconcerting mixture of quantitative
verse forms such as dispersed Alcaics (*see* Glossary, 464). Politicians and the
media may appeal to a consensus, but that supposed middle ground may be
an unrepresentative average (or Peter Reading's 'all equal with nil'). America,
too, is a different country for different groups of people, from the black poet

Langston Hughes reclaiming his own America (326) to factory worker Fred Voss in 'Making America Strong' (326). Voss's satirical snapshot of the American way of life is one of long series of poems he has set in the Goodstone Aircraft Company, an oily amalgam of all the factories where he has sweated it out on the shopfloor, a bastion of male America where bragging men engage in horse-play while turning out faulty parts for the U.S. Air Force.

Many people no longer live in the countries or places of their birth or upbringing, or speak the language of their parents, and poets such as Imtiaz Dharker (327), Jackie Kay (329), Shirley Geok-Lin Lim (329) and Moniza Alvi (330) address the modern condition of exile and displacement as well as the meaning of 'home' for immigrants and people of mixed race.

Poems about countries can be grounded in actual landscapes, but such places can be transformed through the act of poetic imagination. Philip Pacey's portrait of Uffington in Berkshire (306) is from a cycle of poems called *Charged Landscapes*. Like Paul Nash's paintings, they show particular landscapes in a special light that charges the visible world with significance, making connections between Nature and human nature; his sequence begins with an epigraph from the religious thinker Martin Buber: 'Nature needs Man for…its hallowing.' But nowadays Man is more likely to harrow the land and lay waste its wildlife and natural riches: this is the message of poets from Edward Thomas, writing about England in the early years of the last century in 'The Combe' (307), to Cumbria's Norman Nicholson, describing the landscape around Sellafield when that benighted place was called 'Windscale' (307). John Heath-Stubbs writes his elegy for England as 'The Green Man's Last Will and Testament' (308).

Poems about people often relate also to language, faith and betrayal. Anna Akhmatova begins 'Our Own Land' (298) with a defiantly appropriate quotation ('There is no one in the world more tearless,/ more proud, more simple than us') from a poem she wrote 40 years earlier, 'I am not among those who left our land'. In contrast, Glyn Maxwell's perspective in 'We Billion Cheered' (338) is far from clearcut, viewing his people through absences and shifting shades of meaning in a poem of psychological depth which could apply to any country whose sense of nation is informed not by morality but by expediency. Maxwell's menacing account of a country still in transition reminds me of the Greek poet C.P. Cavafy's 'Waiting for the Barbarians' (339). The two poems are unsettling in the way they portray collective disillusionment and public ignorance, but both poets write from inside the crowd, as one of 'we billion'… 'what are we waiting for?' Because they include and implicate themselves, their criticism can be ironically detached without being judgemental or inhuman.

Many poets have had an ambivalent attitude toward writing about political issues, often citing Keats's comment 'We hate poetry that has a palpable design on us' (actually a reaction against Wordsworth's personality) as a justification of lyric poetry. W.B. Yeats believed that the will must not usurp the work of the imagination. In this section of the book, and in the following section on *War and peace*, I have chosen a number of so-called "political" poems. But these particular writers have responded to deeply felt concerns not through political rhetoric or social comment, but in human terms, getting under the skins of their own people to write highly imaginative poetry of transformative power and direct relevance. They have heeded Keats's advice to Shelley: 'Be more of an artist, and load every rift of your subject with ore.'

'The East-West border...'

The East-West border is always wandering,
sometimes eastward, sometimes west,
and we do not know exactly where it is just now:
in Gaugamela, in the Urals, or maybe in ourselves,
so that one ear, one eye, one nostril, one hand, one foot,
one lung and one testicle or one ovary
is on the one, another on the other side. Only the heart,
only the heart is always on one side:
if we are looking northward, in the West;
if we are looking southward, in the East;
and the mouth doesn't know on behalf of which or both
it has to speak.

JAAN KAPLINSKI
translated from the Estonian by the author with Sam Hamill & Riina Tamm

My People

my people
pass through gardens untouched by the toxic pollen of lilies
sway with the pre-factored rhythm of skyscrapers flexing in strong
        wind
thicken the air at night clubs and bus stops and cab ranks with
        their absence

my people
speak with the voices of ten million leaves, of earthquakes and
        dust motes
feed on starlight and moonshine and fallen crumbs of consumed
        dreams
grow with the vegetable fierceness of beansprouts, knowing that
        no growing is death

when they come
outracing planes whose snail trails silver the hollow sphere of the air
from earth where coal can burn twenty years in an underground seam
by sea, with sodium fire in their radiant lungfuls of water

their hands
will greet me with gestures that flux into silent legions of butterflies
will bear astounding weight with the sevenfold strength of ants
will move over me like perfect maggots purging the flesh of wounds

my people
are moving somewhere, trailing in wakes of their purpose the seasons
are wrung by an appetite gnawing at glaciers and atoms and bricks
are tirelessly looking for me, but in the wrong house, or country,
          or century

KONA MACPHEE

Our Own Land

> *There is no one in the world more tearless,*
> *more proud, more simple than us.*
>   1922

We don't wear it in sacred amulets on our chests.
We don't compose hysterical poems about it.
It does not disturb our bitter dream-sleep.
It doesn't seem to be the promised paradise.
We don't make of it a soul
object for sale and barter,
and we being sick, poverty-stricken, unable to utter a word
don't even remember about it.
Yes, for us it's mud on galoshes,
    for us it's crunch on teeth,
    and we mill, mess and crush
    that dust and ashes
    that is not mixed up in anything.
But we'll lie in it and be it,
that's why, so freely, we call it our own.

Leningrad, 1961

ANNA AKHMATOVA
translated from the Russian by Richard McKane

A Summer Morning

Her young employers, having got in late
From seeing friends in town
And scraped the right front fender on the gate,
Will not, the cook expects, be coming down.

She makes a quiet breakfast for herself.
The coffee-pot is bright,
The jelly where it should be on the shelf.
She breaks an egg into the morning light,

Then, with the bread-knife lifted, stands and hears
The sweet efficient sounds
Of thrush and catbird, and the snip of shears
Where, in the terraced backward of the grounds,

A gardener works before the heat of day.
He straightens for a view
Of the big house ascending stony-gray
Out of his beds mosaic with the dew.

His young employers having got in late,
He and the cook alone
Receive the morning on their old estate,
Possessing what the owners can but own.

RICHARD WILBUR

The Heron

A servant's soul. He said I had a servant's soul
    and he spat in the grate
and left me crying here like the wretch that I am.
So I thought then I should never touch him again
    and I hated myself
and I sobbed for an hour alone in the cold room.
    I'd had enough. I'd go.
Though the roads were crueller than he, I would walk home.
Then he knocked and came in with the bird in his hands.

He was red – with the heat of straw and horses on him.
But the anger was gone, and his face oddly still.
      I was certain at last
I should never be quite alone; something of him
      stuck with me, a splinter;
something he didn't want to give that remained yet.
      I said, It's a heron.
And he said, Yes, it was dead by the stable door
at the foot of the wall, in the snow, in the drain.

Its eye, he said, was deep as a fish's eye, its
      wing's grey was my cloth dress.
And what kind of help was left for us, when the bird
he had watched a week as it stalked the river's length
      could be driven to this,
to a heap of frozen rag flung down from the roof,
with the rods of its legs furred white in ice, where the
      horses breathed, where the pond
it had poached from in spring was snapped tight like a gin?

STUART HENSON

A Letter to Dennis
(in memoriam Dennis Potter)

Deep in the strangest pits in England, deep
in the strangest forest, my grandfathers
and yours coughed out their silicotic lungs.
Silicosis. England. Land of phlegm
and stereophonic gobbing, whose last pearls
of sputum on the lips, whose boils and tropes
and hallucinations are making me sick.

The point is how to find a use for fury,
as you have taught, old father,
my old butt, wherever you are.
Still rude, I hope, still raucous and rejoicing
in the most painful erection in heaven
which rises through its carapace of sores
and cracking skin to sing in English.

You are as live to me as the tongue
in my mouth, as the complicated shame
of Englishness. Would you call me lass?
Would you heave up any stars for my crown?

JO SHAPCOTT

Turns

I thought it made me look more 'working class'
(as if a bit of chequered cloth could bridge that gap!)
I did a turn in it before the glass.
My mother said: *It suits you, your dad's cap.*
(She preferred me to wear suits and part my hair:
You're every bit as good as that lot are!)

All the pension queue came out to stare.
Dad was sprawled beside the postbox (still VR),
his cap turned inside up beside his head,
smudged H A H in purple Indian ink
and Brylcreem slicks displayed so folk might think
he wanted charity for dropping dead.

He never begged. For nowt! Death's reticence
crowns his life's, and *me*, I'm opening my trap
to busk the class that broke him for the pence
that splash like brackish tears into our cap.

TONY HARRISON

The Door

Yes, that is the door and behind it they live,
But not grossly as we do. Through a fine sieve
Their people pass the incoming air. They are said
To circulate thoughtfully in walled gardens, the aged –
And they live long – wheeling in chairs. They exchange

301

Nothing but traditional courtesies. Most strange
However is their manner of dying, for they know the hour,
When it comes, as old elephants do. They devour
Their usual breakfast of plovers' eggs and rise
Then or are lifted by the janitors and without goodbyes
They step or are borne aloft through that door there –
And thus they end. For of course meeting the air,
The air we breathe, they perish instantly,
They go all into dust, into dead dust, and Stanley,
The Sweeper, comes with his brush and shovel and little cart
And sweeps them up and shovels them not apart
But into one black plastic bag with dimps, dog-shit
And all our common dirt. But this they intend and it
Signals their gracious willingness to reside
In the poor heart of life, once they have died.

DAVID CONSTANTINE

from Going On

These are the days of the horrible headlines,
Bomb Blast Atrocity, Leak From Reactor,
Soccer Fans Run Amok, Middle East Blood Bath,
PC Knocks Prisoner's Eye Out In Charge Room.
Outside, the newsvendors ululate. Inside,
lovers seek refuge in succulent plump flesh,
booze themselves innocent of the whole shit-works.
Why has the gentleman fallen face-forward
into his buttered asparagus, Garçon?
He and his girlfriend have already drunk two
bottles of Bollinger and they were half-tight
when they arrived at the place half-an-hour since.
Waiters man-handle the gentleman upright,
aim him (with smirks at the lady) towards his
quails (which he misses and slumps in the gravy –
baying, the while, for 'Encore du Savigny').
He is supplied with the Beaune, which he noses,
quaffs deeply, relishes... sinks to the gingham
where he reposes susurrantly. There is

'63 Sandeman fetched to revive him.
Chin on the Pont l'Evêque, elbow in ash-tray,
as from the *Book of the Dead*, he produces
incomprehensible hieroglyphs, bidding
Access surrender the price of his coma
unto the restaurateur, kindly and patient.
These are the days of the **National Health Cuts**,
days of the end of the innocent liver;
they have to pay for it privately, who would seek anaesthetic.

PETER READING

In Britain

The music, on fat bellied instruments.
The fingers, swarming down ladders
into the bubbling cauldrons of sound.
The mouths, greasy, encouraging the prying fingers
with songs of fecund stomachs.
The hands, transferring to the singing mouths
whatever is lifted through the scum.
The choicest morsels, the collops of dog and the
gobbets of pig. The orchestras and bands,
the minstrelsy arranged in tiers,
dripping on each other. The larded steps.
The treacherous floors in the wooden galleries.
The garlands of offal, plopping on heads
from a height of some feet.
The offal sliding off down the front of the face,
or over the neck and ears. The offal reposing like hats.
The curly grey-white tubes, dangling jauntily
above the left eye of the bagpipe player.
The guests, similarly festooned.
The guests at their conversation,
abundance of dogs and pigs in these islands.
The guests at their serious business, lying in pools.
The stories, farting and belching across the puddled boards.
The gross imaginations, bulging with viscera.
The heads full of stories, the stories thwacked like bladders.

The stories steaming in time to the music.
The stories, chewed like lumps of gristle.
The stories describing extravagant herds.
The stories, reasons for killing each other.

PETER DIDSBURY

England Nil

The advance to Hamburg broke with all the plans.
Doug spelled them out in Luton Friday night.
Someone had ballsed it up. A dozen vans
Waited in convoy, ringside. Blue and white
We stumbled through. The beer
When we found it in that piss-hole of jerries
Was all we needed. Who won the war,
Anyway? Who nuked Dresden? Two fairies
Skittered behind the bar, talking Kraut
Or maybe Arabic. We clocked the poison
Smiles and chanted till the SS threw us out.
Stuttgart was a tea-party to this. One
By one they've nicked us, berserk with fear.
You've been Englished but you won't forget it, never.

ANNE ROUSE

Barton in the Beans

For comfort on bad nights,
open out a map of Middle England

and sing yourself to sleep
with a lullaby of English names:

Shouldham Thorpe, in gentle sunshine,
Swadlincote, in a Laura Ashley frock,

Little Cubley, veins running with weak tea,
Kibworth Beauchamp, praying on protestant knees,

Ashby-de-la-Zouch, saying 'Morning',
Wigston Parva, smiling – but not too widely,

Ramsey Mereside, raising an eyebrow,
Eye Kettleby, where they'd rather not talk about it,

Market Overton, echoing with the slamming doors
of Cold Overton, where teenagers flee every night to their rooms,

screaming that from Appleby Magna to Stubbers Green
they never met a soul who understood.

They never met a soul.
At Barton in the Beans, the rain says *Sssshhhhh...*

JOANNE LIMBURG

The Reason

It's because you never left
these endless fields

where an oak tree sails the horizon
like a lost galleon

where rabbits crouch in mad-dog heat
under a sky full of eyes

where a gunshot scatters acres of birds
leaving wires like empty staves

where a road runs straight for hours
towards a shimmering spire

where a man can live all his life
beyond calling distance.

ESTHER MORGAN

Charged Landscape: Uffington

From the eye of the Uffington White Horse
the downs' every feature. Spur, combe
and fluting; lifted by low sun

waves of a fossil sea, surging again
as wind through barley, breaking
on Berkshire's plain. The hand of man

who cleared scrub – yew and juniper; felled
trees below, exposing to view this land's
form, kept cropped by sheep and cultivation.

Cut through turf then, to this sea-horse,
tip of a contour's whip uncoiling,
crack of it – hoove's strike on storm's iron? –

lightning, will loose on earth rain.
At night, the white chalk reflecting, become
moon in the form, mare; fecund

to the sun her stallion. Who depended
for life on these things, each year
came as grooms to her, with hands scarred

by labour scouring flanks of the hill
until, the work done, made celebration in
the scooped hollow its earthen castle.

Come now, from close-to join up
detail to detail, bold
curve of back or foreleg, to an imagined

whole; and, from this eye, look to
the horizon, Harwell's shimmering:
charged with the same power that's here?

PHILIP PACEY

The Combe

The Combe was ever dark, ancient and dark.
Its mouth is stopped with bramble, thorn, and briar;
And no one scrambles over the sliding chalk
By beech and yew and perishing juniper
Down the half precipices of its sides, with roots
And rabbit holes for steps. The sun of Winter,
The moon of Summer, and all the singing birds
Except the missel-thrush that loves juniper,
Are quite shut out. But far more ancient and dark
The Combe looks since they killed the badger there,
Dug him out and gave him to the hounds,
That most ancient Briton of English beasts.

EDWARD THOMAS

Windscale

The toadstool towers infest the shore:
Stink-horns that propagate and spore
    Wherever the wind blows.
Scafell looks down from the bracken band,
And sees hell in a grain of sand,
    And feels the canker itch between his toes.

This is a land where dirt is clean,
And poison pasture, quick and green,
    And storm sky, bright and bare;
Where sewers flow with milk, and meat
Is carved up for the fire to eat,
    And children suffocate in God's fresh air.

NORMAN NICHOLSON

The Green Man's Last Will and Testament

In a ragged spinney (scheduled
For prompt development as a bijou housing estate)
I saw the green daemon of England's wood
As he wrote his testament. The grey goose
Had given him one of her quills for a pen;
The robin's breast was a crimson seal;
The long yellow centipede held a candle.

He seemed like a hollow oak-trunk, smothered with ivy:
At his feet or roots clustered the witnesses,
Like hectic toadstools, or pallid as broom-rape:
Wood-elves – goodfellows, hobs and lobs,
Black Anis, the child-devouring hag,
From her cave in the Dane Hills, saucer-eyed
Phantom dogs, Black Shuck and Barghest, with the cruel nymphs
Of the northern streams, Peg Powler of the Tees
And Jenny Greenteeth of the Ribble,
Sisters of Bellisama, the very fair one.

'I am sick, I must die,' he said. 'Poisoned like Lord Randal
From hedges and ditches. My ditches run with pollution,
My hedgerows are gone, and the hedgerow singers.
The rooks, disconsolate, have lost their rookery:
The elms are all dead of the Dutch pox.
No longer the nightjar churns in the twilit glade,
Nor the owl, like a white phantom, silent-feathered
Glides to the barn. The red-beaked chough,
Enclosing Arthur's soul, is seen no more
Wheeling and calling over the Cornish cliffs.
Old Tod has vacated his deep-dug earth;
He has gone to rummage in the city dustbins.
Tiggy is squashed flat on the M1.

'My delicate deer are culled, and on offshore islands
My sleek silkies, where puffin and guillemot
Smother and drown in oil and tar.
The mechanical reaper has guillotined
Ortygometra, though she was no traitor,
Crouching over her cradle – no longer resounds
Crek-crek, crek-crek, among the wheatfields,
Where the scarlet cockle is missing and the blue cornflower.

My orchids and wild hyacinths are raped and torn,
My lenten lilies and my fritillaries.
Less frequent now the debate
Of cuckoo and nightingale – and where is the cuckoo's maid,
The snake-necked bird sacred to Venus,
Her mysteries and the amber twirling wheel?
In no brightness of air dance now the butterflies –
Their hairy mallyshags are slaughtered among the nettles.
The innocent bats are evicted from the belfries,
'The death-watch remains, and masticates history.

'I'll leave to the people of England
All that remains:
Rags and patches – a few old tales
And bawdy jokes, snatches of song and galumphing dance-steps.
Above all my obstinacy – obstinacy of flintstones
That breed in the soil, and pertinacity
Of unlovely weeds – chickweed and groundsel,
Plantain, shepherd's purse and Jack-by-the-hedge.
Let them keep it as they wander in the inhuman towns.

'And the little children, imprisoned in ogrish towers, enchanted
By a one-eyed troll in front of a joyless fire –
I would have them remember the old games and the old dances:
Sir Roger is dead, Sir Roger is dead,
She raised him up under the apple tree;
Poor Mary is a-weeping, weeping like Ariadne,
Weeping for her husband on a bright summer's day.'

JOHN HEATH-STUBBS

Kith

On the other side of the border
they call this *Scozia Irredenta*:
unredeemed.

      A few coffers of coins
didn't change hands; a battle was lost
instead of won; the in-between land
stays in-between.

A line on a map
moved back through the years
                down to the Tees.
England was never an only child
but has grown to think so. Stone streets dip –
rise. They're burning coal on morning fires
in dark front rooms: smoke gusts over roofs.
Gardens, late coming into flower,
brazen it out with bright aubrietia.

I've followed the hills to Carter Bar
past lost peels, and moors where soaking sheep
stagger between tufts of died-back grass.
Standing in the rain, she's there – harassed,
hurt – a foster-mother, telling me
she hasn't much to offer. I'll take
my chance: I don't believe her.
                                The bends
on the border
                won't make up their minds.
Five times
            they twist me round, but I still
head north.

ROBYN BOLAM

passage

it faced the north with a roar, then
ran snivelling southward, long
green dribbles into the sun
where cattle were happy, men
had called it Alba,
Caledonia, briefly
talked of it as Scotland, now
it empties under our wingtips,
five minutes of wrinkles,

a dusting of snow.

G.F. DUTTON

An Outlying Station

A sea-fog like gunsmoke was cresting The Sound
and our coffee steam making the van windows misty,
the morning the crew was at last leaving town.

I say *town*, but more like a village with bells on:
the streets full of strays, houses glutted with ghosties
and squash full of fuck-ups, like Scoraig or Findhorn.

The worst part of three weeks spent watching the telly
in the one pub-cum-caff which served home brew like toffee;
a bar-bint called Morvern who gives men the willies.

Three weeks of bad drugs, badass jazz, bad religion,
the same German blonde who came on to me nightly
and clipper-scalped DJs who talked revolution.

Was I really the only one here who owned luggage?
They watched as I loaded it onto the trolley,
half the weight of their spurious, spiritual baggage.

We boarded the train at an outlying station.
I woke on the border of some brand new country;
my forehead was prickly with chill perspiration.

RODDY LUMSDEN

from Evagatory

Came to an island farctate with feculence:
chip-papers, Diet-Pepsi cans clattering,
prams, supermarket trolleys, spent mattresses,

bus-rank of steel and rank uriniferous
concrete, a footbridge richly enlivened with
    aerosol squirtings, daubed graffiti,

311

       pustular simian sub-teenagers
hurling abuse and empty bottles
       over the parapet into crowds of
       pensioners waiting for **X-PRESS SERVISS**,

       xylophone tinkle of smashed glass, crackle
under a tyre, a hapless old fart
stanching the flow from freshly sliced flesh.

*

    Avian botulism thriving
(black plastic bin-bags/scavenging *Laridae*);
    sand-eels depleted (over-fishing):

sanitised quondam herring gull colony,
sanitised quondam kittiwake colony –
    all that remains, their last year's shit's stink.

*

53 bus approaching the terminus;
       dapper sartorial English elder
       suited in Manx tweed, close-clipped grey tash:

Too much is wrong, Gibbonian undertones,
    schooling and bread and dress and manners,
era's decline, Elgarian sadnesses;

too much is wrong, duff ticker, insomnia,
    ulcer and thyrotoxicosis,
        end of the world in one's lifetime likely,
flight of a sparrow brief through the feasting hall.

*

Perilous trek, unarmed, unaccompanied:
       set out from Cranium, through uncharted
       swamp, to arrive at Lingua Franca,
thence to this Logaoedic Dependency.

*

Cranial voice loquacious/inadequate
(translationese from life to lingo):

Only a troubled idyll now possible,
pastoral picnic under an ozone hole,
England, *The Times* screwed up in a trash-bucket,
   gliding astern, the Thames, the old prides,
   end of an era, nation, notion,
      Albion urban, devenustated
   (one of those routine periodic
faunal extinctions [cf. the Permian]),
arthropod aberration (posterity).

*

a dreadful, bloody, civil insurrection among the poor mad
islanders brought about because their automobiles, which they
had revered above all else, and which had helped boost their
weak, inferior egos, had been confiscated by their (suddenly
aware and panic-stricken) government. For it seems that, whereas
the manifest absurdity of mayhem on congested tarmac and the
lowering mantle of ferruginous fog had somehow failed to awaken
authoritarian sensibility, this abrupt (albeit long-prognosticated)
termination of a fundamental, unrenewable

*

Newspapers there (the sumps of society,
draining off, holding up for inspection a
   corporate concentrated slurry)
retail, with relish, mayhem and muck of a
      clapped-out, subliterate, scrap-stuffed fake state:
   23.3 million vehicles,
   29.8 million drivers,
300 000 maimed on their ludicrous
   tarmac p.a., 5000 flenched dead –
      fortunate, then, that it doesn't matter
(for they are far too philoprogenitive).

*

Snow-haired, an elder, dulled eyes gum-filled,
tuning a sweet-toned curious instrument,
    gulps from a goblet of local merlot,
sings on a theme whose fame was fabled,
that of a sad realm farctate with feculence
    (patois and translationese alternately):

Gobschighte damapetty,
    gobby Fer-dama,
    getspeeke baggsy,
    getspeeke parly
    comma cul, comma
    malbicker-bicker,
porky getspeeke?, porky?

Wonderful little Madam,
self-mocking Iron Lady,
who some said was a windbag,
some said talked
like an arsehole, like
a termagant – why,
why did some say that?

Pascoz vots clobberjoli,
    vots chevvy-dur dur,
    vots baggsymain chic,
    vots collier-prick,
    cuntyvach twitnit,
    iscst pukkerjoli –
illos jalouz dats porky!

Because your pretty frocks,
your permed-stiff hair,
your smart handbag, your
tight-sharp necklace,
satrapess so marvellous,
were so beautiful –
they were envious, that's it!

Ni iscst vots marrypappa
    grignaleto, ne.
    Mas vots pollytiq
    saggio sauvay
    vots salinsula,
    insulapetty,
et fair tutts egal mit-nochts.

Nor was your spouse
a pipsqueak – far from it!
But your many wise policies
were saving your islet,
your filthy isle, and
made all equal with nil.

PETER READING

After Mr Mayhew's visit

So now the Victorians are all in heaven,
Miss Routledge and the young conservatives
chatting with the vicar, visiting again
the home for incurables who never die.

The old damp soaks through the wallpaper,
there's servant trouble, the cook
fighting drunk at the sherry, and Edith
coughing and consumptive, fainting away.

Only this time it never ends: the master
continually remarking how the weather bites cold,
the brandy flask stands empty, and the poor
are pushing to the windows like the fog.

KEN SMITH

The Nation

The national day
had dawned. Everywhere
the national tree was opening its blossoms
to the sun's first rays, and from all quarters
young and old in national costume
were making their way to the original National
Building, where the national standard already
fluttered against the sky. Some breakfasted
on the national dish as they walked, frequently
pausing to greet acquaintances with a heartfelt
exchange of the national gesture. Many
were leading the national animal; others carried it
in their arms. The national bird
flew overhead; and on every side
could be heard the keen strains
or the national anthem, played on
the national instrument.

Where enough were gathered together,
national feeling ran high, and concerted cries of
'Death to the national foe!' were raised.
The national weapon was brandished. Though
festivities were constrained by the size of
the national debt, the national sport was
vigorously played all day
and the national drink drunk.
And from midday till late in the evening
there arose continually from the rear
of the national prison the sounds of the national
method of execution, dealing out rapid
justice to those who had given way
– on this day of all days –
to the national vice.

ROY FISHER

Everyone Hates the English

Everyone hates the English,
　　Including the English. They sneer
At each other for being so English,
　　So what are they doing here,
The English? It's *thick* with the English,
　　All over the country. Why?
Anyone ever born English
　　Should shut up, or fuck off, or die.

Anyone ever born English
　　Should hold their extraction in scorn
And apologise all over England
　　For ever at all being born,
For that's how it is, being English;
　　Fodder for any old scoff
That England might be a nice country
　　If only the English fucked off!

KIT WRIGHT

A song for England

An' a so de rain a-fall
An' a so de snow a-rain

An' a so de fog a-fall
An' a so de sun a-fail

An' a so de seasons mix
An' a so de bag-o'-tricks

But a so me understan'
De misery o' de Englishman.

ANDREW SALKEY

The Voyeur

what's your favourite word dearie
is it wee
I hope it's wee
wee's such a nice wee word
like a wee hairy dog
with two wee eyes
such a nice wee word to play with dearie
you can say it quickly
with a wee smile
and a wee glance to the side
or you can say it slowly dearie
with your mouth a wee bit open
and a wee sigh dearie
a wee sigh
put your wee head on my shoulder dearie
oh my
a great wee word
and Scottish
it makes you proud

TOM LEONARD

The King and Queen of Dumfriesshire

The King and Queen of Dumfriesshire sit
in their battery-dead Triumph, gazing ahead
at an iced-over windscreen like a gull rolled flat.
They are cast in bronze, with Henry Moore holes
shot in each other by incessant argument;
these are convenient for holding her tartan flask,
his rolled-up *Scotsman*. The hairy skeleton
of a Border terrier sits in the back window,
not nodding. On the back seat rests
their favourite argument, the one about
how he does not permit her to see the old friends
she no longer likes and he secretly misses;
the one which is really about punishing each other
for no longer wanting to make love.
The argument is in the form of a big white bowl
with a black band around it hand-painted with fruit.
It has a gold rim, and in it lies
a brown curl of water from the leaking roof.
Outside, the clouds continue
to bomb the glen with sheep, which bare
their slate teeth as they tumble,
unexpectedly sneering.
The King and Queen of Dumfriesshire sit
like the too-solid bullet-ridden ghosts
of Bonnie and Clyde, not eating their
tinned salmon sandwiches, crustless, still
wrapped in tinfoil, still in the tupperware.
They survey their domain, not glancing at
each other, not removing from the glove compartment
any of the old words they have always used,
words like 'twae', like 'couthy', like 'Kirkcudbright',
which keep their only threat at bay: of separation.

W.N. HERBERT

Reservoirs

There are places in Wales I don't go:
Reservoirs that are the subconscious
Of a people, troubled far down
With gravestones, chapels, villages even;
The serenity of their expression
Revolts me, it is a pose
For strangers, a watercolour's appeal
To the mass, instead of the poem's
Harsher conditions. There are the hills,
Too; gardens gone under the scum
Of the forests; and the smashed faces
Of the farms with the stone trickle
Of their tears down the hills' side.

Where can I go, then, from the smell
Of decay, from the putrefying of a dead
Nation? I have walked the shore
For an hour and seen the English
Scavenging among the remains
Of our culture, covering the sand
Like the tide and, with the roughness
Of the tide, elbowing our language
Into the grave that we have dug for it.

R.S. THOMAS

Synopsis of the Great Welsh Novel

Dai K lives at the end of a valley. One is not quite sure
Whether it has been drowned or not. His Mam
Loves him too much and his Dada drinks.
As for his girlfriend Blodwen, she's pregnant. So
Are all the other girls in the village – there's been a Revival.
After a performance of *Elijah*, the mad preacher
Davies the Doom has burnt the chapel down.

319

One Saturday night after the dance at the Con Club,
With the Free Wales Army up to no good in the back lanes,
A stranger comes to the village; he is, of course,
God, the well-known television personality. He succeeds
In confusing the issue, whatever it is, and departs
On the last train before the line is closed.
The colliery blows up, there is a financial scandal
Involving the most respected citizens; the Choir
Wins at the National. It is all seen, naturally,
Through the eyes of a sensitive boy who never grows up.
The men emigrate to America, Cardiff and the moon. The girls
Find rich and foolish English husbands. Only daft Ianto
Is left to recite the Complete Works of Sir Lewis Morris
To puzzled sheep, before throwing himself over
The edge of the abandoned quarry. One is not quite sure
Whether it is fiction or not.

HARRI WEBB

Westering Home

Though you'd be pressed to say exactly where
It first sets in, driving west through Wales
Things start to feel like Ireland. It can't be
The chapels with their clear grey windows,
Or the buzzards menacing the scooped valleys.
In April, have the blurred blackthorn hedges
Something to do with it? Or possibly
The motorway, which seems to lose its nerve
Mile by mile. The houses, up to a point,
With their masoned gables, each upper window
A raised eyebrow. More, though, than all of this,
It's the architecture of the spirit;
The old thin ache you thought that you'd forgotten –
More smoke, admittedly, than flame;
Less tears than rain. And the whole business
Neither here nor there, and therefore home.

BERNARD O'DONOGHUE

Overheard in County Sligo

I married a man from County Roscommon
and I live at the back of beyond
with a field of cows and a yard of hens
and six white geese on the pond.

At my door's a square of yellow corn
caught up by its corners and shaken,
and the road runs down through the open gate
and freedom's there for the taking.

I had thought to work on the Abbey stage
or have my name in a book,
to see my thought on the printed page,
or still the crowd with a look.

But I turn to fold the breakfast cloth
and to polish the lustre and brass,
to order and dust the tumbled rooms
and find my face in the glass.

I ought to feel I'm a happy woman
for I lie in the lap of the land,
and I married a man from County Roscommon
and I live in the back of beyond.

GILLIAN CLARKE

Inniskeen Road: July Evening

The bicycles go by in twos and threes –
There's a dance in Billy Brennan's barn tonight,
And there's the half-talk code of mysteries
And the wink-and-elbow language of delight.
Half-past eight and there is not a spot
Upon a mile of road, no shadow thrown
That might turn out a man or woman, not
A footfall tapping secrecies of stone.

I have what every poet hates in spite
Of all the solemn talk of contemplation.
Oh, Alexander Selkirk knew the plight
Of being king and government and nation.
A road, a mile of kingdom, I am king
Of banks and stones and every blooming thing.

PATRICK KAVANAGH

The Language Issue

I place my hope on the water
in this little boat
of the language, the way a body might put
an infant

in a basket of intertwined
iris leaves,
its underside proofed
with bitumen and pitch,

then set the whole thing down amidst
the sedge
and bulrushes by the edge
of a river

only to have it borne hither and thither,
not knowing where it might end up;
in the lap, perhaps,
of some Pharaoh's daughter.

NUALA NÍ DHOMHNAILL
translated from the Irish by Paul Muldoon

Break

Soldier boy, dark and tall, sat for a rest
on Crumlish's wall. *Come on over.*

Look at my Miraculous Medal.
Let me punch your bulletproof vest. *Go on, try.*

The gun on your knees is blackened metal.
Here's the place where the bullets sleep.

Here's the catch and here's the trigger.
Let me look through the eye.

Soldier, you sent me for cigs but a woman
came back and threw the money in your face.

I watched you backtrack, alter, cover
your range of vision, shoulder to shoulder.

COLETTE BRYCE

The Toome Road

One morning early I met armoured cars
In convoy, warbling along on powerful tyres,
All camouflaged with broken alder branches,
And headphoned soldiers standing up in turrets.
How long were they approaching down my roads
As if they owned them? The whole country was sleeping.
I had rights-of-way, fields, cattle in my keeping,
Tractors hitched to buckrakes in open sheds,
Silos, chill gates, wet slates, the greens and reds
Of outhouse roofs. Whom should I run to tell
Among all of those with their back doors on the latch
For the bringer of bad news, that small-hours visitant
Who, by being expected, might be kept distant?
Sowers of seed, erectors of headstones...

O charioteers, above your dormant guns,
It stands here still, stands vibrant as you pass,
The invisible, untoppled omphalos.

SEAMUS HEANEY

The Sightseers

My father and mother, my brother and sister
and I, with uncle Pat, our dour best-loved uncle,
had set out that Sunday afternoon in July
in his broken-down Ford

not to visit some graveyard – one died of shingles,
one of fever, another's knees turned to jelly –
but the brand-new roundabout at Ballygawley,
the first in mid-Ulster.

Uncle Pat was telling us how the B-Specials
had stopped him one night somewhere near Ballygawley
and smashed his bicycle

and made him sing the Sash and curse the Pope of Rome.
They held a pistol so hard against his forehead
there was still the mark of an O when he got home.

PAUL MULDOON

Dream Avenue

Monumental, millennial decrepitude,
As tragedy requires. A broad
Avenue with trash unswept,
A few solitary speck-sized figures
Going about their business
In a world already smudged by a schoolboy's eraser.

You've no idea what city this is,
What country? It could be a dream,
But is it yours? You're nothing
But a vague sense of loss,
A piercing, heart-wrenching dread
On an avenue with no name

With a few figures conveniently small
And blurred who, in any case,
Have their backs to you
As they look elsewhere, beyond
The long row of gray buildings and their many windows,
Some of which appear broken.

CHARLES SIMIC

' "next to of course god america i" '

"next to of course god america i
love you land of the pilgrims' and so forth oh
say can you see by the dawn's early my
country 'tis of centuries come and go
and are no more what of it we should worry
in every language even deafanddumb
thy sons acclaim your glorious name by gorry
by jingo by gee by gosh by gum
why talk of beauty what could be more beaut-
iful than these heroic happy dead
who rushed like lions to the roaring slaughter
they did not stop to think they died instead
then shall the voice of liberty be mute?"

He spoke. And drank rapidly a glass of water

E.E. CUMMINGS

I, Too

I, too, sing America.

I am the darker brother.
They send me to eat in the kitchen
When company comes,
But I laugh,
And eat well,
And grow strong.

Tomorrow,
I'll be at the table
When company comes.
Nobody'll dare
Say to me,
'Eat in the kitchen,'
Then.

Besides,
They'll see how beautiful I am
And be ashamed –

I, too, am America.

LANGSTON HUGHES

Making America Strong

We worked nights as machine operators
at Goodstone Aircraft Company, where we made parts
for the Air Force's new bomber, the K-20.
In the parking lot, before work and during lunch break,
we drank and smoked dope and snorted chemicals.
At work we wore sunglasses
and danced in front of our machines.
We picked up bomber parts and blew through them
as if they were saxophones.
We stalked each other with squirt guns,
screaming and laughing and staggering.

We played with the overhead crane,
hoisting each other's tool boxes to the ceiling.
We unscrewed knobs from machine handles
and threw them around like baseballs.
Our foreman snuck drinks
from the bottle of vodka in his toolbox,
and paced about the shop in a daze.
We respected our foreman.
He'd given us some valuable advice.
'Whatever you do,' he'd warned us over and over, 'don't join
the Air Force and fly a K-20. It's gonna CRASH.'

FRED VOSS

They'll say, 'She must be from another country'

When I can't comprehend
why they're burning books
or slashing paintings,
when they can't bear to look
at god's own nakedness,
when they ban the film
and gut the seats to stop the play
and I ask why
they just smile and say,
'She must be
from another country.'

When I speak on the phone
and the vowel sounds are off
when the consonants are hard
and they should be soft,
they'll catch on at once
they'll pin it down
they'll explain it right away
to their own satisfaction,
they'll cluck their tongues
and say,
'She must be
from another country.'

327

When my mouth goes up
instead of down,
when I wear a tablecloth
to go to town,
when they suspect I'm black
or hear I'm gay
they won't be surprised,
they'll purse their lips
and say,
'She must be
from another country.'

When I eat up the olives
and spit out the pits
when I yawn at the opera
in the tragic bits
when I pee in the vineyard
as if it were Bombay,
flaunting my bare ass
covering my face
laughing through my hands
they'll turn away,
shake their heads quite sadly,
'She doesn't know any better,'
they'll say,
'She must be
from another country.'

Maybe there is a country
where all of us live,
all of us freaks
who aren't able to give
our loyalty to fat old fools,
the crooks and thugs
who wear the uniform
that gives them the right
to wave a flag,
puff out their chests,
put their feet on our necks,
and break their own rules.

But from where we are
it doesn't look like a country,

it's more like the cracks
that grow between borders
behind their backs.
That's where I live.
And I'll be happy to say,
'I never learned your customs.
I don't remember your language
or know your ways.
I must be
from another country.'

IMTIAZ DHARKER

In my country

walking by the waters
down where an honest river
shakes hands with the sea,
a woman passed round me
in a slow watchful circle,
as if I were a superstition;

or the worst dregs of her imagination,
so when she finally spoke
her words spliced into bars
of an old wheel. A segment of air.
Where do you come from?
'Here,' I said, 'Here. These parts.'

JACKIE KAY

Modern Secrets

Last night I dreamt in Chinese.
Eating Yankee shredded wheat
I said it in English
To a friend who answered

In monosyllables:
All of which I understood.

The dream shrank to its fiction.
I had understood its end
Many years ago. The sallow child
Ate rice from its ricebowl
And hides still in the cupboard
With the china and tea-leaves.

SHIRLEY GEOK-LIN LIM

Exile

The old land swinging in her stomach
she must get to know this language
better – key words, sound patterns
wordgroups of fire and blood.

Try your classmates with
the English version of your name.
Maria. Try it.
Good afternoon. How are you?

I am fine. Your country –
you see it in a drop of water.
The last lesson they taught you there
was how to use a gun.

And now in stops and starts
you grow a second city in your head.
It is Christmas in this school.
Sarajevo is falling through

a forest of lit-up trees,
cards and decorations.
Mountains split with gunfire
swallow clouds, birds, sky.

MONIZA ALVI

Exile

When the country we have isn't ours
Lost because of silence and renunciation
Even the voice of the sea becomes exile
And the light all around us is like bars

SOPHIA DE MELLO BREYNER
translated from the Portuguese by Richard Zenith

Emigrants

Will know where they are by the absence
of trees, of people – the absence
even of anything to do. All
luggage is in transit; nothing at all
to do but watch from the empty house

through the empty window. The sky
is underlit, and under the sky
a lake, pewter, reflecting; a road.
Yellow buses turn at the end of the road,
if it is an end. Reeds block the view:

this bus is wheel-deep in them; it swims
along the lake's edge and a swan swims
towards it. They pass. And here, at last,
are two people, waiting for the last
bus out, or just standing, as people must

stand here often, leaning on the wind,
deep in reeds, and speechless in the wind
as if lake and sky were foreign words
to them as well: standing without words
but without need of them, being at home.

JANE GRIFFITHS

Epilogue

I have crossed an ocean
I have lost my tongue
from the root of the old one
a new one has sprung

GRACE NICHOLS

In Your Mind

The other country, is it anticipated or half-remembered?
Its language is muffled by the rain which falls all afternoon
one autumn in England, and in your mind
you put aside your work and head for the airport
with a credit card and a warm coat you will leave
on the plane. The past fades like newsprint in the sun.

You know people there. Their faces are photographs
on the wrong side of your eyes. A beautiful boy
in the bar on the harbour serves you a drink – what? –
asks you if men could possibly land on the moon.
A moon like an orange drawn by a child. No.
Never. You watch it peel itself into the sea.

Sleep. The rasp of carpentry wakes you. On the wall,
a painting lost for thirty years renders the room yours.
Of course. You go to your job, right at the old hotel, left,
then left again. You love this job. Apt sounds
mark the passing of the hours. Seagulls. Bells. A flute
practising scales. You swap a coin for a fish on the way home.

Then suddenly you are lost but not lost, dawdling
on the blue bridge, watching six swans vanish
under your feet. The certainty of place turns on the lights
all over town, turns up the scent on the air. For a moment
you are there, in the other country, knowing its name.
And then a desk. A newspaper. A window. English rain.

CAROL ANN DUFFY

Homeland

For a country of stone and harsh wind
For a country of bright perfect light
For the black of its earth and the white of its walls

For the silent and patient faces
Which poverty slowly etched
Close to the bone with the detail
Of a long irrefutable report

And for the faces like sun and wind

And for the clarity of those words
Always said with passion
For their colour and weight
For their clean concrete silence
From which the named things spring
For the nakedness of awed words

Stone river wind house
Lament day song breath
Expanse root water –
My homeland and my centre

The moon hurts me the sea weeps me
And exile stamps the heart of time

SOPHIA DE MELLO BREYNER
translated from the Portuguese by Richard Zenith

Motherland
(after Tsvetayeva)

Language is impossible
in a country like this. Even
the dictionary laughs when I look up
'England', 'Motherland', 'Home'.

It insists on falling open instead
three times out of the nine I try it
at the word 'Distance' –
degree of remoteness, interval of space –

the word is ingrained like pain.
So much for England and so much
for my future to walk into the horizon
carrying distance in a broken suitcase.

The dictionary is the only one
who talks to me now. Says laughing,
'Come back HOME!' but takes me
further and further away into the cold stars.

I am blue, bluer than water
I am nothing, for all I do
is pour syllables over aching brows.

England. It hurts my lips to shape
the word. This country makes me say
too many things I can't say, home
of my rotting pride, my motherland.

JO SHAPCOTT

'That city that I have loved'

That city that I have loved since I was a child
seemed to me today
in its December stillness
to be my squandered inheritance.

Everything that was handed to me spontaneously,
was so easy to give away:
the soul's burning heat, the sounds of prayer,
and the grace of the first song –

all, all carried away in transparent smoke,
turned to ash in the depths of mirrors...
and now a noseless violinist
strikes up a tune from the irrevocable past.

With the curiosity of a foreigner
captivated by everything new
I listened to my Mother Tongue
and watched the sledges race.

Happiness blew in my face
with a wild freshness and force,
as though an eternally dear friend
accompanied me onto the steps.

ANNA AKHMATOVA
translated from the Russian by Richard McKane

from What the Light Teaches

Language is the house with lamplight in its windows,
visible across fields. Approaching, you can hear
music; closer, smell
soup, bay leaves, bread – a meal for anyone
who has only his tongue left.

It's a country; home; family:
abandoned; burned down; whole lines dead, unmarried.
For those who can't read their way in the streets,
or in the gestures and faces of strangers,
language is the house to run to;
in wild nights, chased by dogs and other sounds,
when you've been lost a long time,
when you have no other place.

There are nights in the forest of words
when I panic, every step into thicker darkness,
the only way out to write myself into a clearing,
which is silence.

Nights in the forest of words
when I'm afraid we won't hear each other
over clattering branches, over
both our voices calling.

In winter, in the hour
when the sun runs liquid then freezes,
caught in the mantilla of empty trees;
when my heart listens
through the cold stethoscope of fear,
your voice in my head reminds me
what the light teaches.
Slowly you translate fear into love,
the way the moon's blood is the sea.

ANNE MICHAELS

My Faithful Mother Tongue

Faithful mother tongue,
I have been serving you.
Every night, I used to set before you little bowls of colors
so you could have your birch, your cricket, your finch
as preserved in my memory.
This lasted many years.
You were my native land; I lacked any other.
I believed that you would also be a messenger
between me and some good people
even if they were few, twenty, ten
or not born, as yet.

Now, I confess my doubt.
There are moments when it seems to me I have squandered my life.
For you are a tongue of the debased,
of the unreasonable, hating themselves
even more than they hate other nations,
a tongue of informers,
a tongue of the confused,
ill with their own innocence.

But without you, who am I?
Only a scholar in a distant country,
a success, without fears and humiliations.
Yes, who am I without you?
Just a philosopher, like everyone else.

I understand, this is meant as my education:
the glory of individuality is taken away,
Fortune spreads a red carpet
before the sinner in a morality play
while on the linen backdrop a magic lantern throws
images of human and divine torture.

Faithful mother tongue,
perhaps after all it's I who must try to save you.
So I will continue to set before you little bowls of colors
bright and pure if possible,
for what is needed in misfortune is a little order and beauty.

CZESLAW MILOSZ
translated from the Polish by the author and Robert Hass

Betrayal

The greatest delight, I sense,
is hidden sublimely in the act of betrayal
which can be equal only to fidelity.
To betray a woman, friends, an idea,
to see new light in the eyes
of distant shadows. But choices are
limited: other women, other
ideas, the enemies of our
long-standing friends. If only
we could encounter some quite different
otherness, settle in a country which has
no name, touch a woman before
she is born, lose our memories, meet
a God other than our own.

ADAM ZAGAJEWSKI
translated from the Polish by Renata Gorczynski

We Billion Cheered

We billion cheered.
    Some threat sank in the news and disappeared.
It did because
    Currencies danced and we forgot what it was.

It rose again.
    It rose and slid towards our shore and when
It got to it,
    It laced it like a telegram. We lit

Regular fires,
    But missed it oozing along irregular wires
Towards the Smoke.
    We missed it elbowing into the harmless joke

Or dreams of our
    Loves asleep in the cots where the dolls are.
We missed it how
    You miss an o'clock passing and miss now.

We missed it where
    You miss my writing of this and I miss you there.
We missed it through
    Our eyes, lenses, screen and angle of view.

We missed it though
    It specified where it was going to go,
And when it does,
    The missing ones are ten to one to be us.

We line the shore,
    Speak of the waving dead of a waving war.
And clap a man
    For an unveiled familiar new plan.

Don't forget.
    Nothing will start that hasn't started yet.
Don't forget
    It, its friend, its foe and its opposite.

GLYN MAXWELL

Waiting for the Barbarians

What are we waiting for, assembled in the forum?

    The barbarians are due here today.

Why isn't anything going on in the senate?
Why are the senators sitting there without legislating?

    Because the barbarians are coming today.
    What's the point of senators making laws now?
    Once the barbarians are here, they'll do the legislating.

Why did our emperor get up so early,
and why is he sitting enthroned at the city's main gate,
in state, wearing the crown?

    Because the barbarians are coming today
    and the emperor's waiting to receive their leader.
    He's even got a scroll to give him,
    loaded with titles, with imposing names.

Why have our two consuls and praetors come out today
wearing their embroidered, their scarlet togas?
Why have they put on bracelets with so many amethysts,
rings sparkling with magnificent emeralds?
Why are they carrying elegant canes
beautifully worked in silver and gold?

    Because the barbarians are coming today
    and things like that dazzle the barbarians.

Why don't our distinguished orators turn up as usual
to make their speeches, say what they have to say?

    Because the barbarians are coming today
    and they're bored by rhetoric and public speaking.

Why this sudden bewilderment, this confusion?
(How serious people's faces have become.)
Why are the streets and squares emptying so rapidly
everyone going home lost in thought?

Because night has fallen and the barbarians haven't come.
And some of our men just in from the border say
there are no barbarians any longer.

Now what's going to happen to us without barbarians?
They were, those people, a kind of solution.

C.P. CAVAFY
translated from the Greek by Edmund Keeley & Philip Sherrard

Gare du Midi

A nondescript express in from the South,
Crowds round the ticket barrier, a face
To welcome which the mayor has not contrived
Bugles or braid: something about the mouth
Distracts the stray look with alarm and pity.
Snow is falling. Clutching a little case,
He walks out briskly to infect a city
Whose terrible future may have just arrived.

W.H. AUDEN

The Coming of the Plague

September was when it began.
Locusts dying in the fields; our dogs
Silent, moving like shadows on a wall;
And strange worms crawling; flies of a kind
We had never seen before; huge vineyard moths;
Badgers and snakes, abandoning
Their holes in the field; the fruit gone rotten;
Queer fungi sprouting; the fields and woods
Covered with spiderwebs; black vapors
Rising from the earth – all these,

And more, began that fall. Ravens flew round
The hospital in pairs. Where there was water,
We could hear the sound of beating clothes
All through the night. We could not count
All the miscarriages, the quarrels, the jealousies.
And one day in a field I saw
A swarm of frogs, swollen and hideous,
Hundreds upon hundreds, sitting on each other,
Huddled together, silent, ominous,
And heard the sound of rushing wind.

WELDON KEES

Death by Meteor

The night the meteor struck, the headline writers
were raising point sizes. The ten o'clock news
was brought forward an hour. In restaurants, waiters

ran from table to table. Theatre queues
were issued with free tickets. England was there
for the taking with Scotland and Wales. The pews

remained empty. Too late now for hot air.
This would be phlegmatic, immediate,
dignified, business as usual. Trafalgar Square

was full of pigeons. Trains would run extra late
until the shadow thickened sometime towards dawn
when the noise would be deafening. So they would wait

in streets or in pubs or on the well-kept lawn
of the bowling green, some tanked up with beer,
others with mugs of tea, some of them drawn

to familiar places, others steering clear
of all acquaintance. An Englishman's home
was the castle at the end of a frail pier,

the silence of a haunted aerodrome
where ghosts were running forward into fire.
Already they could hear the distant boom

of the approaching rock over Yorkshire,
the Midlands, Derby and Birmingham
the pitch rising, ever sharper and higher.

GEORGE SZIRTES

Ancient History

The year began with baleful auguries:
comets, eclipses, tremors, forest fires,
the waves lethargic under a coat of pitch
the length of the coastline. And a cow spoke,
which happened last year too, although last year
no one believed cows spoke. Worse was to come.
There was a bloody rain of lumps of meat
which flocks of gulls snatched in mid-air
while what they missed fell to the ground
where it lay for days without festering.
Then a wind tore up a forest of holm-oaks
and jackdaws pecked the eyes from sheep.
Officials construing the Sibylline books
told of helmeted aliens occupying
the crossroads, and high places of the city.
Blood might be shed. Avoid, they warned,
factions and in-fights. The tribunes claimed
this was the usual con-trick
trumped up to stonewall the new law
about to be passed. Violence was only curbed
by belief in a rumour that the tribes
to the east had joined forces and forged
weapons deadlier than the world has seen
and that even then the hooves of their scouts
had been heard in the southern hills.
The year ended fraught with the fear of war.
Next year began with baleful auguries.

JAMIE McKENDRICK

9

War and peace

My subject is War, and the Pity of War.
The Poetry is in the pity...
All a poet can do today is warn.
That is why the true Poets must be truthful

WILFRED OWEN

In the dark times
Will there also be singing?
Yes, there will also be singing.
About the dark times.

BERTOLT BRECHT
from 'Motto'

IN 1917 Hiram Johnson told the U.S. Senate: 'The first casualty when war comes is truth'. Robert Graves's poem 'The Persian Version' (363) tells us how this has always been so; written during the Second World War, its ostensible subject is the Battle of Marathon in 490 BC between the Athenians and the Persians, but it could just as easily apply to the First World War, in which Graves fought. Johnson and Graves could almost be talking about the Gulf War, as described by Tony Harrison in 'Initial Illumination' (364) and glossed by Jo Shapcott in her poem 'Phrase Book' (362), which interweaves lines from an old-fashioned phrase book with phrases used by the military to hide the human consequences of their actions. Geoffrey Hill's 'September Song' (356) was written for an unknown child who died anonymously in one or other concentration camp. Throughout this oblique and understated poem, Hill writes with an acute awareness of how the Nazis perfected the art of mis-using language to disguise the nature of their 'Final Solution', simultaneously masking and revealing the horror behind that phrase through painful irony, awful double-meanings and juxtapositions ('routine cries'), so that the meaning of each line changes, or shifts, with each line-break.

Wilfred Owen (347) and Isaac Rosenberg (348) were killed in the First World War, while Siegfried Sassoon (348) and Robert Graves survived the horrors of the Western Front. Owen's comment above is from a short preface he wrote for a collection not published until after his death; because he was truthful to his own experience, his poetry's warning power is undiminished nearly a century later. 'My subject is War, and the Pity of War' was the stance of those soldier poets of the Great War who refused to write propagandist verse, as did Keith Douglas, who was a tank commander in North Africa during the Second World War and was later killed during the Normandy invasion; the phrase '*Vergissmeinnicht*' in his poem (354) is the German inscription ('Forget-me-not') on a dead soldier's photograph of his sweetheart.

Bertolt Brecht fled to America when the Nazis took over. His poem 'Motto' (343) asserts that poetry will not be silenced in and by the dark times. When the Red Army was fighting to hold back the German advance, Brecht wrote that 'the battle for Smolensk is also a battle for lyric poetry'. David Constantine reads this as meaning that 'a battle is being fought against forces which would annihilate all possibility of lyric poetry because, if they won, they would have annihilated the good in mankind'; the best war poetry or political poetry is truthful art, not propaganda, 'poetry working as poetry, through aesthetic means towards an end which may be called political...the writing of poetry is itself an assertion of hope, a contradicting of the times, an act of opposition'.

Several of the poems here focus on particular wars, but the human situations they describe are common to all wars. The American poets Bruce Weigl (360) and Carolyn Forché (361) write about consequences of the Vietnam War, Weigl as a combatant, Forché as a woman whose lover refuses to be drafted. James Fenton (361) was a war correspondent in South East Asia. The Canadian poet Gwendolyn MacEwen's engagement with the life and times of Lawrence of Arabia was imaginative but no less human in its authenticity; the poems here (352) are from a book-length sequence written in his voice, drawing not only on his writings but on her own mental resources to portray a kindred soul.

Michael Longley's 'Ceasefire' (350) and Paul Durcan's 'The Bloomsday Murders, 16 June 1997' (351) were both written in response to terrorist atrocities, but take very different approaches. Longley's poem is classically precise, formally contained within the tight numbered stanzas of a sonnet, and refers obliquely to the present, while Durcan's anguish and anger are barely restrained, bursting forth in rhetorical flourishes. Longley's theme is forgiveness, while Durcan's is the redemption offered by non-violence and by insistence on the absolute value of every individual human life. Conflating several passages from Homer's *Iliad*, Longley's poem was published in *The Irish Times* two days after the start of the August 1994 ceasefire in Northern Ireland; the last couplet recalls the words of Gordon Wilson, the father from Enniskillen whose daughter was one of those killed when an IRA bomb exploded at a Remembrance Day ceremony in 1987, who publicly forgave her murderers on television in one simple sentence which has never been forgotten in Ireland. Durcan's poem juxtaposes a bombing in which two of his neighbours were killed in Dublin with a book signing in Dublin the same day by the Sinn Féin leader Gerry Adams. Both happened on 16 June 1997, on Bloomsday, when Dubliners remember James Joyce, who set his novel *Ulysses* on 16 June 1904. Joyce's Leopold Bloom is his Jewish everyman figure who parallels Ulysses (Odysseus) in Homer. The comparison of Adams with Joyce's political hero Charles Stewart Parnell and with Abraham Lincoln is one of the poem's many bitter ironies. When Durcan's poem was published at the end of the same week in an Irish Sunday newspaper, the poet received death threats.

War Poetry

The class has dropped its books. The janitor's
disturbed some wasps, broomed the nest
straight off the roof. It lies outside, exotic
as a fallen planet, a burst city of the poor;
its newsprint halls, its ashen, tiny rooms
all open to the air. The insects' buzz
is low-key as a smart machine. They group,
regroup, in stacks and coils, advance
and cross like pulsing points on radar screens.

And though the boys have shaven heads
and football strips, and would, they swear,
enlist at once, given half a chance,
march down Owen's darkening lanes
to join the lads and stuff the Boche –
they don't rush out to pike the nest,
or lap the yard with grapeshot faces.
They watch the wasps through glass,
silently, abashed, the way we all watch war.

KATE CLANCHY

Grass

Pile the bodies high at Austerlitz and Waterloo.
Shovel them under and let me work –
    I am the grass; I cover all.

And pile them high at Gettysburg
And pile them high at Ypres and Verdun.
Shovel them under and let me work.
Two years, ten years, and passengers ask the conductor:
    What place is this?
    Where are we now?

    I am the grass.
    Let me work.

CARL SANDBURG

The fly

She sat on a willow-trunk
watching
part of the battle of Crécy,
the shouts,
the gasps,
the groans,
the tramping and the tumbling.

During the fourteenth charge
of the French cavalry
she mated
with a brown-eyed male fly
from Vadincourt.

She rubbed her legs together
as she sat on a disembowelled horse
meditating
on the immortality of flies.

With relief she alighted
on the blue tongue
of the Duke of Clervaux.

When silence settled
and only the whisper of decay
softly circled the bodies

and only
a few arms and legs
still twitched jerkily under the trees,

she began to lay her eggs
on the single eye
of Johann Uhr,
the Royal Armourer.

And thus it was
that she was eaten by a swift
fleeing
from the fires of Estrées.

MIROSLAV HOLUB
translated from the Czech by George Theiner

Anthem for Doomed Youth

What passing-bells for these who die as cattle?
    – Only the monstrous anger of the guns.
    Only the stuttering rifles' rapid rattle
Can patter out their hasty orisons.
No mockeries now for them; no prayers nor bells;
    Nor any voice of mourning save the choirs, –
The shrill, demented choirs of wailing shells;
    And bugles calling for them from sad shires.

What candles may be held to speed them all?
    Not in the hands of boys but in their eyes
Shall shine the holy glimmers of goodbyes.
    The pallor of girls' brows shall be their pall;
Their flowers the tenderness of patient minds,
And each slow dusk a drawing-down of blinds.

WILFRED OWEN

For Wilfred Owen

Today you would find your distant sad shire
Apparently forgetful of slaughtered innocence
And given wholly to the business of spring.
If you were to approach Habberley for instance,

By way of the stream and erratic plovers,
You would meet a girl in a dedicated mood
Airing the newest generation in a pram
While carefully avoiding the lane's yeasty mud.

And later, the village dog would confront you
With his oddity of one grey eye and one brown
Dancing attendance on your singularity,
Until you stopped by a cottage almost overgrown

With the season and the gardener's art,
Where even the doorway frames an affair
Of flowers fuming in an old tin helmet
Resigned to being always suspended there.

FREDA DOWNIE

Everyone Sang

Everyone suddenly burst out singing;
And I was filled with such delight
As prisoned birds must find in freedom,
Winging wildly across the white
Orchards and dark-green fields; on – on – and out of sight.

Everyone's voice was suddenly lifted;
And beauty came like the setting sun:
My heart was shaken with tears; and horror
Drifted away...O, but Everyone
Was a bird; and the song was wordless; the singing will never
        be done.

SIEGFRIED SASSOON

Returning, we hear the Larks

Sombre the night is.
And though we have our lives, we know
What sinister threat lurks there.

Dragging these anguished limbs, we only know
This poison-blasted track opens on our camp –
On a little safe sleep.

But hark! joy – joy – strange joy.
Lo! heights of night ringing with unseen larks.
Music showering our upturned list'ning faces.

348

Death could drop from the dark
As easily as song –
But song only dropped,
Like a blind man's dreams on the sand
By dangerous tides,
Like a girl's dark hair for she dreams no ruin lies there,
Or her kisses where a serpent hides.

ISAAC ROSENBERG

As the team's head brass

As the team's head brass flashed out on the turn
The lovers disappeared into the wood.
I sat among the boughs of the fallen elm
That strewed an angle of the fallow, and
Watched the plough narrowing a yellow square
Of charlock. Every time the horses turned
Instead of treading me down, the ploughman leaned
Upon the handles to say or ask a word,
About the weather, next about the war.
Scraping the share he faced towards the wood,
And screwed along the furrow till the brass flashed
Once more.
            The blizzard felled the elm whose crest
I sat in, by a woodpecker's round hole,
The ploughman said. 'When will they take it away?'
'When the war's over.' So the talk began –
One minute and an interval of ten,
A minute more and the same interval.
'Have you been out?' 'No.' 'And don't want to, perhaps?'
'If I could only come back again, I should.
I could spare an arm. I shouldn't want to lose
A leg. If I should lose my head, why, so,
I should want nothing more.... Have many gone
From here?' 'Yes.' 'Many lost?' 'Yes, a good few.
Only two teams work on the farm this year.
One of my mates is dead. The second day
In France they killed him. It was back in March,

349

The very night of the blizzard, too. Now if
He had stayed here we should have moved the tree.'
'And I should not have sat here. Everything
Would have been different. For it would have been
Another world.' 'Ay, and a better, though
If we could see all all might seem good.' Then
The lovers came out of the wood again:
The horses started and for the last time
I watched the clods crumble and topple over
After the ploughshare and the stumbling team.

EDWARD THOMAS

Ceasefire

I

Put in mind of his own father and moved to tears
Achilles took him by the hand and pushed the old king
Gently away, but Priam curled up at his feet and
Wept with him until their sadness filled the building.

II

Taking Hector's corpse into his own hands Achilles
Made sure it was washed and, for the old king's sake,
Laid out in uniform, ready for Priam to carry
Wrapped like a present home to Troy at daybreak.

III

When they had eaten together, it pleased them both
To stare at each other's beauty as lovers might,
Achilles built like a god, Priam good-looking still
And full of conversation, who earlier had sighed:

IV

'I get down on my knees and do what must be done
And kiss Achilles' hand, the killer of my son.'

MICHAEL LONGLEY

The Bloomsday Murders, 16 June 1997

– A nation? says Bloom. A nation is the same people
living in the same place.
Ulysses, Bodley Head edition, 1960, p.489

Not even you, Gerry Adams, deserve to be murdered:
You whose friends at noon murdered my two young men,
David Johnston and John Graham;
You who in the afternoon came on TV
In a bookshop on Bloomsday signing books,
Sporting a trendy union shirt
(We vain authors do not wear collars and ties.)

Instead of the bleeding corpses of David and John
We were treated to you gazing up into camera
In bewilderment fibbing like a spoilt child:
'Their deaths diminish us all.'
You with your paterfamilias beard,
Your Fidel Castro street-cred,
Your Parnell martyr-gaze,
Your Lincoln gravitas.
O Gerry Adams, you're a wicked boy.

Only on Sunday evening in sunlight
I met David and John up the park
Patrolling the young mums with prams.
'Going to write a poem about us, Paul?'
How they laughed! How they saluted!
How they turned their backs! Their silver spines!

Had I known it, would I have told them?
That for next Sunday's newspaper I'd compose a poem
How you, Gerry Adams, not caring to see,
Saw two angels in their silver spines shot.

I am a citizen of the nation of Ireland –
The same people living in the same place.
I hope the Protestants never leave our shores.
I am a Jew and my name is Bloom.
You, Gerry Adams, do not sign books in my name.
May God forgive me – lock, stock and barrel.

PAUL DURCAN

from The T.E. Lawrence Poems

Apologies

I did not choose Arabia; it chose me. The shabby money
That the desert offered us bought lies, bought victory.
       What was I, that soiled Outsider, doing
Among them? I was not becoming one of them, no matter
What you think. They found it easier to learn my kind
       of Arabic, than to teach me theirs.
And they were all mad; they mounted their horses and camels
       from the right.

But my mind's twin kingdoms waged an everlasting war;
The reckless Bedouin and the civilised Englishman
       fought for control, so that I, whatever I was,
Fell into a dumb void that even a false god could not fill,
       could not inhabit.

The Arabs are children of the idea; dangle an idea
In front of them, and you can swing them wherever.
       I was also a child of the idea; I wanted
       no liberty for myself, but to bestow it
Upon them. I wanted to present them with a gift so fine
       it would outshine all other gifts in their eyes;
       it would be *worthy*. Then I at last could be
Empty.

You can't imagine how beautiful it is to be empty.
Out of this grand emptiness wonderful things must surely
       come into being.
When we set out, it was morning. We hardly knew
That when we moved we would not be an army, but a world.

Damascus

The dream was dead in me before we reached Damascus;
       it died with your death, and dead love
Was all I carried around with me in the clumsy luggage
       of the desert. But I remember

Entering the city, and the air silk with locusts;
        there was the smell of eternal cookies baking,
And someone ran up to me with a bunch of yellow grapes.

In the crowds, the Arabs smelled of dried sweat,
        and the English had a hot aura of piss
And naptha. For some reason I noticed a sword
        lying unused in a garden, a still garden
Behind a palm tree. And the worthless Turkish money
        was flying crazily through the air.
Later, in the evening, the satiny white sand cooled
        my feet; nowhere else was there such sand.

That night the Turks and Germans burned what was left
        of their ammunition dumps.
They're burning Damascus, I said. And then I fell asleep.

Tall Tales

It has been said that I sometimes lie, or bend the truth
        to suit me. Did I make that four hundred mile
        trip alone in Turkish territory or not?
        I wonder if it is anybody's business
        to know. Syria is still there,
        and the long lie that the war was.

Was there a poster of me offering money for my capture,
        and did I stand there staring at myself,
        daring anyone to know me? Consider
        truth and untruth, consider why they call them
        the *theatres* of war. All of us
        played our roles to the hilt.

Poets only play with words, you know; they too
        are masters of the Lie, the Grand Fiction.
        Poets and men like me who fight for something
        contained in words, but not words.

What if the whole show was a lie, and it bloody well was –
        would I still lie to you? Of course I would.

GWENDOLYN MacEWEN

Vergissmeinnicht

Three weeks gone and the combatants gone
returning over the nightmare ground
we found the place again, and found
the soldier sprawling in the sun.

The frowning barrel of his gun
overshadowing. As we came on
that day, he hit my tank with one
like the entry of a demon.

Look. Here in the gunpit spoil
the dishonoured picture of his girl
who has put: *Steffi. Vergissmeinnicht*
in a copybook gothic script.

We see him almost with content,
abased, and seeming to have paid
and mocked at by his own equipment
that's hard and good when he's decayed.

But she would weep to see today
how on his skin the swart flies move;
the dust upon the paper eye
and the burst stomach like a cave.

For here the lover and killer are mingled
who had one body and one heart.
And death who had the soldier singled
has done the lover mortal hurt.

KEITH DOUGLAS

The Old Naval Airfield

I looked out Henstridge lately,
　　somewhere where it always was,
even then, without maps or signs,
　　and thought of Philip, chief flying instructor,
brave Philip, who soon was dead –
　　long ago, though, many years ago.
Pretty old, bosky old, footpath
　　country, and nothing was familiar
till suddenly the dull lane
　　roused me. A humpbacked bridge
over a disused railway led me
　　to B Camp that was: now a wood and a shed.
Opposite, the Wessex Grain Company –
　　storage silos that hummed
in the afternoon air like planes.
　　On the edge of the field, a bunker gradually
took my eye. A well-turfed barrow?
　　No, dear God, the rusted roof of a hangar
half-fallen in! And over the field, look,
　　Philip's control tower, a tall wreck
marooned in breaking waves of grass!

Survival is a form of murder.
　　My father ran round the garden in the dark
shouting, 'She's dead, and I could've
　　done more for her. I could have, and I didn't.'
She'd said earlier, 'He couldn't do more,
　　that man, best man who ever lived.'
Truth is, you can always do more.
　　You have to survive, that too, but it's murder.
He lived on, as you do if you can.

MAIRI MacINNES

September Song

born 19.6.32 – deported 24.9.42

Undesirable you may have been, untouchable
you were not. Not forgotten
or passed over at the proper time.

As estimated, you died. Things marched,
sufficient, to that end.
Just so much Zyklon and leather, patented
terror, so many routine cries.

(I have made
an elegy for myself it
is true)

September fattens on vines. Roses
flake from the wall. The smoke
of harmless fires drifts to my eyes.

This is plenty. This is more than enough.

GEOFFREY HILL

There is no greater crime than leaving

There is no greater crime than leaving.
In friends, what do you count on? Not on what they do.
You never can tell what they will do. Not on what they are. That
May change. Only on this: their not leaving.
He who cannot leave cannot stay. He who has a pass
In his pocket – will he stay when the attack begins? Perhaps
He will not stay.
If it goes badly with me, perhaps he will stay. But if it goes
Badly with him, perhaps he will leave.

Fighters are poor people. They cannot leave. When the attack
Begins they cannot leave.
He who stays is known. He who left was not known. What left
Is different from what was here.
Before we go into battle I must know: have you a pass
In your coat pocket? Is a plane waiting for you behind the battlefield?
How many defeats do you want to survive? Can I send you away?
Well, then, let's not go into battle.

BERTOLT BRECHT
translated from the German by Frank Jones

September 1, 1939

I sit in one of the dives
On Fifty-Second Street
Uncertain and afraid
As the clever hopes expire
Of a low dishonest decade:
Waves of anger and fear
Circulate over the bright
And darkened lands of the earth,
Obsessing our private lives;
The unmentionable odour of death
Offends the September night.

Accurate scholarship can
Unearth the whole offence
From Luther until now
That has driven a culture mad,
Find what occurred at Linz,
What huge imago made
A psychopathic god:
I and the public know
What all schoolchildren learn,
Those to whom evil is done
Do evil in return.

Exiled Thucydides knew
All that a speech can say
About Democracy,
And what dictators do,
The elderly rubbish they talk
To an apathetic grave;
Analysed all in his book,
The enlightenment driven away,
The habit-forming pain,
Mismanagement and grief:
We must suffer them all again.

Into this neutral air
Where blind skyscrapers use
The full height to proclaim
The strength of Collective Man,
Each language pours its vain
Competitive excuse:
But who can live for long
In an euphoric dream;
Out of the mirror they stare,
Imperialism's face
And the international wrong.

Faces along the bar
Cling to their average day:
The lights must never go out,
The music must always play,
All the conventions conspire
To make this fort assume
The furniture of home;
Lest we should see where we are,
Lost in a haunted wood,
Children afraid of the night
Who have never been happy or good.

The windiest militant trash
Important Persons shout
Is not so crude as our wish:
What mad Nijinsky wrote
About Diaghilev
Is true of the normal heart;
For the error bred in the bone

Of each woman and each man
Craves what it cannot have,
Not universal love
But to be loved alone.

From the conservative dark
Into the ethical life
The dense commuters come,
Repeating their morning vow,
'I *will* be true to the wife,
I'll concentrate more on my work',
And helpless governors wake
To resume their compulsory game:
Who can release them now,
Who can reach the deaf,
Who can speak for the dumb?

All I have is a voice
To undo the folded lie,
The romantic lie in the brain
Of the sensual man-in-the-street
And the lie of Authority
Whose buildings grope the sky:
There is no such thing as the State
And no one exists alone;
Hunger allows no choice
To the citizen or the police;
We must love one another or die.

Defenceless under the night
Our world in stupor lies;
Yet, dotted everywhere,
Ironic points of light
Flash out wherever the Just
Exchange their messages:
May I, composed like them
Of Eros and of dust,
Beleaguered by the same
Negation and despair,
Show an affirming flame.

W.H. AUDEN

On the Anniversary of Her Grace

Rain and low clouds blown through the valley,
rain down the coast raising the brackish
rivers at their high tides too high,
rain and black skies that come for you.

Not excellent and fair,
I wake from a restless night of dreams of her
whom I will never have again
as surely as each minute passing
makes impossible another small fulfilment
until there's only a lingering
I remember, a kiss I had imagined
would come again and again to my face.

Inside me the war had eaten a hole.
I could not touch anyone.
The wind blew through me to the green place
where they still fell in their blood.
I could hear their voices at night.

I could not undress in the light
her body cast in the dark rented room.

I could keep the dragons at the gate.
I could paint my face and hide
as shadow in the triple-canopy jungle.
I could not eat or sleep then walk all day
and all night watch a moonlit path for movement.

I could draw leeches from my skin
with the tip of a lit cigarette
and dig a hole deep enough to save me
before the sun bloodied the hills we could not take
even with our lives
but I could not open my arms to her
that first night of forgiveness.
I could not touch anyone.
I thought my body would catch fire.

BRUCE WEIGL

Selective Service

We rise from the snow where we've
lain on our backs and flown like children,
from the imprint of perfect wings and cold gowns,
and we stagger together wine-breathed into town
where our people are building
their armies again, short years after
body bags, after burnings. There is a man
I've come to love after thirty, and we have
our rituals of coffee, of airports, regret
After love we smoke and sleep
with magazines, two shot glasses
and the black and white collapse of hours.
In what time do we live that it is too late
to have children? In what place
that we consider the various ways to leave?
There is no list long enough
for a selective service card shriveling
under a match, the prison that comes of it,
a flag in the wind eaten from its pole
and boys sent back in trash bags.
We'll tell you. You were at that time
learning fractions. We'll tell you
about fractions. Half of us are dead or quiet
or lost. Let them speak for themselves.
We lie down in the fields and leave behind
the corpses of angels.

CAROLYN FORCHÉ

Cambodia

One man shall smile one day and say goodbye.
Two shall be left, two shall be left to die.

One man shall give his best advice.
Three men shall pay the price.

One man shall live, live to regret.
Four men shall meet the debt.

One man shall wake from terror to his bed.
Five men shall be dead.

One man to five. A million men to one.
And still they die. And still the war goes on.

JAMES FENTON

Phrase Book

I'm standing here inside my skin,
which will do for a Human Remains Pouch
for the moment. Look down there (up here).
Quickly. Slowly. This is my own front room

where I'm lost in the action, live from a war,
on screen. I am an Englishwoman, I don't understand you.
What's the matter? You are right. You are wrong.
Things are going well (badly). Am I disturbing you?

TV is showing bliss as taught to pilots:
Blend, Low silhouette, Irregular shape, Small,
Secluded. (Please write it down. Please speak slowly.)
Bliss is how it was in this very room

when I raised my body to his mouth,
when he even balanced me in the air,
or at least I thought so and yes the pilots say
yes they have caught it through the Side-Looking

Airborne Radar, and through the J-Stars.
I am expecting a gentleman (a young gentleman,
two gentlemen, some gentlemen). Please send him
(them) up at once. This is really beautiful.

Yes they have seen us, the pilots, in the Kill Box
on their screens, and played the routine for
getting us Stealthed, that is, Cleansed, to you and me,
Taken Out. They know how to move into a single room

like that, to send in with Pinpoint Accuracy, a hundred Harms.
I have two cases and a cardboard box. There is another
bag there. I cannot open my case – look out,
the lock is broken. Have I done enough?

Bliss, the pilots say, is for evasion
and escape. What's love in all this debris?
Just one person pounding another into dust,
into dust. I do not know the word for it yet.

Where is the British Consulate? Please explain.
What does it mean? What must I do? Where
can I find? What have I done? I have done
nothing. Let me pass please. I am an Englishwoman.

JO SHAPCOTT

The Persian Version

Truth-loving Persians do not dwell upon
The trivial skirmish fought near Marathon.
As for the Greek theatrical tradition
Which represents that summer's expedition
Not as a mere reconnaissance in force
By three brigades of foot and one of horse
(The left flank covered by some obsolete
Light craft detached from the main Persian fleet)
But as a grandiose, ill-starred attempt
To conquer Greece – they treat it with contempt;
And only incidentally refute
Major Greek claims, by stressing what repute
The Persian Monarch and the Persian nation
Won by this salutary demonstration:
Despite a strong defence and adverse weather
All arms combined magnificently together.

ROBERT GRAVES

Initial Illumination

Farne cormorants with catches in their beaks
shower fishscale confetti on the shining sea.
The first bright weather here for many weeks
for my Sunday G-Day train bound for Dundee,
off to St Andrew's to record a reading,
doubtful, in these dark days, what poems can do,
and watching the mists round Lindisfarne receding
my doubt extends to Dark Age Good Book too.
Eadfrith the Saxon scribe/illuminator
incorporated cormorants I'm seeing fly
round the same island thirteen centuries later
into the *In principio*'s initial I.
Billfrith's begemmed and jewelled boards got looted
by raiders gung-ho for booty and berserk,
the sort of soldiery that's still recruited
to do today's dictators' dirty work,
but the initials in St John and in St Mark
graced with local cormorants in ages,
we of a darker still keep calling Dark,
survive in those illuminated pages.
The word of God so beautifully scripted
by Eadfrith and Billfrith the anchorite
Pentagon conners have once again conscripted
to gloss the cross on the precision sight.
Candlepower, steady hand, gold leaf, a brush
were all that Eadfrith had to beautify
the word of God much bandied by George Bush
whose word illuminated midnight sky
and confused the Baghdad cock who was betrayed
by bombs into believing day was dawning
and crowed his heart out at the deadly raid
and didn't live to greet the proper morning.

Now with noonday headlights in Kuwait
and the burial of the blackened in Baghdad
let them remember, all those who celebrate,
that their good news is someone else's bad
or the light will never dawn on poor Mankind.
Is it open-armed at all that victory V,

that insular initial intertwined
with slack-necked cormorants from black laquered sea,
with trumpets bulled and bellicose and blowing
for what men claim as victories in their wars,
with the fire-hailing cock and all those crowing
who don't yet smell the dunghill at their claws?

TONY HARRISON

Every Day

War is no longer declared,
but rather continued. The outrageous
has become the everyday. The hero
is absent from the battle. The weak
are moved into the firing zone.
The uniform of the day is patience,
the order of merit is the wretched star
of hope over the heart.

It is awarded
when nothing more happens,
when the bombardment is silenced,
when the enemy has become invisible
and the shadow of eternal weapons
covers the sky.

It is awarded
for deserting the flag,
for bravery before a friend,
for the betrayal of shameful secrets
and the disregard
of every command.

INGEBORG BACHMANN
translated from the German by Peter Filkins

from Spain, take away this cup from me

XII *Mass*

At the end of the battle,
with the combatant dead, a man came up
and told him: 'Don't die, I love you so much!'
But the corpse, alas! went on dying.

Two others came up and said to him again:
'Don't leave us! Courage! Come back to life!'
But the corpse, alas! went on dying.

Twenty, a hundred, a thousand, five hundred thousand ran up to him,
crying out: 'So much love and no way of countering death!'
But the corpse, alas! went on dying.

Millions of individuals stood round him,
with a common plea: 'Stay here brother!'
But the corpse, alas! went on dying.

Then all the men on earth
stood round him; the sad corpse saw them, with emotion;
he got up slowly,
embraced the first man; began to walk...

CÉSAR VALLEJO
translated from the Spanish by Ed Dorn & Gordon Brotherston

The End and the Beginning

After every war
someone's got to tidy up.
Things won't pick
themselves up, after all.

Someone's got to shove
the rubble to the roadsides
so the carts loaded with corpses
can get by.

Someone's got to trudge
through sludge and ashes,
through the sofa springs,
the shards of glass,
the bloody rags.

Someone's got to lug the post
to prop the wall,
someone's got to glaze the window,
set the door in its frame.

No sound bites, no photo opportunities
and it takes years.
All the cameras have gone
to other wars.

The bridges need to be rebuilt,
the railroad stations, too.
Shirt sleeves will be rolled
to shreds.

Someone, broom in hand,
still remembers how it was.
Someone else listens, nodding
his unshattered head.
But others are bound to be bustling nearby
who'll find all that
a little boring.

From time to time someone still must
dig up a rusted argument
from underneath a bush
and haul it off to the dump.

Those who knew
what this was all about
must make way for those
who know little.
And less than that.
And at last nothing less
than nothing.

Someone's got to lie there
in the grass that covers up
the causes and effects
with a cornstalk in his teeth,
gawking at clouds.

WISLAWA SZYMBORSKA
translated from the Polish by Stanislaw Baranczak and Clare Cavanagh

The People of the Other Village

hate the people of this village
and would nail our hats
to our heads for refusing in their presence to remove them
or staple our hands to our foreheads
for refusing to salute them
if we did not hurt them first: mail them packages of rats,
mix their flour at night with broken glass.
We do this, they do that.
They peel the larynx from one of our brothers' throats.
We devein one of their sisters.
The quicksand pits they built were good.
Our amputation teams were better.
We trained some birds to steal their wheat.
They sent to us exploding ambassadors of peace.
They do this, we do that.
We canceled our sheep imports.
They no longer bought our blankets.
We mocked their greatest poet
and when that had no effect
we parodied the way they dance
which did cause pain, so they, in turn, said our God
was leprous, hairless.
We do this, they do that.
Ten thousand (10,000) years, ten thousand
(10,000) brutal, beautiful years.

THOMAS LUX

10

Disappearing acts

Poetry is a way of talking about things that frighten you.
MICK IMLAH

This is one sense of poetry. A little concoction of words against
death. It's almost the instinct against death crystallised.
MIROSLAV HOLUB

THOM GUNN has said: 'There's nothing to write about death, unless you believe
in an afterlife.' This paradox lies behind most modern poetry about death.
While there are some writers whose faith offers the solace of the soul's life
after death, many poets are writing as agnostics or unbelievers, and in trying to
make sense of death they are confronting not only loss but fear of extinction.

Seamus Heaney calls Philip Larkin's 'Aubade' (374) 'the definitive post-
Christian English poem, one that abolishes the soul's traditional pretension to
immortality', yet an absence of life after death is as questionable as its presence.
Larkin's poem copes with the eternal subject of death, says Czeslaw Milosz,
'in a manner corresponding to the second half of the twentieth century', and
yet it 'leaves me not only dissatisfied but indignant...poetry by its very essence
has always been on the side of life. Faith in life everlasting has accompanied
man in his wanderings through time and has always been larger and deeper
than religious or philosophical creeds.' Heaney says that in imagining death,
poetry brings human existence into a fuller life.

Poems about death also help others to gain inner strength by sharing in the
writer's experience of facing death and bereavement at a time when they them-
selves are still being tossed on the unpredictable tides of grief. The poems here
by Pamela Gillilan (387), Caroline Smith (388) and Liz Lochhead (389) focus on
what bereaved people see or sense of the dead in their houses, presences they
will feel for many years. The poem can be another repository for grief, and
when those left behind are expected to "get over" or "come to terms" with
their loss after a period of mourning, they can continue to engage with their
feelings through poetry after they no longer feel able to talk about them.

Every poem mourning the death of a loved one is also a poem about love.
Vladimir Holan (400) and Charles Causley (401) relive fond memories of loved
parents in poems about meetings in the afterlife. Theodore Roethke writes
about his continuing love after death in 'She' (392) while Alden Nowlan wants
to be remembered at and after his death for his love (389). Pablo Neruda's

poem 'Dead Woman' (394) was spoken in the film *Truly, Madly, Deeply* by the ghost (played by Alan Rickman) to help his grieving wife (Juliet Stevenson) know their love would never die. 'Yes' (395) is one of a whole book of love poems Tess Gallagher wrote in mourning for her husband Raymond Carver, with an epigraph from Paul Celan: 'The world is gone. I must carry you'. She wrote that the poems were the way she found to carry him forward in her life, to give the love a body and to give the grieving a form. In 'Wake' (390) she lies down beside him, wanting 'that experience of crossing into the death zone, still being in life, and of following the loved one in that way'.

Death is defied in Dylan Thomas's 'Do Not Go Gentle into That Good Night' (379), the anonymous 'Do not stand at my grave and weep' (381), and W.H. Auden's 'Funeral Blues' (380), which featured in the film *Four Weddings and a Funeral*, while living life to the full changes the meaning of death in the poems by Michael Longley (381) and Miroslav Holub (382).

The coupling of desolation with an inability to comprehend the inexplicable is expressed in many poems about loved ones taking their own lives. In 'The Gas-poker' (384) Thom Gunn tries to reimagine the scene 48 years earlier when his mother used a flute-like gas-poker not to breathe music into life but to make herself mute; the discussion of dates at the beginning suggests that poem was triggered by the painful anniversary of her death. There are other poems about suicide in the 'Dead or Alive' section (123-27).

A number of modern poets, such as Andrew Motion (395) and Jo Shapcott (402), have written poems in which they imagine themselves as ghosts after their own deaths, while others deny death by making light of it, as in the blackly humorous poems about ghosts and the lives of the dead by the Americans Billy Collins (397), Stephen Dobyns (399) and August Kleinzahler (405).

Poems on death are followed by poems about disappearances because death is an inexplicable disappearing act. Many poets in the past have written about sleep being a kind of death, and more recently poets have become fascinated with the idea of disappearing, almost as if disappearance were a death rehearsal in which life continues. As Philip Larkin writes in 'Poetry of Departures', those left behind can envy the audacity of people who cut all ties: '*He chucked up everything / And just cleared off.*' The American poet Weldon Kees created an alter ego figure in his edgy, jokey Robinson poems, and in 'Robinson' (411) he imagines the scene after the man's disappearance. A review by Kees mentioning 'human beings murdering themselves – either literally or symbolically' appeared in *The New Republic* on 18 July 1955, on the same day that his car was found abandoned near Golden Gate Bridge in San Francisco; he'd talked to friends of suicide as well as of clearing off to start a new life in Mexico. No one knows what happened to him. His disappearance or death was as much a mystery as why Brownlee left in Paul Muldoon's poem (407), as symbolic as the almost theatrical suicide of Hart Crane, the American poet who on 27 April 1932 walked the length of a steamship in his dressing-gown and stepped off the stern into Gulf of Mexico. His body was never found either; nor was that of Captain Oates, who stepped outside Scott's tent on 15 March 1912, saying 'I am just going outside and may be some time', which Derek Mahon echoes in 'Antarctica' (407) with his villanelle's repeated line 'At the heart of the ridiculous, the sublime'. In all three cases, the date of the person's disappearance is the only certain fact which can be recorded, just as the absolute truth when someone dies is the time and date of their death.

Rain – Birdoswald

I stand under a leafless tree
more still, in this mouse-pattering
    thrum of rain,
than cattle shifting in the field.
    It is more dark than light.
A Chinese painter's brush of deepening grey
    moves in a subtle tide.

    The beasts are darker islands now.
Wet-stained and silvered by the rain
    they suffer night,
marooned as still as stone or tree.
    We sense each other's quiet.

    Almost, death could come
inevitable, unstrange
    as is this dusk and rain,
and I should be no more
    myself, than raindrops
glimmering in last light
    on black ash buds

or night beasts in a winter field.

FRANCES HOROVITZ

Björn Olinder's Pictures

I have learned about dying by looking at two pictures
Björn Olinder needed to look at when he was dying:
A girl whose features are obscured by the fall of her hair
Planting a flower,
              and a seascape: beyond the headland
A glimpse of immaculate sand that awaits our footprints.

MICHAEL LONGLEY

Now Light Congeals

Now light congeals. Soon the late summer air
Will blur upon the hillside and its farms
And darkness speak its language everywhere.
But here in London, from their concrete stems
Clusters of oranges dilute the dark
And far beyond her, etched on violet strings
The swallows brood before they disembark.
A girl swings past me on electric heels,
Walking her body through the streets to home;
The ghost within me now no longer feels
Its scrotum tightening and taking aim
At some faint odour that her flesh conceals.
This also celebrates the coming dark.
My energies, like birds, are returning
Into the haunted centre of a stone
To gather strength before their journeying.
I sense the numinous waver of a line
Weaving through craters to more rigid night
And scrabble debris for some minute sign
That may be relevant, however faint.
Can anything be more appropriate?
There glows the silent onrush of the Thames
Before these oranges on concrete stems
Blink on dead filament, and sputter out.

THOMAS BLACKBURN

Psalm

You've been a long time making up your mind,
O Lord, about these madmen
Running the world. Their reach is long
And their claws must have frightened you.

One of them found me with his shadow.
The day turned chill. I dangled
Between terror and valor
In the darkest corner of my son's bedroom.

I sought with my eyes, You in whom I do not believe.
You've been busy making the flowers pretty,
The lambs run after their mother,
Or perhaps you haven't been doing even that?

It was spring. The killers were full of sport
And merriment, and your divines
Were right at their side, to make sure
Our final goodbyes were said properly.

CHARLES SIMIC

Someone

someone is dressing up for death today, a change of skirt or tie
eating a final feast of buttered sliced pan, tea
scarcely having noticed the erection that was his last
shaving his face to marble for the icy laying out
spraying with deodorant her coarse armpit grass
someone today is leaving home on business
saluting, terminally, the neighbours who will join in the cortège
someone is trimming his nails for the last time, a precious moment
someone's thighs will not be streaked with elastic in the future
someone is putting out milkbottles for a day that will not come
someone's fresh breath is about to be taken clean away
someone is writing a cheque that will be marked 'drawer deceased'
someone is circling posthumous dates on a calendar
someone is listening to an irrelevant weather forecast
someone is making rash promises to friends
someone's coffin is being sanded, laminated, shined
who feels this morning quite as well as ever
someone if asked would find nothing remarkable in today's date
perfume and goodbyes her final will and testament
someone today is seeing the world for the last time
as innocently as he had seen it first

DENNIS O'DRISCOLL

Aubade

I work all day, and get half-drunk at night.
Waking at four to soundless dark, I stare.
In time the curtain-edges will grow light.
Till then I see what's really always there:
Unresting death, a whole day nearer now,
Making all thought impossible but how
And where and when I shall myself die.
Arid interrogation: yet the dread
Of dying, and being dead,
Flashes afresh to hold and horrify.

The mind blanks at the glare. Not in remorse
– The good not done, the love not given, time
Torn off unused – nor wretchedly because
An only life can take so long to climb
Clear of its wrong beginnings, and may never;
But at the total emptiness for ever,
The sure extinction that we travel to
And shall be lost in always. Not to be here,
Not to be anywhere,
And soon; nothing more terrible, nothing more true.

This is a special way of being afraid
No trick dispels. Religion used to try,
That vast moth-eaten musical brocade
Created to pretend we never die,
And specious stuff that says *No rational being
Can fear a thing it will not feel*, not seeing
That this is what we fear – no sight, no sound,
No touch or taste or smell, nothing to think with,
Nothing to love or link with,
The anaesthetic from which none come round.

And so it stays just on the edge of vision,
A small unfocused blur, a standing chill
That slows each impulse down to indecision.
Most things may never happen: this one will,
And realisation of it rages out
In furnace-fear when we are caught without
People or drink. Courage is no good:

It means not scaring others. Being brave
Lets no one off the grave.
Death is no different whined at than withstood.

Slowly light strengthens, and the room takes shape.
It stands plain as a wardrobe, what we know,
Have always known, know that we can't escape,
Yet can't accept. One side will have to go.
Meanwhile telephones crouch, getting ready to ring
In locked-up offices, and all the uncaring
Intricate rented world begins to rouse.
The sky is white as clay, with no sun.
Work has to be done.
Postmen like doctors go from house to house.

PHILIP LARKIN

'Death does not come from outside...'

Death does not come from outside. Death is within.
Born-grows together with us.
Goes with us to kindergarten and school.
Learns with us to read and count.
Goes sledging with us, and to the pictures.
Seeks with us the meaning of life.
Tries to make sense with us of Einstein and Wiener.
Makes with us our first sexual contacts.
Marries, bears children, quarrels, makes up.
Separates, or perhaps not, with us.
Goes to work, goes to the doctor, goes camping,
to the convalescent home and the sanatorium. Grows old,
sees children married, retired,
looks after grandchildren, grows ill, dies
with us. Let us not fear, then. Our death
will not outlive us.

JAAN KAPLINSKI
translated from the Estonian by Hildi Hawkins

'Good creatures...'

Good creatures, do you love your lives
    And have you ears for sense?
Here is a knife like other knives,
    That cost me eighteen pence.

I need but stick it in my heart
    And down will come the sky,
And earth's foundations will depart
    And all you folk will die.

A.E. HOUSMAN

Thrall

The room is sparsely furnished:
A chair, a table and a father.

He sits in the chair by the window.
There are books on the table.
The time is always just past lunch.

You tiptoe past as he eats his apple
And reads. He looks up, angry.
He has heard your asthmatic breathing.

He will read for years without looking up
Until your childhood is over:

Smells, untidiness and boring questions;
Blood, from the first skinned knees
To the first stained thighs;
The foolish tears of adolescent love.

One day he looks up, pleased
At the finished product.
Now he is ready to love you!

So he coaxes you in the voice reserved
For reading Keats. You agree to everything.

Drilled in silence and duty,
You will give him no cause for reproach.
He will boast of you to strangers.

When the afternoon is older
Shadows in a smaller room
Fall on the bed, the books, the father.

You read aloud to him 'La Belle Dame sans Merci'.
You feed him his medicine,
You tell him you love him.

You wait for his eyes to close at last
So you may write this poem.

CAROLYN KIZER

Book Ends (I)

Baked the day she suddenly dropped dead
we chew it slowly that last apple pie.

Shocked into sleeplessness you're scared of bed.
We never could talk much, and now don't try.

You're like book ends, the pair of you, she'd say,
Hog that grate, say nothing, sit, sleep, stare...

The 'scholar' me, you, worn out on poor pay,
only our silence made us seem a pair.

Not as good for staring in, blue gas,
too regular each bud, each yellow spike.

At night you need my company to pass
and she not here to tell us we're alike!

Your life's all shattered into smithereens.

Back in our silences and sullen looks,
for all the Scotch we drink, what's still between 's
not the thirty or so years, but books, books, books.

TONY HARRISON

For My Mother

When does the soul leave the body?
Since early morning you have not moved –
only your head moves, thrown back
with each deliberate breath,
the one sound that matters in the room.
My brother is here, my sister,
two of your sisters, ripples
widening from the bed.
The nurses check and measure,
keeping the many records.

Are you afraid?
Are you dreaming of what is past, lost,
or is this sleep some other preparation?
My sister has put your rings
on my finger; it seems like your hand
stroking the white brow,
unable to release you,
not even after you have asked for death –

And we know nothing about such pain,
except that it has weaned you from us,
and from the reedy, rusted
sunflowers outside the window,
dropping over the snow like tongueless bells.

ELLEN BRYANT VOIGT

Do Not Go Gentle into That Good Night

Do not go gentle into that good night,
Old age should burn and rave at close of day;
Rage, rage against the dying of the light.

Though wise men at their end know dark is right,
Because their words had forked no lightning they
Do not go gentle into that good night.

Good men, the last wave by, crying how bright
Their frail deeds might have danced in a green bay,
Rage, rage against the dying of the light.

Wild men who caught and sang the sun in flight,
And learn, too late, they grieved it on its way,
Do not go gentle into that good night.

Grave men, near death, who see with blinding sight
Blind eyes could blaze like meteors and be gay,
Rage, rage against the dying of the light.

And you, my father, there on the sad height,
Curse, bless, me now with your fierce tears, I pray.
Do not go gentle into that good night.
Rage, rage against the dying of the light.

DYLAN THOMAS

'Do not stand at my grave and weep'

Do not stand at my grave and weep;
I am not there. I do not sleep.
I am a thousand winds that blow.
I am the diamond glints on snow.
I am the sunlight on ripened grain.
I am the gentle autumn rain.

When you awaken in the morning's hush
I am the swift uplifting rush
Of quiet birds in circled flight.
I am the soft stars that shine at night.
Do not stand at my grave and cry;
I am not there. I did not die.

ANONYMOUS *

* Written at least fifty years ago, this poem has been attributed,
at different times, to J.T. Wiggins, Mary E. Fry and Marianne
Reinhardt, and recently to a British soldier killed in Northern
Ireland, Stephen Cummins (who left a copy for his relatives).

Funeral Blues

Stop all the clocks, cut off the telephone,
Prevent the dog from barking with a juicy bone,
Silence the pianos and with muffled drum
Bring out the coffin, let the mourners come.

Let aeroplanes circle moaning overhead
Scribbling on the sky the message He Is Dead,
Put crêpe bows round the white necks of the public doves,
Let the traffic policemen wear black cotton gloves.

He was my North, my South, my East and West,
My working week and my Sunday rest,
My noon, my midnight, my talk, my song;
I thought that love would last for ever: I was wrong.

The stars are not wanted now: put out every one;
Pack up the moon and dismantle the sun;
Pour away the ocean and sweep up the wood.
For nothing now can ever come to any good.

W.H. AUDEN

Death of an Irishwoman

Ignorant, in the sense
she ate monotonous food
and thought the world was flat,
and pagan, in the sense
she knew the things that moved
at night were neither dogs nor cats
but *púcas* and darkfaced men,
she nevertheless had fierce pride.
But sentenced in the end
to eat thin diminishing porridge
in a stone-cold kitchen
she clenched her brittle hands
around a world
she could not understand.
I loved her from the day she died.
She was a summer dance at the crossroads.
She was a card game where a nose was broken.
She was a song that nobody sings.
She was a house ransacked by soldiers.
She was a language seldom spoken.
She was child's purse, full of useless things.

MICHAEL HARTNETT

Water-burn

We should have been galloping on horses, their hoofprints
Splashes of light, divots kicked out of the darkness,
Or hauling up lobster pots in a wake of sparks. Where
Were the otters and seals? Were the dolphins on fire?
Yes, we should have been doing more with our lives.

MICHAEL LONGLEY

The dead

After his third operation, his heart
riddled like an old fairground target,
he woke up on his bed
and said: Now I'll be fine,
fit as a fiddle. And have you ever seen
horses coupling?

He died that night.

And another dragged on through eight insipid years
like a river weed in an acid stream,
as if pushing up his pallid
skewered face over the cemetery wall.

Until that face eventually vanished.

Both here and there the angel of death
quite simply stamped his hobnailed boot
on their medulla oblongata.

I know they died the same way.
But I don't believe they are
dead the same way.

MIROSLAV HOLUB
translated from the Czech by Ewald Osers

Death's Secret

It is not true
that death begins after life.
When life stops
death also stops.

GÖSTA ÅGREN
translated from the Finland Swedish by David McDuff

Death in October

Good to go off in colours.
Scarlet before the sleet;
fuming crimson, shrieking orange
a relaxed butter-pat

yellow. Name them. Anything
is better than flat
worn-out green. Even that
is strangely remote

in frost lying on the white
grass, whiter
edged, each vein
picked out for the last time, crystalline.

G.F. DUTTON

'Pity the drunks'

Pity the drunks in this late April snow.
They drank their hats and coats a week ago.
They touched the sun, they tapped the melting ground,
In public parks we saw them sitting round
The merry campfire of a cider jar
Upon a crocus cloth. Alas, some are
Already stiff in mortuaries who were
Seduced by Spring to go from here to there,
Putting their best foot forward on the road
To Walkden, Camberwell or Leeds. It snowed.
It met them waiting at the roundabout.
They had no hats and coats to keep it out.
They did a lap or two, they caught a cough.
They did another lap and shuffled off.

DAVID CONSTANTINE

Scattering Ashes

The nose of the pick-up lifted
into the sky and then down onto the fell
as we made our way to the spot
he drove to himself to drop hay
in bad winters and as he got lame.
From where we stopped, we could see
the farmhouse and the tops of hills
which for a moment seemed to pour in
on the random heap of an old sheep pen.
Willy fed the ash out like a trail
of gunpowder. It blew among us
taking the words with it: ashes; sacred;
our brother here departed. We stood
fixed awkwardly as hawthorn trees watching
the white ashes of a man who once stamped
this ground, fly off in fancy with the wind.
Arms were wrapped like scarves round shoulders;
and the dog, whistled out of the back,
wove in front of the car a sad reel
as we followed the fresh tracks home
through all the open gates on the land.

DAVID SCOTT

The Gas-poker

Forty-eight years ago
– Can it be forty-eight
Since then? – they forced the door
Which she had barricaded
With a full bureau's weight
Lest anyone find, as they did,
What she had blocked it for.

She had blocked the doorway so,
To keep the children out.
In her red dressing-gown
She wrote notes, all night busy
Pushing the things about,
Thinking till she was dizzy,
Before she had lain down.

The children went to and fro
On the harsh winter lawn
Repeating their lament,
A burden, to each other
In the December dawn,
Elder and younger brother,
Till they knew what it meant.

Knew all there was to know.
Coming back off the grass
To the room of her release,
They who had been her treasures
Knew to turn off the gas,
Take the appropriate measures,
Telephone the police.

One image from the flow
Sticks in the stubborn mind:
A sort of backwards flute.
The poker that she held up
Breathed from the holes aligned
Into her mouth till, filled up
By its music, she was mute.

THOM GUNN

Boy finds tramp dead

But for your comfort, child, who found him curled
With crizzled cheeks, his hands in his own ice,
Among the trapped dead birds and scraps of girls,

His spectacles and broken teeth put by
Along the window with a pile of pence,
Remember this man was the son of nobody,

Father, brother, husband, lover, friend
Of nobody, and so by dying alone
With rats hurt nobody. Perhaps he joined

And mended easily with death between
Newspaper sheets in drink and did not wake
Too soon, at midnight, crying to sleep again,

Alive and hung on cold, beyond the embrace
Of morning, the warm-handed. He was pressed
Together when you found him, child, but names

Had left his lips of wicked men released
Quickly in sunlight and of one who baked
Asleep inside a kiln and many at rest

With cancer in the casual ward or knocked
Under fast wheels. These he conjured with
To Christ as instances of mercy, being racked

Himself on boards beside a prolapsed hearth.
His vermin died. The morning's broken glass
And brightening air could not pick up his breath.

Little by little everything in him froze,
Everything stopped: the blood in the heart's ways,
The spittle in his mouth, his tongue, his voice.

DAVID CONSTANTINE

On a Dark Night

On a dark night
When all the street was hushed, you crept
Out of our bed and down the carpeted stair;
I stirred, unknowing that some light
Within you had gone out, and still I slept.
As if, out of the dark air

Of night, some call
Drew you, you moved in the silent street
Where cars were white in frost. Beyond the gate
You were your shadow on a garage-wall.
Mud on our laneway touched your naked feet.
The dying elms of our estate

Became your bower
And on your neck the chilling airs
Moved freely. I was not there when you kept
Such a hopeless tryst. At this most silent hour
You walked distracted with your heavy cares
On a dark night while I slept.

JOHN F. DEANE

Four Years

The smell of him went soon
from all his shirts.
I sent them for jumble,
and the sweaters and suits.
The shoes
held more of him; he was printed
into his shoes. I did not burn
or throw or give them away.
Time has denatured them now.

Nothing left.
There will never be
a hair of his in a comb.
But I want to believe
that in the shifting housedust
minute presences still drift:
an eyelash,
a hard crescent cut from a fingernail,
that sometimes
between the folds of a curtain
or the covers of a book
I touch
a flake of his skin.

PAMELA GILLILAN

Metamorphosis

Since you died, I notice
the outside seeping in.
There is the smell of damp in my chair.
My skin hangs in loose bracelets of bark
and my fingers scratch against my face
like a branch walked into.
A numbness is spreading up my cold ankles
as my locked feet take root.
The hands on my watch stand
motionless as deer against the trees,
pulling away with long slow strides
dragging the nights into silent days.
I call out, like a startled jay
clattering up through the canopy
of leaves closing over me
as I search the woodland paths
for traces of you.

CAROLINE SMITH

Sorting Through

The moment she died, my mother's dancedresses
turned from the colours they really were
to the colours I imagine them to be.
I can feel the weight of bumptoed silver shoes
swinging from their anklestraps as she swaggers
up the path towards *her* Dad, light-headed
from airman's kisses. Here, at what I'll have to learn
to call *my father's house*, yes every duster prints her
even more vivid than an Ilford snapshot on some seafront
in a white cardigan and that exact frock.
Old lipsticks. Liquid stockings.
Labels like *Harella, Gor-ray, Berketex.*
And, as I manhandle whole outfits into binbags for Oxfam,
every mote in my eye is a utility mark
and this is useful:
the sadness of dispossessed dresses,
the decency of good coats roundshouldered
in the darkness of wardrobes,
the gravitas of lapels,
the invisible danders of skin fizzing off from them
like all that life that will not neatly end.

LIZ LOCHHEAD

This Is What I Wanted to Sign Off With

You know what I'm
like when I'm sick: I'd sooner
curse than cry. And people don't often
know what they're saying in the end.
Or I could die in my sleep.

So I'll say it now. Here it is.
Don't pay any attention
if I don't get it right
when it's for real. Blame that

on terror and pain
or the stuff they're shooting
into my veins. This is what I wanted to
sign off with. Bend
closer, listen, I love you.

ALDEN NOWLAN

Wake

Three nights you lay in our house.
Three nights in the chill of the body.
Did I want to prove how surely
I'd been left behind? In the room's great dark
I climbed up beside you onto our high bed, bed
we'd loved in and slept in, married
and unmarried.

There was a halo of cold around you
as if the body's messages carry farther
in death, my own warmth taking on the silver-white
of a voice sent unbroken across snow just to hear
itself in its clarity of calling. We were dead
a little while together then, serene
and afloat on the strange broad canopy
of the abandoned world.

TESS GALLAGHER

About Death

  1

At the moment of death
what is the correct procedure?

Cut the umbilical, they said.

And with the umbilical cut
how then prepare the body?

Wash it in sacred water.
Dress it in silk for the wedding.

2

I wash and iron for you
your final clothes
(my heart on your sleeve)
wishing to wash your flesh
wishing to close
your sightless eyes

nothing remains to do

I am a vacant house

P.K. PAGE

The Vacuum

The house is so quiet now
The vacuum cleaner sulks in the corner closet,
Its bag limp as a stopped lung, its mouth
Grinning into the floor, maybe at my
Slovenly life, my dog-dead youth.

I've lived this way long enough,
But when my old woman died her soul
Went into that vacuum cleaner, and I can't bear
To see the bag swell like a belly, eating the dust
And the woollen mice, and begin to howl

Because there is old filth everywhere
She used to crawl, in the corner and under the stair.
I know now how life is cheap as dirt,
And still the hungry, angry heart
Hangs on and howls, biting at air.

HOWARD NEMEROV

Inside Our Dreams

Where do people go to when they die?
Somewhere down below or in the sky?
'I can't be sure,' said Grandad, 'but it seems
They simply set up home inside our dreams.'

JEANNE WILLIS

The Reassurance

About ten days or so
After we saw you dead
You came back in a dream.
I'm all right now you said.

And it was you, although
You were fleshed out again:
You hugged us all round then,
And gave your welcoming beam.

How like you to be kind,
Seeking to reassure.
And, yes, how like my mind
To make itself secure.

THOM GUNN

She

I think the dead are tender. Shall we kiss? –
My lady laughs, delighting in what is.
If she but sighs, a bird puts out its tongue.
She makes space lonely with a lovely song.
She lilts a low soft language, and I hear
Down long sea-chambers of the inner ear.

We sing together; we sing mouth to mouth.
The garden is a river flowing south.
She cries out loud the soul's own secret joy;
She dances, and the ground bears her away.
She knows the speech of light, and makes it plain
A lively thing can come to life again.

I feel her presence in the common day,
In that slow dark that widens every eye.
She moves as water moves, and comes to me,
Stayed by what was, and pulled by what would be.

THEODORE ROETHKE

A Glimpse of Starlings

I expect him any minute now although
He's dead. I know he has been talking
All night to his own dead and now
In the first heart-breaking light of morning
He is struggling into his clothes,
Sipping a cup of tea, fingering a bit of bread,
Eating a small photograph with his eyes.
The questions bang and rattle in his head
Like doors and cannisters the night of a storm.
He doesn't know why his days finished like this
Daylight is as hard to swallow as food
Love is a crumb all of him hungers for.
I can hear the drag of his feet on the concrete path
The close explosion of his smoker's cough
The slow turn of the Yale key in the lock
The door opening to let him in
To what looks like release from what feels like pain
And over his shoulder a glimpse of starlings
Suddenly lifted over field, road and river
Like a fist of black dust pitched in the wind.

BRENDAN KENNELLY

Dead Woman

If suddenly you do not exist,
if suddenly you no longer live,
I shall live on.

I do not dare,
I do not dare to write it,
if you die.

I shall live on.

For where a man has no voice,
there shall be my voice.

Where blacks are flogged and beaten,
I cannot be dead.
When my brothers go to prison
I shall go with them.

When victory,
not my victory,
but the great victory
comes,
even if I am dumb I must speak;
I shall see it coming even if I am blind.

No, forgive me.
If you no longer live,
if you, beloved, my love,
if you
have died,
all the leaves will fall on my breast,
it will rain on my soul night and day,
the snow will burn my heart,
I shall walk with frost and fire and death and snow,
my feet will want to walk to where you are sleeping,
but
I shall stay alive,
because above all things you wanted me

indomitable,
and, my love, because you know that I am not only a man
but all mankind.

PABLO NERUDA
translated from the Spanish by Brian Cole

Yes

Now we are like that flat cone of sand
in the garden of the Silver Pavilion in Kyōto
designed to appear only in moonlight.

Do you want me to mourn?
Do you want me to wear black?

Or like moonlight on whitest sand
to use your dark, to gleam, to shimmer?

I gleam. I mourn.

TESS GALLAGHER

Close

The afternoon I was killed
I strolled up the beach from the sea
where the big wave had hit me,
helped my wife and kids
pack up their picnic things,
then took my place in the car
for the curving journey home
through almost-empty lanes.

I had never seen the country
looking so beautiful –
furnace red in the poppies
scribbled all over the fields;
a darker red in the rocks
which sheltered the famous caves;
and pink in the western sky
which bode us well for tomorrow.

Nobody spoke about me
or how I was no longer there.
It was odd, but I understood why:
when I had drowned I was only
a matter of yards out to sea
(not too far out – too close),
still able to hear the talk
and have everything safe in view.

My sunburned wife, I noticed,
was trying to change for a swim,
resting her weight on one leg
as if she might suddenly start
to dance, or jump in the air,
but in fact snaking out of her knickers –
as shy as she was undressing
the first time we went to bed.

ANDREW MOTION

Inscription

When I die I will return to seek
The moments I did not live by the sea

SOPHIA DE MELLO BREYNER
translated from the Portuguese by Richard Zenith

'Buffalo Bill 's'

Buffalo Bill 's
defunct
     who used to
     ride a watersmooth-silver
          stallion
and break onetwothreefourfive pigeonsjustlikethat
               Jesus

he was a handsome man
         and what i want to know is
how do you like your blueeyed boy
Mister Death

E.E. CUMMINGS

The Dead

The dead are always looking down on us, they say,
while we are putting on our shoes or making a sandwich,
they are looking down through the glass-bottom boats of heaven
as they row themselves slowly through eternity.

They watch the tops of our heads moving below on earth,
and when we lie down in a field or on a couch,
drugged perhaps by the hum of a warm afternoon,
they think we are looking back at them,

which makes them lift their oars and fall silent
and wait, like parents, for us to close our eyes.

BILLY COLLINS

Proofs

Death will not correct
a single line of verse
she is no proof-reader
she is no sympathetic
lady editor

a bad metaphor is immortal

a shoddy poet who has died
is a shoddy dead poet

a bore bores after death
a fool keeps up his foolish chatter
from beyond the grave

TADEUSZ RÓZEWICZ
translated from the Polish by Adam Czerniawski

On Walking Backwards

My mother forbad us to walk backwards. That is how the dead
walk, she would say. Where did she get this idea? Perhaps from a
bad translation. The dead, after all, do not walk backwards but
they do walk behind us. They have no lungs and cannot call out
but would love for us to turn around. They are victims of love,
many of them.

ANNE CARSON

Cemetery Nights

Sweet dreams, sweet memories, sweet taste of earth:
here's how the dead pretend they're still alive –
one drags up a chair, a lamp, unwraps
the newspaper from somebody's garbage,
then sits holding the paper up to his face.
No matter if the lamp is busted and his eyes
have fallen out. Or some of the others
group together in front of the TV, chuckling
and slapping what's left of their knees.
No matter if the screen is dark. Four more
sit at a table with glasses and plates,
lift forks to their mouths and chew. No matter
if their plates are empty and they chew only air.
Two of the dead roll on the ground,
banging and rubbing their bodies together
as if in love or frenzy. No matter if their skin
breaks off, that their genitals are just a memory.

The head cemetery rat calls in all the city rats,
who pay him what rats find valuable –
the wing of a pigeon or ear of a dog.
The rats perch on tombstones and the cheap
statues of angels and, oh, they hold their bellies
and laugh, laugh until their guts half break;
while the stars give off the same cold light
that all these dead once planned their lives by,
and in someone's yard a dog barks and barks
just to see if some animal as dumb as he is
will wake from sleep and perhaps bark back.

STEPHEN DOBYNS

Father, Mother, Robert Henley who hanged himself in the ninth grade, et al

I've sensed ghosts more than once,
    their presence
a kind of plucking from the memorious air.

Always they reveal themselves as lost,
    surviving
on what's loose in me, some last words

I never said, some I did. I've heard
    they can't live
if fully embraced, if taken fully in,

yet I do nothing but listen to their
    wingless hovering,
the everything they never say.

If only I could give them what they need,
    no, if only
I could convince myself these things

must die as naturally as apples
    on the apple tree...
but that's in Nature, which is never

wrong, just thoughtless and without shame.

STEPHEN DUNN

Resurrection

Is it true that after this life of ours we shall one day be awakened
by a terrifying clamour of trumpets?
Forgive me, God, but I console myself
that the beginning and resurrection of all of us dead
will simply be announced by the crowing of the cock.

After that we'll remain lying down a while...
The first to get up
will be Mother... We'll hear her
quietly laying the fire,
quietly putting the kettle on the stove
and cosily taking the teapot out of the cupboard.
We'll be home once more.

VLADIMÍR HOLAN
translated from the Czech by George Theiner

Eden Rock

They are waiting for me somewhere beyond Eden Rock:
My father, twenty-five, in the same suit
Of Genuine Irish Tweed, his terrier Jack
Still two years old and trembling at his feet.

My mother, twenty-three, in a sprigged dress
Drawn at the waist, ribbon in her straw hat,
Has spread the stiff white cloth over the grass.
Her hair, the colour of wheat, takes on the light.

She pours tea from a Thermos, the milk straight
From an old H.P. sauce bottle, a screw
Of paper for a cork; slowly sets out
The same three plates, the tin cups painted blue.

The sky whitens as if lit by three suns.
My mother shades her eyes and looks my way
Over the drifted stream. My father spins
A stone along the water. Leisurely,

They beckon to me from the other bank.
I hear them call, 'See where the stream-path is!
Crossing is not as hard as you might think.'

I had not thought that it would be like this.

CHARLES CAUSLEY

When I Died

I'm coming back on All Saints' Day
for your olives, old peanuts and dodgy sherry,
dirty dancing. I'll cross-dress at last
pirouette and flash, act pissed.
You'll have to look for me hard:
search for my bones in the crowd.
Or lay a pint and a pie on my grave to tempt me out
and a trail of marigolds back to the flat,
where you'll leave the door ajar
and the cushions plumped in my old armchair.

JO SHAPCOTT

All Souls'

Suppose there is no heaven and no hell,
And that the dead can never leave the earth,
That, as the body rots, the soul breaks free,
Weak and disabled in its second birth.

And then invisible, rising to the light,
Each finds a world it cannot touch or hear,
Where colors fade and, if the soul cries out,
The silence stays unbroken in the air.

How flat the ocean seems without its roar,
Without the sting of salt, the bracing gust.
The sunset blurs into a grayish haze.
The morning snowfall is a cloud of dust.

The pines that they revisit have no scent.
They cannot feel the needled forest floor.
Crossing the stream, they watch the current flow
Unbroken as they step down from the shore.

They want their voices to become the wind –
Intangible like them – to match its cry,
Howling in treetops, covering the moon,
Tumbling the storm clouds in a rain-swept sky

But they are silent as a rising mist,
A smudge of smoke dissolving in the air.
They watch the shadows lengthen on the grass.
The pallor of the rose is their despair.

DANA GIOIA

from Lessons

Between us and the farthest star
lie the unthinkable distances –
lines, tracks, paths. If there
is a place beyond this space
it would be there he disappeared:
neither farther nor less far
but in another space, abstracted
beyond measure. The ruler laid
from us to him lost continuity
like a sword broken across the knee.

*

'Who will help me? No one can come this far.
Holding my hands won't stop them shaking,
shading my eyes won't stop them seeing,
being close to me day and night like a coat
can do nothing against this heat, this cold.
I can at least confirm there is a wall here
that no invading force will ever destroy.
There's nothing for it now but the longest and worst.'

Is this what he whispers to the narrowing night?

*

It's over us now
like a mountainous shadow.

An icy shadow in which
we can only pray and vomit.

It's hard to watch.

Something buries itself in him to kill.
The pity of it
when the other world sinks its blade
in a living body!

Don't ask me
to forge light from this iron.

Our heads against the mountain
In the cold dawn,
we are filled with, horror and pity.

In the dawn bristling with birds.

*

If it should be, and who can ever be sure,
that he still has some kind of existence today,
of consciousness even, not too far away,
would it be here that he would stay,
in the garden rather than out in the pasture?
Might he be waiting there, as if
by arrangement, 'beside the stone'?
Might he have need of our voices, our tears?
I don't know; but one day or another will see
these stones buried by the eternal grass,
sooner or later there will be no one left
to visit the grave, which will be buried too,
not even shadows in that shadowless place.

PHILIPPE JACCOTTET
translated from the French by Derek Mahon

Where Souls Go

No telling where: down the hill
and out of sight –
soapbox derby heroes in a new dimension.
Don't bother to resurrect them
unless some old newsreel clip
catches them shocked
with a butter knife in the toaster.
Countless snaps and episodes in space
once you hit the viewfinder that fits.
It's a lie anyway, all Hollywood –
the Mind is a too much thing
cleansing itself like a great salt sea.
Rather, imagine them in the eaves

among pigeons
or clustered round the D train's fan
as we cross the bridge to Brooklyn.
And make that a Friday night
July say. We are walking past
the liquor store to visit our love.
Two black boys are eating Corn Doodles
in the most flamboyant manner possible.
She waits, trying
to have the best song on as we arrive.
The moon is blurred.
Our helicopters are shooting at fieldworkers.
The Mets are down 3-1 in the 6th.

AUGUST KLEINZAHLER

A Mosquito

The lady whines, then dines; is slapped and killed;
Yet it's her killer's blood that has been spilled.

BRAD LEITHAUSER

The Wild Iris

At the end of my suffering
there was a door.

Hear me out: that which you call death
I remember.

Overhead, noises, branches of the pine shifting.
Then nothing. The weak sun
flickered over the dry surface.

It is terrible to survive
as consciousness
buried in the dark earth.

Then it was over: that which you fear, being
a soul and unable
to speak, ending abruptly, the stiff earth
bending a little. And what I took to be
birds darting in low shrubs.

You who do not remember
passage from the other world
I tell you I could speak again: whatever
returns from oblivion returns
to find a voice:

from the center of my life came
a great fountain, deep blue
shadows on azure seawater.

LOUISE GLÜCK

Antarctica

'I am just going outside and may be some time.'
The others nod, pretending not to know.
At the heart of the ridiculous, the sublime.

He leaves them reading and begins to climb,
Goading his ghost into the howling snow;
He is just going outside and may be some time.

The tent recedes beneath its crust of rime
And frostbite is replaced by vertigo:
At the heart of the ridiculous, the sublime.

Need we consider it some sort of crime,
This numb self-sacrifice of the weakest? No,
He is just going outside and may be some time –

In fact, for ever. Solitary enzyme,
Though the night yield no glimmer there will glow,
At the heart of the ridiculous, the sublime.

He takes leave of the earthly pantomime
Quietly, knowing it is time to go.
'I am just going outside and may be some time.'
At the heart of the ridiculous, the sublime.

DEREK MAHON

Why Brownlee Left

Why Brownlee left, and where he went,
Is a mystery even now.
For if a man should have been content
It was him; two acres of barley,
One of potatoes, four bullocks,
A milker, a slated farmhouse.
He was last seen going out to plough
On a March morning, bright and early.

By noon Brownlee was famous;
They had found all abandoned, with
The last rig unbroken, his pair of black
Horses, like man and wife,
Shifting their weight from foot to
Foot, and gazing into the future.

PAUL MULDOON

Sleep with a Suitcase

I slept with a suitcase last night.
It didn't snore. It was half-packed
and there was a map on the floor.
Outside, snow covered the roof
of my tanked-up car. I kept
my clothes on and the heating up,
and the phone off the hook.
I wanted no one and nothing
between me and the morning.
I set my alarm for the dawn.
The poison I fed the cat
was working in the dark kitchen.
The mailbox was in the trash.
I left a note on the oven
saying I was dead, forgotten,
and the house was my son's.
He would sleep for three days
then wake with a headache.
I left him aspirin and water,
and his father's phone number,
or the last one I knew.

MATTHEW SWEENEY

As It Should Be

We hunted the mad bastard
Through bog, moorland, rock, to the star-lit west
And gunned him down in a blind yard
Between ten sleeping lorries
And an electricity generator.

Let us hear no idle talk
Of the moon in the Yellow River.
The air blows softer since his departure.

Since his tide burial during school hours
Our kiddies have known no bad dreams.
Their cries echo lightly along the coast.

This is as it should be.
They will thank us for it when they grow up
To a world with method in it.

DEREK MAHON

How to Disappear

First rehearse the easy things.
Lose your words in a high wind,
walk in the dark on an unlit road,
observe how other people mislay keys,
their diaries, new umbrellas.
See what it takes to go unnoticed
in a crowded room. Tell lies:
I love you. I'll be back in half an hour.
I'm fine.

Then childish things.
Stand very still behind a tree,
become a cowboy, say you've died,
climb into wardrobes, breathe on a mirror

until there's no one there, and practise magic,
tricks with smoke and fire –
a flick of the wrist and the victim's lost
his watch, his wife, his ten pound note. Perfect it.
Hold your breath a little longer every time.

The hardest things.
Eat less, much less, and take a vow of silence.
Learn the point of vanishing, the moment
embers turn to ash, the sun falls down,
the sudden white-out comes.
And when it comes again – it will –
just walk at it, walk into it, and walk,
until you know that you're no longer
anywhere.

AMANDA DALTON

Folderol

I have been walking by the harbour
where I see it's recently sprayed
that *Fred loves Freda*, and *Freda cops Fred*.
Which reminds me of you, and the twenty-four

words for 'nonsense' I wrote on your thighs and back
(the night you came home from her house with some cock-
and-bull story of missed connections and loose ends)
with passion-fruit lipstick and mascara pens.

Including, for the record: blather, drivel, trash,
prattle, palaver, waffle, balderdash, gibberish, shit.
Thinking I had made a point of sorts, but not
so sure when I woke up to find my own flesh

covered with your smudged disgrace
while you, of course, had vanished without trace.

VONA GROARKE

Robinson

The dog stops barking after Robinson has gone.
His act is over. The world is a gray world,
Not without violence, and he kicks under the grand piano,
The nightmare chase well under way.

The mirror from Mexico, stuck to the wall,
Reflects nothing at all. The glass is black.
Robinson alone provides the image Robinsonian.

Which is all of the room-walls, curtains,
Shelves, bed, the tinted photograph of Robinson's first wife,
Rugs, vases, panatellas in a humidor.
They would fill the room if Robinson came in.

The pages in the books are blank,
The books that Robinson has read. That is his favorite chair,
Or where the chair would be if Robinson were here.

All day the phone rings. It could be Robinson
Calling. It never rings when he is here.

Outside, white buildings yellow in the sun.
Outside, the birds circle continuously
Where trees are actual and take no holiday.

WELDON KEES

Night and the House

Night reunites the house and its silence
From the foundations up
To the still flower
Only the ticking of time's clock is heard

Night reunites the house and its destiny

Now nothing is scattered nothing divided
Everything watches like the vigilant cypress

Emptiness walks in its living spaces

SOPHIA DE MELLO BREYNER
translated from the Portuguese by Richard Zenith

Distant howling

In Alsace,
on 6th July 1885,
a rabid dog knocked down
the nine-year-old Joseph Meister
and bit him fourteen times.

Meister was the first patient
saved by Pasteur
with his vaccine, in thirteen
progressive doses
of the attenuated virus.

Pasteur died of ictus
ten years later.
The janitor Meister
fifty-five years later
committed suicide
when the Germans occupied
his Pasteur Institute
with all those poor dogs.

Only the virus
remained above it all.

MIROSLAV HOLUB
translated from the Czech by Ewald Osers

11

Me, the Earth, the Universe

Poetry has to do with the non-rational parts of man.
For a poet, a human being is a mystery...
this is a religious feeling.

CZESLAW MILOSZ

Poetry is what makes the invisible appear.

NATHALIE SARRAUTE

THESE SMALL POEMS are about the big questions: about time, matter, gravity, life and the nature of the universe. All are questioning poems whether written out of wonder or disquiet, faith or fury, belief or unbelief. Edna Longley has described how modern poetry is full of displaced or redirected religion: 'Christianity shapes the vision and forms even of poets who disown it, like Thomas Hardy. Yeats was drawn to poetry as compensation for the loss of God. Conversely, *The Waste Land* can be read as a search for God...A post-religious sense of loss gives modern poetry its persistent metaphysical dimension.'

Seamus Heaney's deceptively simple poem from his sequence *Lightenings* (418) makes an imaginative bridge between the world of our everyday lives and that of our aspirations. He has called it a parable about 'the way consciousness can be alive in two different and contradictory dimensions of reality and still find a way of negotiating between them...within our individual selves we can reconcile two orders of knowledge which we might call the practical and the poetic; to affirm also that each form of knowledge redresses the other and that the frontier between them is there for the crossing.'

Heaney's poem is effective *as a poem* because his story engages the reader's imagination. The abstract is grounded in the actual. By contrast, in Wallace Stevens's 'The Snow Man' (428), what the poem describes is subservient to what the poet says it means. Stevens uses particulars as illustrations of general truths. Goethe's view was that 'It makes a great difference whether the poet seeks the particular in relation to the universal or contemplates the universal in the particular'. This is where modern poetry differs from Romanticism. The contemporary poet usually seeks meaning *in* the particular.

The three poems by Gwyneth Lewis are from her sequence *Zero Gravity* (433). This traces an inner journey, confronting the self and death, while outwardly describing a space mission by her astronaut cousin.

Homage to Isaac Newton

We commit what we do not commit,
and we do not commit what we commit.
Somewhere there is a terrible silence.
Towards that we gravitate.

JÁNOS PILINSZKY
translated from the Hungarian by Peter Jay

New Gravity

Treading through the half-light of ivy
and headstone, I see you in the distance
as I'm telling our daughter
about this place, this whole business:
a sister about to be born,
how a life's new gravity suspends in water.
Under the oak, the fallen leaves
are pieces of the tree's jigsaw;
by your father's grave you are pressing acorns
into the shadows to seed.

ROBIN ROBERTSON

Moment

Clear moments are so short.
There is much more darkness. More
ocean than firm land. More
shadow than form.

ADAM ZAGAJEWSKI
translated from the Polish by Renata Gorczynski

Morning

She opened the shutters. She hung the sheets over the sill.
     She saw the day.
A bird looked at her straight in the eyes. 'I am alone,' she whispered.
'I am alive.' She entered the room. The mirror too is a window.
If I jump from it I will fall into my arms.

YANNIS RITSOS
translated from the Greek by Nikos Stangos

The Other Room

This is the room reflected in the window.
Walk inside, explore it for yourself.
The fire is glacial crimson.

The walls are filmy, not like walls at all.
These are the most densely populated
living-rooms on earth.

But who lives in them. The souls
settle here in their multitudes,
visit the spines of weightless books,

the floating hands of clocks.
Sink into armchairs in the snow.
Lose interest in us, even

as they beat so fiercely
against our bolder rooms,
the glass of the world.

MONIZA ALVI

Brief reflection on accuracy

Fish
    always accurately know where to move and when,
    and likewise
    birds have an accurate built-in time sense
    and orientation.

Humanity, however,
    lacking such instincts resorts to scientific
    research. Its nature is illustrated by the following
    occurrence.

A certain soldier
    had to fire a cannon at six o'clock sharp every evening.
    Being a soldier he did so. When his accuracy was
    investigated he explained:

I go by
    the absolutely accurate chronometer in the window
    of the clockmaker down in the city. Every day at seventeen
    forty-five I set my watch by it and
    climb the hill where my cannon stands ready.
    At seventeen fifty-nine precisely I step up to the cannon
    and at eighteen hours sharp I fire.

And it was clear
    that this method of firing was absolutely accurate.
    All that was left was to check that chronometer. So
    the clockmaker down in the city was questioned about
    his instrument's accuracy.

Oh, said the clockmaker,
    this is one of the most accurate instruments ever. Just imagine,
    for many years now a cannon has been fired at six o'clock sharp.
    And every day I look at this chronometer
    and always it shows exactly six.

So much for accuracy.
    And fish move in the water, and from the skies
    comes a rushing of wings while

Chronometers tick and cannon boom.

MIROSLAV HOLUB
translated from the Czech by Ewald Osers

Zoom!

It begins as a house, an end terrace
in this case
but it will not stop there. Soon it is
an avenue
which cambers arrogantly past the Mechanics' Institute,
turns left
at the main road without even looking
and quickly it is
a town with all four major clearing banks,
a daily paper
and a football team pushing for promotion.

On it goes, oblivious of the Planning Acts,
the green belts,
and before we know it it is out of our hands:
city, nation,
hemisphere, universe, hammering out in all directions
until suddenly,
mercifully, it is drawn aside through the eye
of a black hole
and bulleted into a neighbouring galaxy, emerging
smaller and smoother
than a billiard ball but weighing more than Saturn.

People stop me in the street, badger me
in the check-out queue
and ask 'What is this, this that is so small
and so very smooth
but whose mass is greater than the ringed planet?'
It's just words
I assure them. But they will not have it.

SIMON ARMITAGE

from **Lightenings**

The annals say: when the monks of Clonmacnoise
Were all at prayers inside the oratory
A ship appeared above them in the air.

The anchor dragged along behind so deep
It hooked itself into the altar rails
And then, as the big hull rocked to a standstill,

A crewman shinned and grappled down the rope
And struggled to release it. But in vain.
'This man can't bear our life here and will drown,'

The abbot said, 'unless we help him.' So
They did, the freed ship sailed, and the man climbed back
Out of the marvellous as he had known it.

SEAMUS HEANEY

On the Uncountable Nature of Things
(meditation)

I

Thus, not the thing held in memory, but this:
    The fruit tree with its scars, thin torqued branches;

The high burnished sheen of morning light
    Across its trunk; the knuckle-web of ancient knots,

II

The swift, laboring insistence of insects –
    Within, the pulse of slow growth in sap-dark cores,

And the future waiting, latent in fragile cells:
    The last, terse verses of curled leaves hanging in air –

And the dry, tender arc of the fruitless branch.

III

Yes, the tree's spine conditioned by uncountable
　　　　Days of rain and drought: all fleeting coordinates set

Against a variable sky – recounting faithfully
　　　　The thing as it is – transient, provisional, changing

Constantly in latitude – a refugee not unlike
　　　　Us in this realm of exacting, but unpredictable, time.

IV

And once only a branch laden with perfect
　　　　Fruit – only once daybreak weighed out perfectly by

The new bronze of figs, *not things in memory*,
　　　　But as they are here: the roar and plough of daylight,

The perfect, wild cacophony of the present –
　　　　Each breath measured and distinct in a universe ruled

V

By particulars – each moment a universe:
　　　　As when under night heat – passion sparks, unique –

New in time – and hands, obedient, divine,
　　　　As Desire dilates eye – pulse the blue-veined breast,

Touch driving, forging the hungering flesh:
　　　　To the far edge of each moment's uncharted edge

VI

For the flesh too is wind, desire storm to the marrow –
　　　　Still – *the dream of simplicity in the midst of motion*:

Recollection demanding a final tallying of accounts,
　　　　The mind, loyal clerk, driven each moment to decide –

Even as the tree's wood is split and sweat still graces
　　　　The crevices of the body, which moment to weigh in,

For memory's sake, on the mobile scales of becoming.

ELLEN HINSEY

The Sun Underfoot among the Sundews

An ingenuity too astonishing
to be quite fortuitous is
this bog full of sundews, sphagnum-
lined and shaped like a teacup.
                              A step
down and you're into it; a
wilderness swallows you up:
ankle-, then knee-, then midriff-
to-shoulder-deep in wetfooted
understory, an overhead
spruce-tamarack horizon hinting
you'll never get out of here.
                              But the sun
among the sundews, down there,
is so bright, an underfoot
webwork of carnivorous rubies,
a star-warm thick as the gnats
they're set to catch, delectable
double-faced cockleburs, each
hair-tip a sticky mirror
afire with sunlight, a million
of them and again a million,
each mirror a trap set to
unhand unbelieving,
                              that either
a First Cause said once, 'Let there
be sundews,' and there were, or they've
made their way here unaided
other than by that backhand, round-
about refusal to assume responsibility
known as Natural Selection.
                              But the sun
underfoot is so dazzling
down there among the sundews,
there is so much light
in the cup that, looking,
you start to fall upward.

AMY CLAMPITT

'I stretch my arms'

I stretch my arms like a swan flying
And watch, weightless, the world turning
So high up I can see – endlessly it seems
Rome and white mountains rising beyond,
Triremes at anchor in still Alexandria
Pearl-divers practising from rocks
The wind wandering through the wilderness.
The sun casts no shadow of the compass.
I am rooted to the spot, rotting inside
I had no choice but to choose this perch
And now I cannot choose any more
Each choice I made was like a nail
Fixing my arms to embrace the world.

JAMES HARPUR

A Downward Look

Seen from above, the sky
Is deep. Clouds float down there,

Foam on a long, luxurious bath.
Their shadows over limbs submerged in 'air',

Over protuberances, faults,
A delta thicket, glide. On high, the love

That drew the bath and scattered it with salts

Still radiates new projects old as day,
And hardly registers the tug

When, far beneath, a wrinkled, baby hand
Happens upon the plug.

JAMES MERRILL

I Am the Song

I am the song that sings the bird.
I am the leaf that grows the land.
I am the tide that moves the moon.
I am the stream that halts the sand.
I am the cloud that drives the storm.
I am the earth that lights the sun.
I am the fire that strikes the stone.
I am the clay that shapes the hand.
I am the word that speaks the man.

CHARLES CAUSLEY

from Games

He

Some bite off the others'
Arm or leg or whatever

Take it between their teeth
Run off as quick as they can
Bury it in the earth

The others run in all directions
Sniff search sniff search
Turn up all the earth

If any are lucky enough to find their arm
Or leg or whatever
It's their turn to bite

The game goes on briskly

As long as there are arms
As long as there are legs
As long as there is anything whatever

VASKO POPA
translated from the Serbo-Croat by Anne Pennington

422

Earth

Let the day grow on you upward
through your feet,
the vegetal knuckles,

to your knees of stone,
until by evening you are a black tree;
feel, with evening,

the swifts thicken your hair,
the new moon rising out of your forehead,
and the moonlit veins of silver

running from your armpits
like rivulets under white leaves.
Sleep, as ants

cross over your eyelids.
You have never possessed anything
as deeply as this.

This is all you have owned
from the first outcry
through forever;

you can never be dispossessed.

DEREK WALCOTT

Waking

When Lazarus
Was helped from his cold tomb
Into air cut by bird-calls,
While a branch swayed
And the ground felt unsteady:
I must, like him, with all force possible
Try out my tongue again.

SHEILA WINGFIELD

Places We Love

Places we love exist only through us,
Space destroyed is only illusion in the constancy of time,
Places we love we can never leave,
Places we love together, together, together,

And is this room really a room, or an embrace,
And what is beneath the window: a street or years?
And the window is only the imprint left by
The first rain we understood, returning endlessly,

And this wall does not define the room, but perhaps the night
Your son began to move in your sleeping blood,
A son like a butterfly of flame in your hall of mirrors,
The night you were frightened by your own light,

And this door leads into any afternoon
Which outlives it, forever peopled
With your casual movements, as you stepped,
Like fire into copper, into my only memory;

When you go, space closes over like water behind you,
Do not look back: there is nothing outside you,
Space is only time visible in a different way,
Places we love we can never leave.

IVAN V. LALIC
translated from the Serbo-Croat by Francis R. Jones

Moorland

It is beautiful and still;
            the air rarefied
as the interior of a cathedral

expecting a presence. It is where, also,
            the harrier occurs,
materialising from nothing, snow-

424

soft, but with claws of fire,
          quartering the bare earth
for the prey that escapes it;

hovering over the incipient
          scream, here a moment, then
not here, like my belief in God.

R.S. THOMAS

Three Ways of Looking at God

1

A claustrophobia of sand and stone: a walled heat.
The light bleaches and curves like a blade, isolates
the chirr of crickets, seed-pods detonating,
the valley waiting in a film of flame.
A bird finds an open channel in the air
and follows it without exertion to the branch.

2

The sky is slashed like a sail. Night folds
over the shears, the dye, the docked tails.
We listen to the rumours of the valley:
goats' voices, gear-changes, the stirring of dogs.
In the green light, lambs with rouged cheeks
skitter from their first communion, calling for home.

3

Lightning flexes: a man chalked on a board, reeling,
exact, elementary, flawed; at each kick, birds flinch
and scatter from the white lawn.
The long trees bend to the grain of the gale,
streaming the dark valley like riverweed.
All night: thunder, torn leaves; a sheathing of wings.

ROBIN ROBERTSON

The Avatar

Listen, this is the trinity, he said, tramping the wet road
in the thin well-being of a winter morning:
God the curlew, God the eider,
God the cheese-on-toast.
To his right a huddle of small blue mountains
squatted together discussing the recent storm.
To his left the sea washed.

I thought it was whimsical, what he said,
I condemned it as fey.
Then I saw that he meant it; that, unlike me,
he had no quarrel
with himself, could see his own glory
was young enough for faith still in flesh and in being.
He was not attracted by awe

or a high cold cleanness
but imagined a god as intimate
as the trickles of blood and juice that coursed about inside him,
a god he could eat or warm his hands on,
a low god for winter:
belly-weighted, with the unmistakable call
of the bog curlew or the sea-going eider.

KERRY HARDIE

Sacrament

God, I have sought you as a fox seeks chickens,
curbing my hunger with cunning.
The times I have tasted your flesh
there was no bread and wine between us,
only night and the wind beating the grass.

ALDEN NOWLAN

Journey of the Magi

'A cold coming we had of it,
just the worst time of the year
For a journey, and such a long journey:
The ways deep and the weather sharp,
The very dead of winter.'
And the camels galled, sore-footed, refractory,
Lying down in the melting snow.
There were times we regretted
The summer palaces on slopes, the terraces,
And the silken girls bringing sherbet.
Then the camel men cursing and grumbling
And running away, and wanting their liquor and women,
And the night-fires going out, and the lack of shelters,
And the cities hostile and the towns unfriendly
And the villages dirty and charging high prices:
A hard time we had of it.
At the end we preferred to travel all night,
Sleeping in snatches,
With the voices singing in our ears, saying
That this was all folly.

Then at dawn we came down to a temperate valley,
Wet, below the snow line, smelling of vegetation,
With a running stream and a water-mill beating the darkness,
And three trees on the low sky.
And an old white horse galloped away in the meadow.
Then we came to a tavern with vine-leaves over the lintel,
Six hands at an open door dicing for pieces of silver,
And feet kicking the empty wine-skins.
But there was no information, and so we continued
And arrived at evening, not a moment too soon
Finding the place; it was (you may say) satisfactory.

All this was a long time ago, I remember,
And I would do it again, but set down
This set down
This: were we led all that way for
Birth or Death? There was a Birth, certainly,
We had evidence and no doubt. I had seen birth and death,
But had thought they were different; this Birth was
Hard and bitter agony for us, like Death, our death.

We returned to our places, these Kingdoms,
But no longer at ease here, in the old dispensation,
With an alien people clutching their gods.
I should be glad of another death.

T.S. ELIOT

The Snow Man

One must have a mind of winter
To regard the frost and the boughs
Of the pine trees crusted with snow;

And have been cold a long time
To behold the junipers shagged with ice,
The spruces rough in the distant glitter

Of the January sun; and not to think
Of any misery in the sound of the wind,
In the sound of a few leaves,

Which is the sound of the land
Full of the same wind
That is blowing in the same bare place

For the listener, who listens in the snow,
And, nothing himself, beholds
Nothing that is not there and the nothing that is.

WALLACE STEVENS

Sanctity

To be a poet and not know the trade,
To be a lover and repel all women;
Twin ironies by which great saints are made,
The agonising pincer-jaws of Heaven.

PATRICK KAVANAGH

Via Negativa

Why no! I never thought other than
That God is that great absence
In our lives, the empty silence
Within, the place where we go
Seeking, not in hope to
Arrive or find. He keeps the interstices
In our knowledge, the darkness
Between stars. His are the echoes
We follow, the footprints he has just
Left. We put our hands in
His side hoping to find
It warm. We look at people
And places as though he had looked
At them, too; but miss the reflection.

R.S. THOMAS

To the One Upstairs

Boss of all bosses of the universe.
Mr know-it-all, wheeler-dealer, wire-puller,
And whatever else you're good at.
Go ahead, shuffle your zeros tonight.
Dip in ink the comets' tails.
Staple the night with starlight.

You'd be better off reading coffee dregs,
Thumbing the pages of the Farmer's Almanac.
But no! You love to put on airs,
And cultivate your famous serenity
While you sit behind your big desk
With zilch in your in-tray, zilch
In your out-tray,
And all of eternity around you.

Doesn't it give you the creeps
To hear them begging you on their knees,
Sputtering endearments,
As if you were an inflatable, life-size doll?
Tell them to button up and go to bed.
Stop pretending you're too busy to notice.

Your hands are empty and so are your eyes.
There's nothing to put your signature to,
Even if you knew your own name,
Or believed the ones I keep inventing,
As I scribble this note to you in the dark.

CHARLES SIMIC

Tracks

2 a.m.: moonlight. The train has stopped
out in the middle of the plain. Far away, points of light in a town,
flickering coldly at the horizon.

As when a man has gone into a dream so deep
he'll never remember having been there
when he comes back to his room.

As when someone has gone into an illness so deep
everything his days were becomes a few flickering points, a swarm,
cold and tiny at the horizon.

The train is standing quite still.
2 a.m.: bright moonlight, few stars.

TOMAS TRANSTRÖMER
translated from the Swedish by Robin Fulton

Delay

The radiance of that star that leans on me
Was shining years ago. The light that now
Glitters up there my eye may never see,
And so the time lag teases me with how

Love that loves now may not reach me until
Its first desire is spent. The star's impulse
Must wait for eyes to claim it beautiful
And love arrived may find us somewhere else.

ELIZABETH JENNINGS

Summer farm

Straws like tame lightnings lie about the grass
And hang zigzag on hedges. Green as glass
The water in the horse-trough shines.
Nine ducks go wobbling by in two straight lines.

A hen stares at nothing with one eye,
Then picks it up. Out of an empty sky
A swallow falls and, flickering through
The barn, dives up again into the dizzy blue.

I lie, not thinking, in the cool, soft grass,
Afraid of where a thought might take me – as
This grasshopper with plated face
Unfolds his legs and finds himself in space.

Self under self, a pile of selves I stand
Threaded on time, and with metaphysic hand
Lift the farm like a lid and see
Farm within farm, and in the centre, me.

NORMAN MacCAIG

Tinily a star goes down

Tinily a star goes down
behind a black cloud.

Odd that your wristwatch still should lie
on the shiny dressing-table

its tick so faint I cannot hear
the universe at its centre.

IAIN CRICHTON SMITH

Star Whisper

If you dare breathe out in Verkhoyansk
You'll get the sound of life turning to frost
As if it were an untuned radio,
        A storm of dust.

It's what the stars confess when all is silence
– Not to the telescopes, but to the snow.
It hangs upon the trees like silver berries
        – Iced human dew.

Imagine how the throat gets thick with it,
How many *versts* there are until the spring,
How close the blood is, just behind the lips
        And tongue, to freezing.

Here, you could breathe a hundred times a minute,
And from the temperate air still fail to draw
Conclusions about whether you're alive
        – If so, what for.

CAROL RUMENS

from Zero Gravity

VI

Last suppers, I fancy, are always wide-screen.
I see this one in snapshot: your brothers are rhymes
with you and each other. John has a shiner
from surfing. Already we've started counting time
backwards to zero. The Shuttle processed
out like an idol to its pagan pad.
It stands by its scaffold, being tended and blessed
by priestly technicians. You refuse to feel sad,
can't wait for your coming wedding with speed
out into weightlessness. We watch you dress
in your orange space suit, a Hindu bride,
with wires like henna for your loveliness.
You carry your helmet like a severed head.
We think of you as already dead.

X

Drew trips over his shadow by the pool
but picks himself up. We keep TVs on
like memorial flames, listen as Mission Control
gives cool instructions. You are a sun
we follow, tracking your time over Africa,
a fauvist desert. We see you fall
past pointillist clouds in the Bahamas,
past glaciers, silent hurricanes, the Nile.
We're all provincials when it comes to maps
so we look out for Florida. The world's a road
above you – but you have no 'up',
only an orbit as you dive towards
an opal Pacific, now you see dawn
every ninety minutes. The Shuttle's a cliff
that's shearing, you on it, every way's 'down',
vertiginous plunging. It is yourself
you hold on to, till you lose your grip
on that, even. Then your soul's the ship.

XI

The second time the comet swung by
the knife went deeper. It hissed through the sky,

phosphorus on water. It marked a now,
an only-coming-once, a this-ness we knew

we'd keep forgetting. Its vapour trails
mimicked our voyage along ourselves,

our fire with each other, the endless cold
which surrounds that burning. Don't be fooled

by fireworks. It's no accident that *leave*
fails but still tries to rhyme with *love*.

GWYNETH LEWIS

Rent

If you want my apartment, sleep in it
but let's have a clear understanding:
the books are still free agents.

If the rocking chair's arms surround you
they can also let you go,
they can shape the air like a body.

I don't want your rent, I want
a radiance of attention
like the candle's flame when we eat,

I mean a kind of awe
attending the spaces between us –
Not a roof but a field of stars.

JANE COOPER

Full Moon

My bands of silk and miniver
Momently grew heavier;
The black gauze was beggarly thin;
The ermine muffled mouth and chin;
I could not suck the moonlight in.

Harlequin in lozenges
Of love and hate, I walked in these
Striped and ragged rigmaroles;
Along the pavement my footsoles
Trod warily on living coals.

Shouldering the thoughts I loathed,
In their corrupt disguises clothed,
Mortality I could not tear
From my ribs, to leave them bare
Ivory in silver air.

There I walked, and there I raged;
The spiritual savage caged
Within my skeleton, raged afresh
To feel, behind a carnal mesh,
The clean bones crying in the flesh.

ELINOR WYLIE

Preparation for the big emptiness

Smudges of moon in the morning –
fingerprints of the moon-eaters

A new core gathers for the evening
to be plucked and crumbled by other hands

Sometimes, there is blue in between
Sometimes, there is no one

You must prepare for the big
emptiness to come

It has come

When it comes
you must spread yourself thinly,
transparently,
to fill what can't be filled

It has come

Unlike the moon you must do it
without breaking

KAPKA KASSABOVA

The Shampoo

The still explosions on the rocks,
the lichens, grow
by spreading, gray, concentric shocks.
They have arranged
to meet the rings around the moon, although
within our memories they have not changed.

And since the heavens will attend
as long on us,
you've been, dear friend,
precipitate and pragmatical;
and look what happens. For Time is
nothing if not amenable.

The shooting stars in your black hair
in bright formation
are flocking where,
so straight, so soon?
– Come, let me wash it in this big tin basin,
battered and shiny like the moon.

ELIZABETH BISHOP

Mountains

Something is in the line and air along edges,
which is in woods when the leaf changes
and in the leaf-pattern's gives and gauges,
the water's tension upon ledges.
Something is taken up with entrances,
which turns the issue under bridges.
The moon is between places.
An outlet fills the space between two horses.

Look through a holey stone. Now put it down.
Something is twice as different. Something gone
accumulates a queerness. Be alone.
Something is side by side with anyone.

And certain evenings, something in the balance
falls to the dewpoint where our minds condense
and then inslides itself between moments
and spills the heart from its circumference;
and this is when the moon matchlessly opens
and you can feel by instinct in the distance
the bigger mountains hidden by the mountains,
like intentions among suggestions.

ALICE OSWALD

The Other Side of the Mountain

The bear barged into the boozer
To see what he could see.
And what do you think he saw
Behind the boozer door?

The other bar of the boozer
On the other side of the boozer,
The other side of the boozer
On the other side of the bar.

Which he had seen before.

So

The bear barged out of the boozer,
He didn't get too far.
And what do you think he saw
Outside the boozer door?

The door of another boozer
Outside the door of the boozer,
Outside the door of the boozer
A boozer door ajar.

So

The bear barged into the boozer
To see what he could see
And what do you think he saw
Behind the boozer door?

Another bear in the boozer,
The bar of the other boozer,
Another bear in the boozer
Whom he had seen before.

For

The other bear in the boozer,
The bear in the other boozer,
(The boozer outside the boozer)
Was not another boozer
But a bear inside the bear.

KIT WRIGHT

12

The art of poetry

If I knew where poems came from, I'd go there.

MICHAEL LONGLEY

Spend the day with yourself
Let nothing distract you
A poem emerges so young and so old
You can't know how long it has lived in you

SOPHIA DE MELLO BREYNER
'Day'

POETS ARE OFTEN asked where poems come from, and Eamon Grennan's 'Detail' (448) gives a vivid illustration of W.S. Graham's comment that 'the poem is more than the poet's intention' (460). Recreating a sparrowhawk's sudden seizure of a bird he is watching (this robin is the larger American bird, a member of the thrush family), Grennan casts the whole poem in one long sentence, so that everything leads to the 'terrible truth' at the very end, when he realises that he has just seen what he himself experiences in the act of writing a poem when unconscious or outside forces come into play. He seems to have picked up this narrative trick from his friend Michael Longley (228), whose own technique owes much to a reading of Latin poetry. Meaning is drawn out in the course of the poem, revealed through its structure and syntactical complexity, as it is also in the poetry of W.B. Yeats and in the prose of the novelist Henry James. All poets learn to write by reading and listening attentively, and writers such as Yeats and James, as well as Eliot and Auden, have given many contemporary poets their primary lessons in poetic grammar.

In 'The Painter Dreaming in the Scholar's House' (450), a meditation on art and life, American poet Howard Nemerov achieves a remarkable fusion of clarity and mystery. The poem is written in blank verse, and Nemerov handles his iambic pentameter line with such seeming ease that it carries his narrative forward like the undertow of a river. Michael Blumenthal has described how 'very delicately, never pompously or self-consciously, it dares to take on the "great" themes – the conflict of spirit and sense, the transience of life itself and of its small but meaningful exercises of virtue, the hoped-for redemptions of art as an act of faith'. Spirit and sense as well as form and meaning are unified through Nemerov's transformative poetry.

439

from Songs from Below

It's easy to talk, and writing words on the page
doesn't involve much risk as a general rule:
you might as well be knitting late at night
in a warm room, in a soft, treacherous light.
The words are all written in the same ink,
'flower' and 'fear' are nearly the same for example,
and I could scrawl 'blood' the length of the page
without splashing the paper or hurting
myself at all.

After a while it gets you down, this game,
you no longer know what it was you set out to achieve
instead of exposing yourself to life
and doing something useful with your hands.

That's when you can't escape,
when pain is a figure tearing the fog
that shrouds you, striking away
the obstacles one by one, covering
the swiftly decreasing distance, now
so close you can make out nothing
but his mug wider than the sky.

To speak is to lie, or worse: a craven
insult to grief or a waste
of the little time and energy at our disposal.

*

Might there be things which lend themselves
more readily to words, and live with them
– those glad moments gladly found in poems,
light that releases words
as if erasing them; while other things
resist them, change them, destroy them even –

as if language resisted death,
or rather, as if death consumed
even the words?

PHILIPPE JACCOTTET
translated from the French by Derek Mahon

Ars Poetica

A poem should be palpable and mute
As a globed fruit,

Dumb
As old medallions to the thumb,

Silent as the sleeve-worn stone
Of casement ledges where the moss has grown –

A poem should be wordless
As the flight of birds.

                *

A poem should be motionless in time
As the moon climbs,

Leaving, as the moon releases
Twig by twig the night-entangled trees,

Leaving, as the moon behind the winter leaves,
Memory by memory the mind –

A poem should be motionless in time
As the moon climbs.

                *

A poem should be equal to:
Not true.

For all the history of grief
An empty doorway and a maple leaf

For love
The leaning grasses and two lights above the sea –

A poem should not mean
But be.

ARCHIBALD MacLEISH

The Beast in the Space

Shut up. Shut up. There's nobody here.
If you think you hear somebody knocking
On the other side of the words, pay
No attention. It will be only
The great creature that thumps its tail
On silence on the other side.
If you do not even hear that
I'll give the beast a quick skelp
And through Art you'll hear it yelp.

The beast that lives on silence takes
Its bite out of either side.
It pads and sniffs between us. Now
It comes and laps my meaning up.
Call it over. Call it across
This curious necessary space.
Get off, you terrible inhabiter
Of silence. I'll not have it. Get
Away to whoever it is will have you.

He's gone and if he's gone to you
That's fair enough. For on this side
Of the words it's late. The heavy moth
Bangs on the pane. The whole house
Is sleeping and I remember
I am not here, only the space
I sent the terrible beast across.
Watch. He bites. Listen gently
To any song he snorts or growls
And give him food. He means neither
Well or ill towards you. Above
All, shut up. Give him your love.

W.S. GRAHAM

An Exchange of Gifts

As long as you read this poem
I will be writing it.
I am writing it here and now
before your eyes,
although you can't see me.
Perhaps you'll dismiss this
as a verbal trick,
the joke is you're wrong;
the real trick
is your pretending
this is something
fixed and solid,
external to us both.
I tell you better:
I will keep on
writing this poem for you
even after I'm dead.

ALDEN NOWLAN

Note to the reader: this is not a poem

The pictures are falling from my walls
because the paint is too heavy.
Illusionary landscapes are real landscapes now.

No need for tonality or warmth of colour.
Now I write another poem that nobody will read.
There is loneliness in these words

I tell you the supposed reader in plain terms.
There is no need to hide behind poetry.
I won't try to be clever with you.

HELEN IVORY

Meditation at Lagunitas

All the new thinking is about loss.
In this it resembles all the old thinking.
The idea, for example, that each particular erases
the luminous clarity of a general idea. That the clown-
faced woodpecker probing the dead sculpted trunk
of that black birch is, by his presence,
some tragic falling off from a first world
of undivided light. Or the other notion that,
because there is in this world no one thing
to which the bramble of *blackberry* corresponds,
a word is elegy to what it signifies.
We talked about it late last night and in the voice
of my friend, there was a thin wire of grief, a tone
almost querulous. After a while I understood that,
talking this way, everything dissolves: *justice,
pine, hair, woman, you* and *I*. There was a woman
I made love to and I remembered how, holding
her small shoulders in my hands sometimes,
I felt a violent wonder at her presence
like a thirst for salt, for my childhood river
with its island willows, silly music from the pleasure boat,
muddy places where we caught the little orange-silver fish
called *pumpkinseed*. It hardly had to do with her.
Longing, we say, because desire is full
of endless distances, I must have been the same to her.
But I remember so much, the way her hands dismantled bread,
the thing her father said that hurt her, what
she dreamed. There are moments when the body is as numinous
as words, days that are the good flesh continuing.
Such tenderness, those afternoons and evenings,
saying *blackberry, blackberry, blackberry*.

ROBERT HASS

'Once I got a postcard...'

Once I got a postcard from the Fiji Islands
with a picture of sugar cane harvest. Then I realised
that nothing at all is exotic in itself.
There is no difference between digging potatoes
                                in our Muriku garden
and sugar cane harvesting in Viti Levu.
Everything that is is very ordinary
or, rather, neither ordinary nor strange.
Far-off lands and foreign peoples are a dream,
a dreaming with open eyes
somebody does not wake from.
It's the same with poetry – seen from afar
it's something special, mysterious, festive.
No, poetry is even less
special than a sugar cane plantation or potato field.
Poetry is like sawdust coming from under the saw
or soft yellowish shavings from a plane.
Poetry is washing hands in the evening
or a clean handkerchief that my late aunt
never forgot to put in my pocket.

JAAN KAPLINSKI
translated from the Estonian by the author with Sam Hamill & Riina Tamm

From March 1979

Weary of all who come with words, words but no language
I make my way to the snow-covered island.
The untamed has no words.
The unwritten pages spread out on every side!
I come upon the tracks of deer in the snow.
Language but no words.

TOMAS TRANSTRÖMER
translated from the Swedish by Robin Fulton

Animal Languages

In snow, all tracks
– animal and human –
speak to one another,

a long conversation that keeps breaking off
then starting up again.

I want to read those pages
instead of the kind
made of human words.

I want to write in the language of those
who have been to that place before me.

CHASE TWICHELL

The story of a story

Once upon a time there was a story

Its end came
Before its beginning
And its beginning came
After its end

Its heroes entered it
After their death
And left it
Before their birth

Its heroes talked
About some earth about some heaven
They said all sorts of things

Only they didn't say
What they themselves didn't know
That they are only heroes in a story

In a story whose end comes
Before its beginning
And whose beginning comes
After its end

VASKO POPA
translated from the Serbo-Croat by Anne Pennington

Not Ideas about the Thing but the Thing Itself

At the earliest ending of winter,
In March, a scrawny cry from outside
Seemed like a sound in his mind.

He knew that he heard it,
A bird's cry, at daylight or before,
In the early March wind.

The sun was rising at six,
No longer a battered panache above snow...
It would have been outside.

It was not from the vast ventriloquism
Of sleep's faded papier-mâché...
The sun was coming from outside.

That scrawny cry – it was
A chorister whose c preceded the choir.
It was part of the colossal sun,

Surrounded by its choral rings,
Still far away. It was like
A new knowledge of reality.

WALLACE STEVENS

Detail

I was watching a robin fly after a finch – the smaller bird
chirping with excitement, the bigger, its breast blazing, silent
in light-winged earnest chase – when, out of nowhere
over the chimneys and the shivering front gardens,
flashes a sparrowhawk headlong, a light brown burn
scorching the air from which it simply plucks
like a ripe fruit the stopped robin, whose two or three
cheeps of terminal surprise twinkle in the silence
closing over the empty street when the birds have gone
about their own business, and I began to understand
how a poem can happen: you have your eye on a small
elusive detail, pursuing its music, when a terrible truth
strikes and your heart cries out, being carried off.

EAMON GRENNAN

Ö

Shape the lips to an *o*, say *a*.
That's *island*.

One word of Swedish has changed the whole neighborhood.
When I look up, the yellow house on the corner
is a galleon stranded in flowers. Around it

the wind. Even the high roar of a leaf-mulcher
could be the horn-blast from a ship
as it skirts the misted shoals.

We don't need much more to keep things going.
Families complete themselves
and refuse to budge from the present,
the present extends its glass forehead to sea
(backyard breezes, scattered cardinals)

and if, one evening, the house on the corner
took off over the marshland,
neither I nor my neighbor
would be amazed. Sometimes

a word is found so right it trembles
at the slightest explanation.
You start out with one thing, end
up with another, and nothing's
like it used to be, not even the future.

RITA DOVE

Eating Poetry

Ink runs from the corners of my mouth.
There is no happiness like mine.
I have been eating poetry.

The librarian does not believe what she sees.
Her eyes are sad
and she walks with her hands in her dress.

The poems are gone.
The light is dim.
The dogs are on the basement stairs and coming up.

Their eyeballs roll,
their blond legs burn like brush.
The poor librarian begins to stamp her feet and weep.

She does not understand.
When I get on my knees and lick her hand,
she screams.

I am a new man.
I snarl at her and bark.
I romp with joy in the bookish dark.

MARK STRAND

The Painter Dreaming in the Scholar's House

in memory of the painters Paul Klee and Paul Terence Feeley

I

The painter's eye follows relation out.
His work is not to paint the visible,
He says, it is to render visible.

Being a man, and not a god, he stands
Already in a world of sense, from which
He borrows, to begin with, mental things
Chiefly, the abstract elements of language:
The point, the line, the plane, the colors and
The geometric shapes. Of these he spins
Relation out, he weaves its fabric up
So that it speaks darkly, as music does
Singing the secret history of the mind.
And when in this the visible world appears,
As it does do, mountain, flower, cloud, and tree,
All haunted here and there with the human face,
It happens as by accident, although
The accident is of design. It is because
Language first rises from the speechless world
That the painterly intelligence
Can say correctly that he makes his world,
Not imitates the one before his eyes.
Hence the delightsome gardens, the dark shores,
The terrifying forests where nightfall
Enfolds a lost and tired traveler.

And hence the careless crowd deludes itself
By likening his hieroglyphic signs
And secret alphabets to the drawing of a child.
That likeness is significant the other side
Of what they see, for his simplicities
Are not the first ones, but the furthest ones,
Final refinements of his thought made visible.
He is the painter of the human mind
Finding and faithfully reflecting the mindfulness
That is in things, and not the things themselves.

For such a man, art is an act of faith:
Prayer the study of it, as Blake says,

And praise the practice; nor does he divide
Making from teaching, or from theory.
The three are one, and in his hours of art
There shines a happiness through darkest themes,
As though spirit and sense were not at odds.

II

The painter as an allegory of the mind
At genesis. He takes a burlap bag,
Tears it open and tacks it on a stretcher.
He paints it black because, as he has said,
Everything looks different on black.

Suppose the burlap bag to be the universe,
And black because its volume is the void
Before the stars were. At the painter's hand
Volume becomes one-sidedly a surface,
And all his depths are on the face of it.

Against this flat abyss, this groundless ground
Of zero thickness stretched against the cold
Dark silence of the Absolutely Not,
Material worlds arise, the colored earths
And oil of plants that imitate the light.

They imitate the light that is in thought,
For the mind relates to thinking as the eye
Relates to light. Only because the world
Already is a language can the painter speak
According to the grammar of the ground.

It is archaic speech, that has not yet
Divided out its cadences in words;
It is a language for the oldest spells
About how some thoughts rose into the mind
While others, stranger still, sleep in the world.

So grows the garden green, the sun vermilion.
He sees the rose flame up and fade and fall.
And be the same rose still, the radiant in red.
He paints his language, and his language is
The theory of what the painter thinks.

III

The painter's eye attends to death and birth
Together, seeing a single energy
Momently manifest in every form,
As in the tree the growing of the tree
Exploding from the seed not more nor less
Than from the void condensing down and in,
Summoning sun and rain. He views the tree,
The great tree standing in the garden, say,
As thrusting downward its vast spread and weight,
Growing its green height from dark watered earth,
And as suspended weightless in the sky,
Haled forth and held up by the hair of its head.
He follows through the flowing of the forms
From the divisions of the trunk out to
The veinings of the leaf, and the leaf's fall.
His pencil meditates the many in the one
After the method in the confluence of rivers,
The running of ravines on mountainsides,
And in the deltas of the nerves; he sees
How things must be continuous with themselves
As with whole worlds that they themselves are not,
In order that they may be so transformed.
He stands where the eternity of thought
Opens upon perspective time and space;
He watches mind become incarnate; then
    He paints the tree.

IV

These thoughts have chiefly been about the painter Klee,
About how he in our hard time might stand to us
Especially whose lives concern themselves with learning
As patron of the practical intelligence of art,
And thence as model, modest and humorous in sufferings,
For all research that follows spirit where it goes.

That there should be much goodness in the world,
Much kindness and intelligence, candor and charm,
And that it all goes down in the dust after a while,
This is a subject for the steadiest meditations
Of the heart and mind, as for the tears
That clarify the eye toward charity.

So may it be to all of us, that at some times
In this bad time when faith in study seems to fail,
And when impatience in the street and still despair at home
Divide the mind to rule it, there shall some comfort come
From the remembrance of so deep and clear a life as his
Whom I have thought of, for the wholeness of his mind,
As the painter dreaming in the scholar's house,
His dream an emblem to us of the life of thought,
The same dream that then flared before intelligence
When light first went forth looking for the eye.

HOWARD NEMEROV

Epilogue

Those blessèd structures, plot and rhyme –
why are they no help to me now
I want to make
something imagined, not recalled?
I hear the noise of my own voice:
The painter's vision is not a lens,
it trembles to caress the light.
But sometimes everything I write
with the threadbare art of my eye
seems a snapshot,
lurid, rapid, garish, grouped,
heightened from life,
yet paralysed by fact.
All's misalliance.
Yet why not say what happened?
Pray for the grace of accuracy
Vermeer gave to the sun's illumination
stealing like the tide across a map
to his girl solid with yearning.
We are poor passing facts,
warned by that to give
each figure in the photograph
his living name.

ROBERT LOWELL

Oatmeal

I eat oatmeal for breakfast.
I make it on the hot plate and put skimmed milk on it.
I eat it alone.
I am aware it is not good to eat oatmeal alone.
Its consistency is such that it is better for your mental health if somebody
    eats it with you.
That is why I often think up an imaginary companion to have breakfast with.
Possibly it is even worse to eat oatmeal with an imaginary companion.
Nevertheless, yesterday morning, I ate my oatmeal with John Keats.
Keats said I was right to invite him: due to its glutinous texture, gluey
    lumpishness, hint of slime, and unusual willingness to disintegrate,
    oatmeal must never be eaten alone.
He said it is perfectly OK, however, to eat it with an imaginary companion,
and he himself had enjoyed memorable porridges with Edmund Spenser
    and John Milton.
He also told me about writing the 'Ode to a Nightingale'.
He wrote it quickly, he said, on scraps of paper, which he then stuck in
    his pocket,
but when he got home he couldn't figure out the order of the stanzas,
    and he and a friend spread the papers on a table, and they made
    some sense of them, but he isn't sure to this day if they got it right.
He still wonders about the occasional sense of drift between stanzas,
and the way here and there a line will go into the configuration of a
    Moslem at prayer, then raise itself up and peer about, then lay
    itself down slightly off the mark, causing the poem to move
    forward with God's reckless wobble.
He said someone told him that later in life Wordsworth heard about
    the scraps of paper on the table, and tried shuffling some stanzas
    of his own, but only made matters worse.
When breakfast was over, John recited 'To Autumn'.
He recited it slowly, with much feeling, and he articulated the words
    lovingly, and his odd accent sounded sweet.
He didn't offer the story of writing 'To Autumn', I doubt if there is
    much of one.
But he did say the sight of a just-harvested oat field got him started on it
and two of the lines, 'For Summer has o'er-brimmed their clammy cells'
    and 'Thou watchest the last oozings hours by hours', came to him
    while eating oatmeal alone.
I can see him – drawing a spoon through the stuff, gazing into the
    glimmering furrows, muttering – and it occurs to me:

maybe there is no sublime, only the shining of the amnion's tatters.
For supper tonight I am going to have a baked potato left over from
   lunch.
I'm aware that a leftover baked potato can be damp, slippery, and
   simultaneously gummy and crumbly,
and therefore I'm going to invite Patrick Kavanagh to join me.

GALWAY KINNELL

Consider the Grass Growing

Consider the grass growing
As it grew last year and the year before,
Cool about the ankles like summer rivers
When we walked on a May evening through the meadows
To watch the mare that was going to foal.

PATRICK KAVANAGH

Note

This sonnet
I have divided into parts to make
the meaning clearer. In the first
I explain how the mountains seem
to detach the night from the walls; in the second,
I describe how a charcoal burner walks through the snow
with a lantern, thus referring to human
experience. The third is a sudden vision
of life as an imaginary sweepstake.
The second begins here: The tree-stump, devoured
by the vegetation; and the third here: With rigid mane,
a horse rises from the sea.

JOAN BROSSA
translated from the Catalan by Arthur Terry

Postscript

And some time make the time to drive out west
Into County Clare, along the Flaggy Shore,
In September or October, when the wind
And the light are working off each other
So that the ocean on one side is wild
With foam and glitter, and inland among stones
The surface of a slate-grey lake is lit
By the earthed lightning of a flock of swans,
Their feathers roughed and ruffling, white on white,
Their fully grown headstrong-looking heads
Tucked or cresting or busy underwater.
Useless to think you'll park and capture it
More thoroughly. You are neither here nor there,
A hurry through which known and strange things pass
As big soft buffetings come at the car sideways
And catch the heart off guard and blow it open.

SEAMUS HEANEY

Late Fragment

And did you get what
you wanted from this life, even so?
I did.
And what did you want?
To call myself beloved, to feel myself
beloved on the earth.

RAYMOND CARVER

Appendices

The Sound of Poetry

There is a widely held but totally unfounded belief that poetry *has* to rhyme, or it's not poetry. This enables the uninformed to dismiss much modern poetry as some kind of aberration. Yet rhyme has *never* been the defining characteristic of poetry. But when you look at the kinds of books used in schools over the past hundred years, you begin to see how their narrowness has helped make people's knowledge of poetry so oddly selective.

The essence of all poetry has always been *rhythm* – NOT rhyme – and in many languages rhyme isn't used at all. English poetry didn't use rhyme until the time of Chaucer, when the fashion for rhyming verse was copied from French and Italian writers. Much of Shakespeare is written in blank verse, which doesn't rhyme. Wordsworth may have rhymed his 'Daffodils', but he used blank verse in his great epic poem *The Prelude*. Keats's 'Hyperion' doesn't rhyme. Whitman managed to sing his 'Body Electric' without making it rhyme, and his great American epic 'Song of Myself' doesn't rhyme. Robert Browning's 'Home Thoughts From Abroad' ('Oh, to be in England now that April's there') is one of our best-known rhyming poems, but a great deal of Browning's poetry doesn't rhyme at all. The extended dramatic monologues of both Browning and Tennyson wouldn't work in rhymed verse.

Most of Milton's poetry doesn't use rhyme. And not only did he *not* rhyme *Paradise Lost*, but in its preface he was quite definite – in the 1660s – about this 'troublesome and modern bondage of rhyming'. He pointed out that 'rhyme was no necessary Adjunct or true Ornament of a Poem or good Verse...' and went so far as to call it 'trivial' – 'the Invention of a barbarous Age, to set off wretched matter and lame Meeter'.

It is for the poet to choose whether or not rhyme is appropriate in each particular poem. But if you write traditional rhyming verse, you also have to follow a rhythmical pattern, the metre. The metre dictates not just the number of syllables in a line but also which of those syllables should be stressed. The most common metres in formal English verse are iambic (usually with alternating unstressed and stressed syllables), such as the five-feet iambic pentameter line (*dee-dum dee-dum dee-dum dee-dum dee-dum*) and the often thumping four- and three-feet ballad metre. But poets have a wide range of different metres to choose from. In the glossary, I've given notes on many of these, with examples of poems from this anthology. If you want to work out what metre is used in traditional formal verse, read the poem aloud and note which syllables are stressed in natural English speech. In the examples below, the stressed syllables are underlined and marked above with a slash, with a cross over the unstressed syllables. I've added an alternative notation below the line showing how syllable length is marked in quantitative verse, but very few poets use quantitative metres (see Glossary).

We don't actually read poetry like robots, which makes all this seem rather artificial, but these notations help you see what the poet is doing with the language, and you soon realise that most poets don't follow metres like click-clock metronomes but work the rhythm against all kinds of variations, such as reversing the first or fourth foot in iambic pentameter (as in the second example below):

ROBERT FROST (73), iambic tetrameter (rhyming):

```
     x    /     x    /    x  /     x   /
| Whose woods | these are | I think | I know |
|    ⌣    —  |   ⌣   —  | ⌣  —  | ⌣   —  |
```

EDWARD THOMAS (349), iambic pentameter (unrhymed):

```
   / x    x    /      x    /     x    /      x    /
| After | the plough | share and | the stumb | ling team. |
|  — ⌣  |  ⌣    —   |   ⌣   —  |  ⌣   —   |  ⌣    —   |
```

The vertical line is similar to the bar-line in musical notation, and the metrical foot is sometimes called a measure, as in music. In the introduction I quote some of Basil Bunting's comments on how poetry, like music, must be heard. He also said poetry 'deals in sound – long sounds and short sounds, heavy beats and light beats, the tone relations of vowels, the relations of consonants to one another which are like instrumental colour in music. Poetry lies dead on the page, until some voice brings it to life, just as music, on the stave, is no more than instructions to the player.' Because spoken English approximates naturally to iambic rhythm, a good poet will ensure that the language is heightened through formal framing, which gives the line its music and helps intensify the emotional effect. Writers who don't have sufficient sensitivity to the music of language write stilted verse which slavishly follows a regular metre because they lack the ear needed to gauge how the language should be set off by the metre.

As an editor, most of the bad poetry I receive is fatally flawed (in Bunting's phrase, 'dead on the page') by a lack of rhythmical control, often with meaning contorted or word-order inverted to make a line fit a metre or a rhyme scheme. Milton complained that rhyme ('the jingling sound of like endings') was too often a constraint and hindrance which made poets express themselves differently 'and for the most part worse than else they would have expressed them'.

A poet's choice of forms is inextricably linked to how that poet thinks and feels. Just as rhyme shouldn't be used as an ornament, so too what is called the writer's "style" is not something added to the poetry. Martin Amis once characterised the novelist's "style" in a way applicable just as much to poets, particularly those in that transitional stage of "finding their voice": '...what a writer regards as his essence is his perceptual manner, his imaginative habits and the way his language answers to these. This essence is sometimes dismissively referred to as [prose-]style. But "style" is not something grafted on to ordinary language: it is inherent in the way a writer sees the world.' And Julian Barnes has written (drawing on Flaubert): 'Style is a function of theme. Style is not imposed on subject-matter, but arises from it. Style is truth to thought.'

Adrienne Rich wrote that the formalism of her early poetry 'was part of the strategy – like asbestos gloves it allowed me to handle materials I couldn't pick up barehanded'. The poet's engagement with language in the poem embodies the way that writer sees the world. This is what makes each poet different and distinctive, what defines an individual voice. It's also what makes the poem, as W.S. Graham says, 'more than the poet's intention. The poet does not write what he knows but what he does not know...He has to explore the imagination by using the language as his pitch.'

Sylvia Plath described how this unity of form and content is *felt* in the poem: 'The poets I delight in are possessed by their poems as by the rhythms of their own breathing. Their finest poems seem born all-of-a-piece, not put together by hand; certain poems in Robert Lowell's *Life Studies*, for instance; Theodore Roethke's greenhouse poems; some of Elizabeth Bishop and a very great deal of Stevie Smith ('Art is a wild cat and quite separate from civilisation').

People who are unfamiliar with the subtle language of contemporary poetry think that free verse is no more than prose chopped into lines. My kid could write that, they say, and they are right in one respect, for what their teachers get their kids to write at school is, of course, prose chopped into lines, and much of what passes for poetry, even in print, is staccato prose. What it lacks is poetic rhythm. To write any kind of poetry well, whether in metre or free verse, you need an ear and a sensitivity to language, just as you need a sense of rhythm to play a musical instrument. There's an obvious difference between a Mozart prelude done as a practice piece by a beginner and the same prelude played by a concert pianist.

No writer can develop the sensitivity needed to write good poetry, whether metrical or in freer forms, without reading vast amounts of poetry by other writers. Poetry is a craft learned through much reading, but you need an ear to write poetry as much as to compose or play music, and in modern poetry, "free verse" wouldn't *be* poetry without sound rhythmical control. However, you can't *teach* the skill of writing well-wrought free verse; the sense of how to do it well is something which comes naturally, after time, as an intuitive element in the poet's engagement with language. Robert Frost described 'The figure a poem makes. It begins in delight and ends in wisdom. The figure is the same as for love.'

Frost also said that 'writing free verse is like playing tennis with the net down'. He himself needed to write with the net or frame of metre. Thom Gunn is one of the few writers able to write poetry both in free verse and in metrical or syllabic verse: 'Metrical verse is ultimately allied to song, and I like the connection. Free verse is ultimately allied to conversation, and I like that connection too. Not many poets can mix the two.' But it's also true that much free verse is ghosted by a metrical undertow, and you see this especially in Modernist poets like T.S. Eliot, who said of free verse that there was 'no such thing to the man who wants to do a good job'.

All well-wrought 'free verse' is subject to formal discipline, showing the poet's shaping spirit in the rhythms, sounds and texture of the language. Rita Dove calls poetry the purest of the language arts: 'It's the tightest cage, and if you can get it to sing in that cage it's really really wonderful.' She herself doesn't use the tight cage of metre but employs other kinds of formal discipline in her work.

The main reason why contemporary poetry is generally ignored or misunderstood is historical. The reading public lost touch with poetry when modern poets lost touch with their audience early in the 20th century. This separation can be traced back to the response of the earlier Romantic poets to the Industrial Revolution, which saw men mastering Nature without God's help, leading to that canny Calvinist identification of spiritual salvation with business success. The poets' reaction to a world driven by industrial expansion and to its accommodation by religious apologists was to reject both. 'To the poet, what mattered was his inner self, a limitless world for private exploration,' in Stanley Burnshaw's analysis. But the poet intent on pushing language to its limits was faced 'with an irreducible choice between "clarity" and "truth": he can retain one at the sacrifice of the other. Dare he allow the "understandable" statement to remain when it is not what he feels he must say? If, faced with such a choice, he decided to keep the obscure version, it is only because the clear statement is unacceptable as untrue.'

Influenced by the experiments of Symbolism, the innovative Modernist poets of the early 20th century rejected traditional forms and realism as well as consensus between author and reader, producing highly complex work in response to an awareness, prompted by Freud, Jung and others, of the unconscious and the irrational. Trying to make sense of the mad modern world, poets such as Eliot and Pound tried to 'make it new', just as Picasso was distorting his portraits, fragmenting his figures to mirror the horrors of war while Stravinsky was composing a new music of discord and disharmony.

That particular 'making it new' happened over seventy years ago. Poetry has not stood still since then but has moved with the times, although unacknowledged by the wider public, whose understanding of poets is two hundred years out of date and whose awareness of poetry is either a hundred years behind the times or else still stuck in the 1960s. The quotation by Wordsworth on page 18 is from the Preface to the *Lyrical Ballads* (1800), which states the case for the personal in poetry. It is followed by T.S. Eliot's response from his influential essay "Tradition and the Individual Talent" (1919). Eliot rejects Romantic individualism, arguing that modern poetry should be 'impersonal', engaged with the great poetry of the past but dissociated from contemporary life. Two hundred years on from Wordsworth, and nearly a hundred years after Eliot, poetry now is neither personal nor impersonal but reconnected. Fifty years ago, Auden's age of anxiety gave way to an age of responsibility.

The Second World War and the Holocaust ended all notions of the separateness of poetry. The immediate response was alienation or silence: Adorno's 'no poetry after Auschwitz'. But fifty years later, writers have continued to respond to what George Steiner called the 'legacy' of 'that Central European humanism, *c.* 1860-1930, which Nazism and Stalinism all but obliterated'. In 1968, Steiner wrote: 'Language is a fantastically complex and vulnerable structure; it probably defines man's humanity. Where it is damaged, it is not easy to repair.' In many ways, the best poets of today are repairers of language, restorers of humanity whose books of poems have greater relevance to our ordinary lives than what we read in newspapers, especially in their search for unity, balance and wholeness.

Much damage has also been done to the public's perception of poetry by attempts to *make* poetry more "relevant". In the 1960s, encouraged by charlatans and mad mavericks of poetry and rock 'n' roll to believe that *anyone* could write poetry, the avant-garde's 'free verse' was hijacked under the banner of self-expression, and has since has been giving poetry a bad name through outpourings of rhythmless prose chopped into lines, much of it published in the less discriminating poetry magazines. Free verse came out of the *vers libre* of the French Symbolist poets, beginning with Rimbaud, and then Laforgue (an influence on Eliot), and announced to the world in Viélé-Griffin's declaration in 1889 that '*Le vers est libre*'. But as Eliot and many other poets have insisted, again and again, no poetry is 'free'. Whereas English speech is stress-timed, French is syllabic, and French poets were wanting to replace their rhymed syllable-timed line with a totally different pattern – what Burnshaw calls 'an accent of meaning'. However, for free verse to work in English, there needs to be an almost organic relationship in the language of the poem between natural word-stress and meaning. 'The problem with most free verse,' according to Glyn Maxwell, 'is that it locates wisdom in the self and not in the language.'

Many academic purists assert the primacy of early Modernism in today's poetry, conveniently ignoring both what the poets have actually been writing as well as the fact that a broader version of Modernism (in which European influences are as significant as American models) continues to enrich the imaginative range of most contemporary poets. The American poet Richard Wilbur has rebutted another Modernist fallacy, 'that metre and stanza are intrinsically repressive and right-wing, whereas free verse is liberating and democratic. The idea that free verse is forever original and venturesome, that it is somehow "experimental" to imitate Pound or [Carlos] Williams decade after decade.' Wilbur is one of the supreme formal technicians of our age, and a key influence on later writers such as Michael Longley, Derek Mahon and Michael Donaghy, whose highly expressive poetry combines intellectual complexity with narrative simplicity and decorous music. It's possible to trace a poetic line from Hardy, Yeats, Edward Thomas and Robert Frost, through Auden and MacNeice, through Larkin, Plath and Bishop, to Seamus Heaney and younger writers of the present time who draw on traditional formal techniques but often adapt or subvert conventions to express responses to changed times and cultures.

Poets have many different opinions about how poetry "should" be written, but because there are so many different approaches, the poetry of the past few decades has been more varied than at any time in the history of literature. This means there are many different kinds of poems for the reader to enjoy, whether in free verse or metre (with or without rhyme). Form itself has been questioned, subverted and reinvented. And so has poetry. But the essence of poetry is still an interplay of thought and feeling expressed through the sound and rhythm of language.

GLOSSARY

The following terms are those either commonly used in discussions of poetic technique, or expressions whose glossing is particularly helpful in illuminating formal aspects of poems in this anthology. Where possible, examples are given (with page references) of poems in *Staying Alive*.

Accent: Intensity of emphasis placed on a syllable. In strict terms, *accent* refers to emphasis demanded by the language and *stress* to metrical stress, as in a line of poetry. *See also* **foot**.

Accentual verse: *See* **metre**.

Alcaic strophe: Four-line Greek stanza of the aeolic type used by the Latin poet Horace, and in English poetry by Clough and Swinburne. Lines 1 and 2 ('Greater Alcaic') contain 11 syllables, line 3 contains 9 syllables, and line 4 ('Lesser Alcaic') 10 syllables. In *Evagatory* (311) Peter Reading uses 'dispersed alcaics', the stanza indents marking the varied length lines. His Alcaic line *'flight of a sparrow brief through the feasting hall'* recalls Bede's image of a man's life.

Aeolic verse (after the Greek dialect of Alcaeus and Sappho): set of metres combining dactyls and trochees, as in **alcaics** (above).

Alcmanic verse: Metre used in Greek drama consisting of catalectic dactylic tetrameters. Revived with remarkable incantatory effect by Peter Reading to catalogue more modern horrors in *Going On* (302): 'These are the days of the horrible headlines' | – ∨ ∨ | – ∨ ∨ | – ∨ ∨ | – – |.

Alexandrine: Twelve-syllable hexameter line, the standard metre of French poetry. In English poetry, the alexandrine contains six stress accents rather than the fluid four (or three) in French. Unwieldy for narrative, alexandrines are sometimes used to close off a passage in iambic pentameter, but few English poems are written entirely in alexandrines (Browning and Bridges made valiant attempts). Many of the lines in Randall Jarrell's 'Thinking of the Lost World' (211) are alexandrines, but mixed with shorter lines for a more relaxed effect.

Alliteration: Repetition of initial sounds (usually consonants) in neighbouring words, producing a noticeable sound effect to reinforce meaning or imitate a characteristic of the thing described, as in Ken Smith's 'It goes against the grain' ('Against the grain', 135). *See also* **stress metre**.

Ambiguity: Defined by William Empson as 'any verbal nuance, however slight, which gives room for alternative reactions to the same piece of language', a concentration of meanings is characteristic of 18th century Augustan poetry, as well as of the 17th century Metaphysical poets who influenced many contemporary poets, including Michael Donaghy (*see* **conceit**) and Geoffrey Hill. Every adjective in Hill's short poem 'September Song' (356) shows painfully weighted ambiguity ('so many *routine* cries...').

Amphibrach: A three-syllable foot consisting of a middle stressed syllable with unstressed syllables on either side, e.g. 'arrángement' (x / x). The only modern poem in amphibrachic tetrameter is the editor's sestina 'A Month in the Country' (not included here); its title scans as two amphibrachs.

Anapaest: A foot consisting of two unstressed (or short) syllables followed by a stressed (or long) one, as in 'interrúpt'. Poems using anapaestic metres are rare. Examples include Byron's 'The Destruction of Sennacherib' ('The Assyrian came down like a wolf on the fold,/ And his cohorts were gleaming in purple and gold...')

Anthology: A selection of work by many different writers (literally, 'gathered flowers'), as opposed to a collection, the term for a book of poems by a single poet. This anthology brings together poems from many different collections.

Assonance: Repetition of identical (or similar) vowel sounds, sometimes called 'vocalic rhyme'. Many modern poets use assonance and consonance as musical effects in preference to end-rhymes, e.g. Simon Armitage in 'Poem' (57); or to bind and underline meaning, or to create a unifying musical "texture", as in Richard Murphy's 'Seals at High Island' (242), whose first stanza, for example, has a high concentration of 'a' sounds ('calamity...caverns...malice...clacking ...sadness').

Ballad metre: Alternating iambic tetrameter and trimeter, as in Gillian Clarke's 'Overheard in Co. Sligo' (321).

Blank verse: Iambic pentameter that does not rhyme, as in Shakespeare's verse drama and Milton's *Paradise Lost*. Examples: Robert Frost, 'Directive' (71); Edward Thomas, 'As the team's head-brass' (349); Howard Nemerov, 'The Painter Dreaming in the Scholar's House' (450).

Caesura: In modern prosody, a rhythmic break or pause within the poetic line, dictated not by metrics but by meaning or natural speech patterns and used for investing strict metres with the movement of informal speech.

Catalectic foot: Foot with a missing syllable. The first foot of anapaestic lines is often catalectic, as is the final foot of most trochaic lines (except in humorous verse) and Alcmanic dactylic tetrameters (see above).

Conceit: Unexpected comparison between two dissimilar things or ideas. A favoured device of 17th century English Metaphysical poets ('the most heterogenous ideas are yoked by violence together' was Johnson's description of their wit), and of contemporary poets influenced by them, e.g. Michael Donaghy (81).

Consonance: Repetition of similar or identical consonants whose vowels differ. Half-rhyme is consonance of the final consonants e.g. 'lost/cast'.

Dactyl: (Greek: 'finger') A foot consisting of one stressed and two unstressed syllables ($/ x x$), e.g. 'nástiness' (Reading, 133).

Dimeter: A line consisting of two feet.

Dramatic monologue: Poem usually set in a specific situation and written as if spoken to someone. Browning and Tennyson established the dramatic monologue as a powerful mode in English poetry, influencing many later poets including T.S. Eliot, whose 'Journey of the Magi' (427) is "spoken" by one of the three wise men. It should never be assumed that the 'I' speaker of a modern poem is the poet. The persona may be a clearly identified narrator, as in Gwendolyn MacEwen's *T.E. Lawrence Poems* (352) and 'Anne Sexton's Last Letter to God' by Tracey Herd (126), but it could equally be an animal (as in Les Murray's 'Pigs', 218) or an unspecified speaker, such as Galway Kinnell's hunter in 'The Bear' (63), Peter Didsbury's phantasmagorical explorer in 'The Drainage' (161) and American poet Anne Rouse's English football hooligan in 'England Nil' (304). The fact that the speaker is a persona and not the poet writing in the first person singular may be apparent only from the tone or a particular modulation of voice or from the revelations of the narrative, as in Matthew Sweeney's 'Sleep with a Suitcase' (408) and Derek Mahon's 'As It Should Be' (409). Novelists aren't the only writers of fiction.

Elegiac distich: Classical stanza based on dactyls and spondees, traditionally used for elegy. Peter Reading revives this form in his *Ukulele Music* (133) to give classical gravitas and elegiac cadence to his evocations of tragic, modern times. The dactylic hexameter is followed by a dactylic pentameter: 'What do they

think they're playing at, then, these Poetry Wallahs?' | – ˘ ˘ | – – | – ˘ ˘ | – – |
– ˘ ˘ | – – | 'Finger found stuck on barbed wire. Too black and over the top.'
| – ˘ ˘ | – ˘ ˘ | – | | – ˘ ˘ | – ˘ ˘ | – . The hexameter usually has five dactyls and
one spondee. For a retarding effect, dactyls are often substituted by spondees,
as shown above.

Elegy: Poem of lament or of grave meditation, such as those by Dylan Thomas
(379), W.H. Auden (380) and Michael Hartnett (381). Originally a poem on
any subject composed in the elegiacs used in Greek and Roman poems of
mourning, the term was later applied to a meditation on sentiments, such as
Thomas Gray's 'Elegy in a Country Churchyard', and Rilke's highly influential
Duino Elegies (see extract on page 44), the lament of unearthly powers over
human weakness in penetrating and transfiguring reality.

End-stopped: When both meaning and metre undergo a pause at the end of
the line, it is *end-stopped*, the rhythmic line acting as a unit of sense. The *heroic
couplet* is often end-stopped, when it is sometimes called a 'closed couplet'. A
succession of end-stopped lines produces an emphatic effect, as in Christopher
Logue's 'Be Not Too Hard' (98) and Vachel Lindsay's 'The Leaden-Eyed' (130).

Enjambement: Run-on line: when the sense continues on from the end of
one line into the next, as in Robert Frost's 'He will not see me stopping here/
To see his woods fill up with snow' (73).

Epigram: Short, usually witty statement, often rhymed, such as Brad Leit-
hauser's mosquito poem (405). Epigrammatic statements can occur as part of
longer pieces, such as Pope's essay poems; in 'An Essay on Man', 'Know then
thyself, presume not God to scan,/ The proper study of mankind is man.'

Epigraph: A resonant quotation placed at beginning of book or poem. Adrienne
Rich starts her poem 'Integrity' (61) with a definition from Webster's Dictionary
while the unattributed phrase 'the withness of the body' encapsulates the whole
thrust of Delmore Schwartz's 'The Heavy Bear Who Goes with Me' (66). An
epigraph is often a quotation which has prompted a poem, or one which stands
at one remove from the poem, as if to signal another way in, like Derek Mahon's
line from Seferis, 'Let them not forget us, the weak souls among the asphodels'
at the start of 'A Disused Shed in Co. Wexford' (166). Epigraphs were much
used in Modernist poetry, often with no source given because the reader was
expected to recognise the fragment. Anna Akhmatova begins 'Our Own Land'
(298) with a defiantly appropriate quotation from a poem she wrote 40 years
earlier, 'I am not among those who left our land' from *Anno Domini*, which
Russian readers would recognise immediately. Geoffrey Hill's 'September Song'
(356) remembers an unknown ten-year-old child who died anonymously some
time after 24 September 1942 in one or other Nazi concentration camp. These
bare facts are given only in the epigraph ('born 19.6.32 – deported 24.9.42').
Born in 1932, the same year as Hill, the child could have been him ('an elegy
for myself') or any of us. Epigraphs are over-used in modern poetry, often as
a short-cut or show-off, but these five examples – the only ones used in all
the poems in this book – show the compression and force of the well chosen
epigraph.

Eye rhyme: Near rhyme of two words pronounced differently but spelled alike,
such as 'love' and 'prove'. When pronunciations change and once-rhyming
words become eye rhymes, these are called historical rhymes, although such
rhymes may often remain full in some dialects of English. 18th century Londoners
would have relished the appropriately full rhyme in Pope's couplet: 'Good-
nature and good-sense must ever *join*;/ To err is human, to forgive, di*vine*.'

In Wordsworth's Cumbrian English, 'water' rhymed with 'matter', as Tony Harrison points out in his poem 'Them and [uz]', while reading Keats in the poet's own Cockney voice will preserve other full rhymes. In Harrison's 'Initial Illumination' (364), the monk Eadfrith's *brush* rhymes fully with 'George *Bush*' in the poet's Yorkshire speech.

Feminine rhyme: Rhyme of a stressed followed by an unstressed syllable, as in 'rattle'/'battle', while 'over/lover' is a feminine eye rhyme.

Foot: A foot is a unit in a line of metrical verse. An iambic foot is an unstressed followed by an accented (or stressed) syllable – e.g. 'The cur' is the first foot in 'The cur|few tolls|the knell| of pass| ing day...' (Gray).

Free verse: Poetry based not on the recurrence of stress accent in a regular, strictly measurable pattern, but rather on the irregular rhythmic cadences of phrases and image patterns. All practitioners agree that free verse is far from free in the formal demands it makes on the writer. In free verse, the measure is loosened to give expressive play to vocabulary and syntax, and so to the mind in its excursions. The bracket of the customary foot is expanded to admit more syllables, words or phrases into its confines; the new unit thus created has been described by poets such as William Carlos Williams as the "variable foot". The measure of free verse varies with the idiom and tonality of each individual poem. Anyone who attempts to write free verse but without the necessary formal or rhythmical awareness will only succeed in producing chopped-up prose. Well modulated free verse poems whose phrasing and rhythms are totally unified include Denise Levertov's 'Living' (31) and Ellen Bryant Voigt's 'Daughter' (185). See discussion on pages 458-63.

Heroic couplet: Rhymed pairs of five iambic feet. Robert Graves uses heroic couplets for 'The Persian Version' (363).

Hexameter: A line consisting of six feet.

Hypermetric: When a measure has an extra foot or part of a foot. A foot with an extra syllable (usually at end of line) is called an hypermetric foot: *see also* **Catalectic.**

Iamb: A foot consisting of unstressed and stressed syllables. e.g. 'beneath'.

Iambic pentameter: Five-foot line in iambic metre. Despite Pound's battle cry 'To break the pentameter', iambic pentameter has lasted several centuries because it is a flexible metre well-suited to carrying the modulations of English speech rhythms· the right measure not just for Elizabethan blank verse drama, Shakespeare's sonnets and Milton's epics but for the neatly rational couplets of Pope and Dryden, and many other kinds of poetry, rhymed and unrhymed. Examples of rhymed iambic pentameter: Gjertrud Schnackenberg, 'Supernatural Love' (191), and James McAuley, 'Because' (286); of unrhymed blank verse, Howard Nemerov, 'The Painter Dreaming in the Scholar's House' (450).

Iambic tetrameter: Four-foot line in iambic metre, e.g. Robert Frost, 'My November Guest' (128), and Richard Wilbur, 'April 5, 1974' (153).

Imagery: Figurative language, including **metaphor** and **simile**. Imagery refers to images produced in the mind by language. When Archibald MacLeish writes in 'Ars Poetica' (441) that a poem should be 'Dumb/ As old medallions to the thumb', he expresses the importance of imagery in poetry by using imagery: a poem engages the imagination, not the intellect. A controlling image is a single image dominating a passage or whole poem.

Irony: 'Saying one thing and meaning another' (Peter Sansom). **Romantic irony** mingles self-pity with self-mockery, while **tragic irony** acknowledges the contradictions of experience and apparent incompatibles, as in Yeats's almost masochistic, lifelong balancing act: 'Now that my ladder's gone,/ I must lie down where all the ladders start,/ In the foul rag-and-bone shop of the heart' ('The Circus Animals' Desertion'). Zagajewski's 'Betrayal' (337) and Auden's 'Gare du Midi' (340) are poems of tragic irony.

Lyric: Originally a poem composed to be sung or appropriate for singing and expressive of personal feeling, now more generally used as a term for a short, highly compressed personal poem with strong musical qualities.

Masculine rhyme: Rhyme on final, stressed syllable, as in the Yeats couplet quoted above: 'start'/'heart'.

Metaphor: Device implying a relationship between two things which changes our apprehension of either or both.

Metre: Regular or schematised rhythm. The four main kinds of metre are stress metre, syllabics, quantitative metre (these three are all separately glossed), and accentual or syllabic stress, the most commonly used measurement in English metrics (with iambic pentameter the most popular form of **accentual verse**). In his preface to the *Lyrical Ballads*, Wordsworth says pain is better 'endured in metrical composition, especially in rhyme, than in prose'.

Near rhyme: Repetition in accented syllables of the final consonant-sound but with no correspondence in the preceding vowel, as in much of Emily Dickinson's poetry (e.g. she rhymes 'port' with 'chart'). P.K. Page's 'Cross' (287) uses both near rhymes and full rhymes.

Octave: Stanza of eight lines; opening of an Italian sonnet.

Ode: Formal, ceremonious poem of elaborate design.

Pararhyme: Repetition of two pairs of consonants bracketing different vowel sounds. A device of Welsh poetry, pararhymes were adapted by Wilfred Owen for war poems that required full rhyme to be shied away from, such as 'Strange Meeting'. Paul Muldoon likes the slippery quality of pararhyme, as in 'The Sightseers' (324), which rhymes 'July' with 'jelly'.

Pentameter: Five-foot line introduced into English poetry by Chaucer.

Persona: The narrator or speaker of a poem. *See* **dramatic monologue**.

Prose: Ordinary language without metrical structure or rhythmical patterning.

Prose poem: A short composition having features of the lyric poem but not using the line unit or line-breaks, distinguished in particular by sonorous effects, imagery and density of expression. The first practitioners were 19th century French poets, chiefly Bertrand, Baudelaire, Rimbaud and Mallarmé. See prose poems by Anne Carson (398), Zbigniew Herbert (291) and Charles Simic (201, 225).

Quantitative metre: Line based on syllable length as in the classical prosody of Greek and Latin verse; in the classical foot, a long syllable occupies twice the time of a short one. Although used by poets such as Spenser, Coleridge and Tennyson, very few contemporary poets use quantitative metrics, but these include some of the supreme technicians, such as Peter Reading, whose examples in this anthology are glossed in relation to specific metres: *see* Alcaic strophe, Alcmanic verse, Elegiac distich.

Quatrain: Four-line stanza.

Rhyme: Repetition of sounds, whether vowels, consonants or both, in one or more syllables, usually stressed and recurring at determined and recognisable intervals. End-rhyme is a feature of the last stressed syllable, being **masculine** where the sound is common to single syllables and **feminine** where it relates to two syllables, the first stressed and the second unstressed. Rhyme is usually taken to refer to full rhyme, but there are many other varieties, including half-rhyme, near-rhyme and **pararhyme**. See discussion on pages 458-63.

Rhyme scheme: Pattern of rhyme set up in a poem. Usually we letter each line, giving the same letter to lines which rhyme, as in the analysis below of different varieties of sonnet.

Rhythm: Rhythm is the essence of poetry, whether worked through a metrical pattern or in freer forms. See discussion on page 458-63.

Sestina: Elaborate form from 13th century Provençal troubadour poetry consisting of six sestets with a concluding tercet, the end words of the first stanza imposing a pattern in which the same words are repeated in a strict order: 123456, 615243, 364125, 532614, 451362, 246531, 531 (with 246 repeated within the tercet). The rotated words emphasise key elements in the poem's argument, the form being well-suited to explorations of repetitive conditions, imprisonment, lack of choice etc, as in Kona Macphee's 'IVF' (178).

Sestet: Six-line stanza. Concluding section of an Italian sonnet.

Simile: A comparison of one thing with another, explicitly announced by the use of 'like' or 'as'. More explicit but less expressive than metaphor, a simile joins two separate images or ideas, whereas the relationship in a metaphor is more complex and inclusive.

Sonnet: Traditionally, a 14-line lyric poem in iambic pentameter following one of several prescribed rhyme-schemes, comprising an octave and a sestet and expressing two successive phrases of one thought. **Italian or Petrarchan sonnet:** octave rhymes *abbaabba*, sestet commonly rhymes *cdcdcd* or *cdecde* or *cdedce*, but the difficulty of using only two rhymes in eight lines in English led to the adoption of a looser octave rhyming *abbacddc*, as in Elizabeth Daryush's 'I saw the daughter of the sun...' (96) **English or Shakespearian sonnet:** three quatrains plus couplet, *abab cdcd efef gg* (with variants including *abab cdcd effe gg*), as in Patrick Kavanagh's 'Iniskeen Road: July Evening' (321) and Wilfred Owen's 'Anthem for Doomed Youth' (347). Anne Rouse's 'England Nil' (304) follows the English rhyme scheme but does away with the octave/sestet progression. Carol Ann Duffy's 'Prayer' (43) is an English sonnet with the final couplet reprising the first rhyme. Hayden Carruth's vernacular 'Sonnet' (100) has a Petrarchan octave rhyming *abbaabba* with no break before a sestet rhyming *cddcee*. Poems not obviously sonnets include e.e. cummings's 'next to of course god america i' (325) which rhymes *ababcdcdefgef/g*; Paul Muldoon's two half-rhyme sonnets, 'Quoof' (213), rhyming *abcddbca efgegf,* and 'The Sightseers' (324), rhyming *abcd bcca bcb ede*; and Michael Longley's 'Ceasefire' (350), a modified Shakespearian sonnet with numbered stanzas. Simon Armitage's 'Poem' (57) uses monotonous assonances to bind each quatrain, giving a more repetitive effect than full rhyme would have achieved. Other forms less popular with contemporary poets include Spenserian and Miltonic sonnets. **Meredithian sonnet:** 16-line sonnet invented by George Meredith for his *Modern Love* sonnet sequence and adapted by Tony Harrison for his *School of Eloquence*, as in 'Turns' (301) and 'Book Ends' (377). Seamus Heaney objects to the usual formal description of a sonnet, calling it instead 'a system of muscles and enjambements and age and sex, and it's got a waist and a middle – it is a form ...there are indeed fourteen lines and there are indeed rhyme words...I would like a distinction between form which is an act of living principle and shape which is discernible on the page, but inaudible, and kinetically, muscularly available. Poetry is a muscular response also, I feel. If you read a Shakespearian sonnet, a beloved Shakespearian sonnet, it's a dance within yourself.'

Spondee: A foot consisting of two long syllables, as in 'á-mén'. Spondees are found as variant feet in place of dactyl, iamb, trochee or anapaest, as in 'The lóng|dáy wánes;|the slów|móon clímbs' (Tennyson), where the second and fourth iambs are replaced by spondees.

Stanza: Alternative word for a verse in a poem.

Stress: Accent or emphasis.

Stress metre: Also called strong stress metre or accentual verse, this earliest of English metres is based on stress not syllable. In Anglo-Saxon poetry – which doesn't use rhyme – the two main stressed words are alliterated in the first half of the line, and the third or fourth in the second half. Anglo-Saxon poems like *Beowulf* and *The Wanderer* are echoed in the stress-timed lines and cadences of poets such as Ken Smith, as in 'Being the third song of Urias' (171).

Syllabics: Verse based on syllable count, not stress, as in 'Considering the Snail' (229), where Thom Gunn uses his seven-syllable line to help enact the movement of the snail. More elaborate syllabic stanza patterns have been used by poets such as Marianne Moore.

Symbol: Word or image signifying something other which carries connotations even when denoting something actual. The Irish painter Colin Middleton defined the symbol as 'the bridge between the known and the unknown, the link between conscious and unconscious'.

Syntax: Arrangement of words in a sentence; sentence construction or its rules.

Tercet: Three-line stanza.

Terza rima: Tercet stanzas chain-rhyming *aba,bcb,cdc*, etc. This Italian form gives a strong sense of continuity, helpful for extended narrative, the most famous example being Dante's *Divine Comedy*. English examples include Shelley's 'Ode to the West Wind', Auden's *The Sea and the Mirror*, and Randall Jarrell's *The Lost World* sequence recalling his childhood, from which 'A Night with Lions' (206) is taken (he uses the rhyme scheme, not the stanzas).

Tetrameter: A line consisting of four feet.

Trimeter: A line consisting of three feet.

Triplet: Sometimes (loosely) same as tercet; sometimes a rhythmic measure of three syllables, e.g. 'company'.

Trochee: Foot of one stressed and one unstressed syllable as in 'ópen', most commonly used in trochaic tetrameter: 'Earth, receive an honoured guest;/ William Yeats is laid to rest' (Auden).

Villanelle: French form (adapted from a round sung by farm labourers) with two rhymes running through nineteen lines in six stanzas, and with the first and third lines of the opening tercet recurring alternately at the end of the other tercets, with both repeated at the end of the concluding quatrain, so that two entire lines are repeated four times each. See examples: William Empson, 'Missing Dates' (101); Weldon Kees, 'Villanelle' (101); Theodore Roethke, 'The Waking' (106); Elizabeth Bishop, 'One Art' (118); Dylan Thomas, 'Do Not Go Gentle into That Good Night' (379); Derek Mahon, 'Antarctica' (407).

FURTHER READING

INDIVIDUAL POETS

The acknowledgements pages give details of selected and collected editions by poets represented in this anthology as well as some key individual collections. Readers can also obtain informative catalogues from the main specialist poetry publishers in Britain and Ireland (Bloodaxe, Carcanet, Anvil and Gallery) and from the main publishers with poetry lists (Faber, Cape and Picador).

ANTHOLOGIES

Many poetry anthologies are useless to readers who aren't already familiar with the territory. Like reviews in newspapers, they are produced by poets with other poets – not readers – in mind. But I recommend these books for their range or content or because their introductions or notes are helpful to new readers.

Neil Astley: *Being Alive: the sequel to* Staying Alive (Bloodaxe, 2004). This equally lively companion volume gives readers an even wider selection of brilliantly diverse poetry from around the world.

Neil Astley: *Being Human* (Bloodaxe, 2006). The forthcoming third volume in the series: a companion volume to both *Staying Alive* and *Being Alive.*

Edna Longley: *The Bloodaxe Book of 20th Century Poetry from Britain & Ireland* (Bloodaxe, 2000): The key 60 poets introduced with informative notes.

Seamus Heaney & Ted Hughes: *The Rattle Bag* (Faber, 1982): Classic and modern poems, including poetry in translation and from oral traditions.

Jo Shapcott & Matthew Sweeney: *Emergency Kit: Poems for Strange Times* (Faber, 1996). Lively selection of contemporary English-language poetry.

Ruth Padel: *52 Ways of Looking at a Poem* (Chatto, 2002). Short essays from her newspaper column which strip poems down to their nuts and bolts.

Mark Strand & Eavan Boland: *The Making of a Poem* (Norton, 2000). Traces the evolution of forms through the poems themselves, from early to modern.

J.D. McClatchy: *The Vintage Book of Contemporary American Poetry* (Vintage, 1990): More comprehensive and recent than similarly titled anthologies from Faber and Penguin: selections from 65 poets with editorial notes on each.

J.D. McClatchy: *The Vintage Book of Contemporary World Poetry* (Vintage, 1996): Poets from four continents translated from two dozen languages.

Jeni Couzyn: *The Bloodaxe Book of Contemporary Women Poets* (Bloodaxe, 1985): Large selections – with essays on their work – by eleven leading poets.

Linda France: *Sixty Women Poets* (Bloodaxe, 1993): Selections by the main British and Irish women poets from the 1970s to the early 90s.

Michael Hulse, David Kennedy & David Morley: *The New Poetry* (Bloodaxe, 1993): The first anthology of the new British and Irish poets of the 1980s and 90s – multicultural, politicised, witty, often urban.

Sean O'Brien: *The Firebox: Poetry in Britain and Ireland after 1945* (Picador, 1999): Small selections of numerous poets, with helpful editorial headnotes.

Simon Armitage & Robert Crawford: *The Penguin Book of Poetry from Britain and Ireland since 1945* (Penguin, 1998). Similar selection to O'Brien's *Firebox*, with a fuller selection of Scottish and Welsh poets, but limited notes.

E.A. Markham: *Hinterland: Caribbean Poetry from the West Indies & Britain* (Bloodaxe, 1989): 14 poets with photos, interviews and autobiographical essays.

Patrick Crotty: *Modern Irish Poetry* (Blackstaff, 1995). Nearly 50 writers, each introduced with helpful notes, including some Irish language poets.

Selina Guinness: *The New Irish Poets* (Bloodaxe, 2004). In-depth selections of work by over 30 poets, with photos and editorial commentaries.

ESSAYS & HANDBOOKS

As with the anthologies, most critical guides to modern poetry are produced by writers who have little interest in helping new readers. Many books on modern poetry issued by academic publishers are written in a jargon-studded private language which even highly intelligent readers find baffling, so avoid any book of literary criticism published by a university press, and any book which refers to poems as *texts* or which uses the expressions *decode* or *foregrounding*. The following books are among the few exceptions:

W.N. Herbert & Matthew Hollis: *Strong Words: modern poets on modern poetry* (Bloodaxe, 2000): Absolutely indispensable: essential reading for poets as well as for readers, critics, teachers and students of creative writing. This judicious and comprehensive selection of manifestos starts with Yeats, Eliot, Pound, Auden, Stevens, Lowell, Plath and other key figures, then adds over 30 newly commissioned essays by contemporary poets.

Paul Hyland: *Getting into Poetry: A Readers; and Writers' Guide to the Poetry Scene*, 2nd edition (Bloodaxe, 1996): Hyland has written the book he wanted to read when he started getting into poetry, a handbook to help readers, writers and teachers to hack their way into the jungle of modern poetry.

Peter Sansom: *Writing Poems* (Bloodaxe, 1994). Practical guide with examples drawn from Sansom's long experience of running workshops and courses.

Seamus Heaney: *Finders Keepers: Selected Prose 1971-2001* (Faber, 2002). Essays on many essential poets, including work from *Preoccupations*, *The Government of the Tongue* and *The Redress of Poetry*. All Heaney's readings are informed by his insistence on the unity of poetry and life.

Dennis O'Driscoll: *Troubled Thoughts, Majestic Dreams: Selected Prose Writings* (Gallery Press, 2001). The most perceptive and knowledgeable critic of modern poetry, O'Driscoll is an excellent guide unhampered by critical baggage.

Randall Jarrell: *Poetry and the Age* (1955; Faber, 1973). America's most acute poet-critic, a savager of cant and a salvager of humanity. His essays on poetry and criticism are essential reading for anyone who cares about the art.

Joseph Brodsky: *Less Than Zero: Selected Essays* (1986; Penguin, 1987). Essays on poets of substance, with a 50-page analysis of Auden's 'September 1, 1939'.

Sean O'Brien: *The Deregulated Muse: Essays on Contemporary British & Irish Poetry* (Bloodaxe, 1998). Densely written studies of 20 poets, with shorter comments on another dozen: not the best starting-point for new readers, but the least offputting, despite its male bias and overpoliticised readings.

Clare Brown & Don Paterson: *Don't Ask Me What I Mean: poets in their own words* (Picador, 2003). Short essays commissioned by the Poetry Book Society. The PBS offers readers a Choice and four Recommendations each quarter, all five titles discussed by the poets themselves in the *PBS Bulletin* (their short commentaries are far more illuminating than reviews of poetry). Joining the PBS is one of the easiest and most enjoyable ways of gaining a better knowledge of contemporary poetry. The PBS is at Book House, 45 East Hill, London SW18 2QZ. The PBS's new on-line book ordering service will supply any in-print book of contemporary poetry published in Britain (not just the PBS's own selections): see www.poetrybooks.co.uk.

NOTE: My editorial commentaries include quotations from some of the above books, and from: David Constantine: 'The Usefulness of Poetry', *Brecht's Poetry of Political Exile*, ed. Ronald Speirs (CUP, 2000), and *As the Poet Said*, ed. Tony Curtis & Dennis O'Driscoll (Poetry Ireland/Poetry Society, 1997).

ACKNOWLEDGEMENTS

The poems in this anthology are reprinted from the following books, all by permission of the publishers listed unless stated otherwise. Thanks are due to all the copyright holders cited below for their kind permission:

Robert Adamson: *Reading the River: Selected Poems* (Bloodaxe Books, 2004), by permission of Golvan Arts Management; **Fleur Adcock:** *Poems 1960-2000* (Bloodaxe Books, 2000); **Gösta Ågren:** *A Valley in the Midst of Violence*, tr. David McDuff (Bloodaxe Books, 1992), by permission of author and translator; **Conrad Aiken:** *Collected Poems* (Oxford University Press, Inc., New York, 1953, 1970); **Anna Akhmatova:** *Selected Poems*, tr. Richard McKane (Bloodaxe Books, 1989); **Gillian Allnutt:** *Lintel* (Bloodaxe Books, 2001); **Moniza Alvi:** *Carrying My Wife* (Bloodaxe Books, 2000), *Souk* (Bloodaxe Books, 2002); **Simon Armitage:** *Zoom!* (Bloodaxe Books, 1989), *Kid* (Faber & Faber, 1992); **W.H. Auden:** *Collected Poems*, ed. Edward Mendelson (Faber & Faber, 1991), *The English Auden*, ed. Edward Mendelson (Faber & Faber, 1977).

Ingeborg Bachmann: *Songs in flight: Collected Poems*, tr. Peter Filkins (Marsilio Publishers, New York); **Leland Bardwell:** *Dostoevsky's Grave* (Dedalus Press, Dublin, 1991); **Elizabeth Bartlett:** *Two Women Dancing: New & Selected Poems*, ed. Carol Rumens (Bloodaxe Books, 1995); **Meg Bateman:** *Lightness and Other Poems* (Polygon, 1997); **James K. Baxter:** *Collected Poems* (Oxford University Press, NZ, 1979), by permission of Mrs Jacquie C. Baxter; **Connie Bensley:** *The Back and the Front of It* (Bloodaxe Books, 2000); **John Berryman:** *The Dream Songs* (Faber & Faber, 1993); **Sujata Bhatt:** *Monkey Shadows* (Carcanet Press, 1991); **Elizabeth Bishop:** *The Complete Poems 1927-1979* (Chatto & Windus, 1983), by permission of Farrar, Straus & Giroux, Inc; **Thomas Blackburn:** *Selected Poems*, ed. Julia Blackburn (Carcanet Press, 2001); **Robert Bly:** *Selected Poems* (Harper & Row Publishers, Inc, New York, 1983); **Robyn Bolam:** see Marion Lomax; **Bertolt Brecht:** *Poems 1913-1956*, ed. John Willett & Ralph Manheim (Methuen, 2000), © 1976; **Joseph Brodsky:** *Collected Poems in English*, ed. Ann Kjellberg (Carcanet, 2001); **Joan Brossa:** 'Note', from *Poemes de seny i cabell* (Ariel, Barcelona, 1977), translated by Arthur Terry from *Words are Things: Poems, Objects and Installations* (Riverside Studios, London, 1992); **Eleanor Brown:** *Maiden Speech* (Bloodaxe Books, 1996); **Colette Bryce:** *The Heel of Bernadette* (Picador, 2000), by permission of Macmillan Publishers Ltd; **Basil Bunting:** *Complete Poems* (Bloodaxe Books, 2000); **John Burnside:** *A Normal Skin* (Jonathan Cape, 1997), by permission of the Random House Group Ltd.

Hayden Carruth: *Collected Shorter Poems, 1946-1991* (Copper Canyon Press, USA, 1991); **Anne Carson:** *Glass and God* (Jonathan Cape, 1998), *Men in the Off Hours* (Jonathan Cape, 2000), by permission of Burnes & Clegg, Inc; **Raymond Carver:** *All of Us: Collected Poems* (Harvill Press, 1996), by permission of International Creative Management, Inc., copyright © 1996 Tess Gallagher; **Nina Cassian:** *Life Sentence: Selected Poems*, ed. William Jay Smith (Anvil Press Poetry, 1990); **Charles Causley:** *Collected Poems 1951-2000* (Picador, 2000), by permission of David Higham Associates Ltd; **C.P. Cavafy:** *Collected Poems*, tr. Edmund Keeley & Philip Sherrard (Hogarth Press, 1990), by permission of the estate of C.P. Cavafy and Random House Group Ltd; **Amy Clampitt:** *Collected Poems* (Faber & Faber, 1996), **Kate Clanchy:** *Samarkand* (Picador, 1999), by permission of Macmillan Publishers Ltd; **Polly Clark:** *Kiss* (Bloodaxe Books, 2000); **Gillian Clarke:** *Collected Poems* (Carcanet Press, 1997); **Lucille Clifton:** *Good Woman: Poems and a Memoir 1969-1980* (BOA Editions, 1987); **Billy Collins:** *Taking Off Emily Dickinson's Clothes:*

Selected Poems (Picador, 2000), by permission of Macmillan Publishers Ltd; **Stewart Conn:** *Stolen Light: Selected Poems* (Bloodaxe Books, 1999); **David Constantine:** *Collected Poems* (Bloodaxe Books, 2004); **Jane Cooper:** *The Flashboat: Poems Collected and Reclaimed* (W.W. Norton & Company, 2000); **Julia Copus:** *The Shuttered Eye* (Bloodaxe Books, 1995) and *In Defence of Adultery* (Bloodaxe Books, 2003); **Hart Crane:** *The Complete Poems*, ed. Marc Simon (Liveright Books, 2000), by permission of Liveright Publishing Corporation; **E.E. Cummings:** *Complete Poems 1904-1962* (Liveright, 1994), by permission of W.W. Norton & Company, copyright © 1991 by the Trustees for the E.E. Cummings Trust and George James Firmage.

Amanda Dalton: *How to Disappear* (Bloodaxe Books, 1999); **Elizabeth Daryush:** *Collected Poems* (Carcanet Press, 1976); **John F. Deane:** *Toccata and Fugue: New & Selected Poems* (Carcanet Press, 2000); **Sophia de Mello Breyner:** *Log Book: Selected Poems*, tr. Richard Zenith (Carcanet Press, 1997); **Imtiaz Dharker:** *I Speak for the Devil* (Bloodaxe Books, 2001); **James Dickey:** *The Whole Motion: Collected Poems 1945-1992* (Wesleyan University Press, USA, 1992); **Peter Didsbury:** *Scenes from a Long Sleep: New & Collected Poems* (Bloodaxe Books, 2003); **Stephen Dobyns:** *Velocities: New & Selected Poems* (Penguin Books, USA, 1994; Bloodaxe Books, 1996); **Michael Donaghy:** *Conjure* and *Dances Learned Last Night: Poems 1975-1995* (both Picador, 2000), by permission of Macmillan Publishers Ltd; **Katie Donovan:** *Entering the Mare* (Bloodaxe Books, 1997); **Maura Dooley:** *Sound Barrier: Poems 1982-2002* (Bloodaxe Books, 2002); **Keith Douglas:** *Complete Poems*, ed. Desmond Graham (Faber & Faber, 2000), **Rita Dove:** *Selected Poems* (Pantheon Books, 1993) by permission of the author; **Freda Downie:** *Collected Poems*, ed. George Szirtes (Bloodaxe Books, 1995); **Nick Drake:** *The Man in the White Suit* (Bloodaxe Books, 1999); **Carol Ann Duffy:** *The Other Country* (Anvil Press Poetry, 1990), *Mean Time* (Anvil Press Poetry, 1993); **Helen Dunmore:** *Out of the Blue: Poems 1975-2001* (Bloodaxe Books, 2001); **Douglas Dunn:** *Selected Poems* (Faber & Faber, 1986); **Stephen Dunn:** *Between Angels* (W.W. Norton & Company, New York, 1989); **Jane Duran:** *Breathe Now, Breathe* (Enitharmon Press, 1995); **Paul Durcan:** *A Snail in My Prime: New & Selected Poems* (The Harvill Press, 1993), *Greetings to Our Friends in Brazil* (The Harvill Press, 1999); **G.F. Dutton:** *The Bare Abundance: Selected Poems 1970-2001* (Bloodaxe Books, 2002).

T.S. Eliot: *The Complete Poems and Plays* (Faber, & Faber 1969); **Alistair Elliot:** *My Country: Collected Poems* (Carcanet Press, 1989); **Menna Elfyn:** *Cusan Dyn Dall / Blind Man's Kiss* (Bloodaxe Books, 2001); **William Empson:** *Collected Poems* (Hogarth Press, 1984), by permission of Lady Empson and the Hogarth Press; **Gavin Ewart:** *The Collected Ewart: 1933-1980* (Hutchinson, 1980), by permission of Mrs Margo Ewart and the Random House Group Ltd.

Ruth Fainlight: *Selected Poems* (Sinclair-Stevenson, 1995), by permission of the author; **U.A. Fanthorpe:** *Safe as Houses* (Peterloo Poets, 1995); **Vicki Feaver:** *The Handless Maiden* (Jonathan Cape, 1994), by permission of the Random House Group Ltd; **James Fenton:** *The Memory of War and Children in Exile: Poems 1968-1983* (Penguin, 1983), *Out of Danger* (Penguin, 1993), by permission of Peters, Fraser & Dunlop Group Ltd; **Roy Fisher:** *The Long and the Short of It: Poems 1955-2005* (Bloodaxe Books, 2005); **Leontia Flynn:** *These Days* (Jonathan Cape, 2004), by permission of the author; **Carolyn Forché:** *The Country Between Us* (Jonathan Cape, 1983), by permission of the Virginia Barber Literary Agency, Inc.; **Linda France:** *The Gentleness of the Very Tall* (Bloodaxe Books, 1994); **Robert Frost:** *The Poetry of Robert Frost*, ed. Edward Connery Lathem (Jonathan Cape, 1967), by permission of Random House Group Ltd.

Tess Gallagher: *My Black Horse: New & Selected Poems* (Bloodaxe Books, 1995); **Elizabeth Garrett:** *A Two-Part Invention* (Bloodaxe Books, 1998); **Pamela**

Gillilan: *All-Steel Traveller: New & Selected Poems* (Bloodaxe Books, 1994); **Dana Gioia**: *The Gods of Winter* (Peterloo Poets, 1991); **Louise Glück**: *Firstborn* (1968), *The Triumph of Achilles* (1985) and *Ararat* (1990), reprinted in *The First Five Books of Poems* (Carcanet Press, 1997); *The Wild Iris* (Carcanet Press, 1992); **Jorie Graham**: *The Dream of the Unified Field: Selected Poems 1974-1994* (Carcanet Press, 1996); **W.S. Graham**: *Collected Poems* (Faber, 1979), by permission of Michael & Margaret Snow; **Robert Graves**: *Complete Poems*, ed. Beryl Graves and Dunstan Ward (Carcanet Press, 1995-1999); **Andrew Greig**: *Into You* (Bloodaxe Books, 2001); **Chris Greenhalgh**: *Of Love, Death and the Sea-Squirt* (Bloodaxe Books, 2000); **Lavinia Greenlaw**: *Night Photograph* (Faber & Faber, 1993); **Eamon Grennan**: *Still Life with Waterfall* (Gallery Press, 2001); **Jane Griffiths**: *A Grip on Thin Air* (Bloodaxe Books, 2000); **Philip Gross**: *Changes of Address: Poems 1980-1998* (Bloodaxe Books, 2001); **Vona Groarke**: *Other People's Houses* (Gallery Press, 1999), *Flight* (Gallery Press, 2002), **Thom Gunn**: *The Man with Night Sweats* (Faber & Faber, 1992), *Collected Poems* (Faber & Faber, 1993) and *Boss Cupid* (Faber & Faber, 2000).

Kerry Hardie: *A Furious Place* (Gallery Press, 1996); **James Harpur**: *Oracle Bones* (Anvil Press Poetry, 2001); **Tony Harrison**: *Selected Poems* (Penguin, 1987), *The Gaze of the Gorgon* (Bloodaxe Books, 1992), by permission of Gordon Dickerson and the author; **Michael Hartnett**: *Collected Poems* (Gallery Press, 2001); **Kevin Hart**: *Flame Tree: Selected Poems* (Bloodaxe Books, 2002); **Gwen Harwood**: *The Lion's Bride* (Angus & Robertson, 1981), by permission of John Harwood; **Robert Hass**: *Praise* (HarperCollins Publishers Inc., 1990); **Robert Hayden**: *Angle of Ascent: New & Selected Poems* (Liveright Publishing Corporation, 1966, 1975); **Seamus Heaney**: *The Spirit Level* (Faber & Faber, 1996), *Opened Ground: Poems 1966-1996* (Faber & Faber, 1998); **John Heath-Stubbs**: *Selected Poems* (Carcanet Press, 1990), by permission of David Higham Associates; **Stuart Henson**: *Ember Music* (Peterloo Poets, 1994); **W.N. Herbert**: *Cabaret McGonagall* (Bloodaxe Books, 1996), *The Big Bumper Book of Troy* (Bloodaxe Books, 2002); **Zbigniew Herbert**: *Selected Poems*, tr. John & Bogdana Carpenter (Oxford University Press, 1991), by permission of Oxford University Press; **Tracey Herd**: *No Hiding Place* (Bloodaxe Books, 1996), *Dead Redhead* (Bloodaxe Books, 2001); **Rita Ann Higgins**: *Sunny Side Plucked: New & Selected Poems* (Bloodaxe Books, 1996); **Geoffrey Hill**: *Collected Poems* (Penguin, 1985); **Selima Hill**: *A Little Book of Meat* (Bloodaxe Books, 1993); **Ellen Hinsey**: *The White Fire of Time* (Wesleyan University Press, 2002); **Vladimír Holan**: *Selected Poems*, tr. Ian & Jarmila Milner (Penguin Books, 1971); **Miroslav Holub**: *Poems Before & After: Collected English Translations* (Bloodaxe Books, 1990); **Frances Horovitz**: *Collected Poems*, ed. Roger Garfitt (Bloodaxe Books, 1985); **A.E. Housman**: *The Collected Poems* (Jonathan Cape, 1939), by permission of the Society of Authors as the literary representative of the Estate of A.E. Housman; **Frieda Hughes**: *Wooroloo* (Bloodaxe Books, 1999), *Stonepicker* (Bloodaxe Books, 2001); **Langston Hughes**: *The Collected Poems of Langston Hughes* (Knopf, NY, 1994), by permission of David Higham Associates; **Ted Hughes**: poems from *New Selected Poems* (Faber & Faber, 1995), reprinted from his Faber collections *The Hawk in the Rain* (1957), *Wodwo* (1967) and *Cave Birds* (1975).

Helen Ivory: *The Double Life of Clocks* (Bloodaxe Books, 2002).

Philippe Jaccottet: *Selected Poems*, tr. Derek Mahon (Penguin, 1987) and *Words in the Air*, tr. Derek Mahon (Gallery Press, 1998), by permission of Gallery Press; **Kathleen Jamie**: *Mrs and Mrs Scotland Are Dead: Poems 1980-1994* (Bloodaxe Books, 2002), *Jizzen* (Picador, 1999), by permission of Macmillan Publishers Ltd; **Randall Jarrell**: *The Complete Poems* (Faber & Faber, 1971); **Elizabeth Jennings**: *New Collected Poems* (Carcanet Press, 2002), by permission of David Higham Associates; **Jenny Joseph**: *Selected Poems* (Bloodaxe Books, 1992), by permission of John Johnson Ltd.

Jaan Kaplinski: *The Wandering Border*, tr. the author with Sam Hamill & Riina Tamm (Copper Canyon Press, USA, 1987; Harvill, 1992), *Through the Forest*, tr. Hildi Hawkins (Harvill Press, 1996); **Kapka Kassabova:** *Dismemberment* (Auckland University Press, NZ, 1998), by permission of the author; **Patrick Kavanagh:** *Selected Poems*, ed. Antoinette Quinn (Penguin, 1996), reprinted here by permission of the Trustees of the Estate of the late Katherine B. Kavanagh, and through the Jonathan Williams Literary Agency; **Jackie Kay:** *Other Lovers* (Bloodaxe Books, 1993); **Weldon Kees:** *The Collected Poems of Weldon Kees*, ed. Donald Justice (University of Nebraska Press, 1975); **Brendan Kennelly:** *Familiar Strangers: New & Selected Poems 1960-2004* (Bloodaxe Books, 2004); **Galway Kinnell:** *Selected Poems* (Houghton Mifflin, USA, 2000; Bloodaxe Books, 2001); **John Kinsella:** *The Hunt* (FACP, Australia; Bloodaxe Books, 1998); **Carolyn Kizer:** *Cool, Calm and Collected: Poems 1960-2000* (Copper Canyon Press, USA, 2001); **August Kleinzahler:** *Live from the Hong Kong Nile Club: Poems 1975-1990* (Faber & Faber, 2000); **Stephen Knight:** *Dream City Cinema* (Bloodaxe Books, 1996).

Ivan V. Lalic: *A Rusty Needle*, tr. Francis R. Jones (Anvil Press Poetry, 1996); **Philip Larkin:** *Collected Poems*, ed. Anthony Thwaite (Faber & Faber, 1990); **Brad Leithauser:** *Between Leaps: Poems 1972-1985* (OUP, 1987), by permission of Carcanet Press; **Denise Levertov:** *New & Selected Poems* (Bloodaxe Books, 2003); **Tom Leonard:** *Intimate Voices: Selected Work 1965-1983* (Vintage, 1985), by permission of the author; **Gwyneth Lewis:** *Zero Gravity* (Bloodaxe Books, 1998); **Vachel Lindsay:** *Collected Poems* (New York, 1925), out of copyright; **Joanne Limburg:** *Femenismo* (Bloodaxe Books, 2000); **Shirley Geok-lin Lim:** *Modern Secrets* (Dangaroo Press, 1989); **Liz Lochhead:** 'Sorting Through', uncollected poem by permission of the author; **Christopher Logue:** *Selected Poems* (Faber & Faber, 1996); **Marion Lomax [Robyn Bolam]:** *Raiding the Borders* (Bloodaxe Books, 1996); **Michael Longley:** *Selected Poems* (Jonathan Cape, 1998), *The Weather in Japan* (Jonathan Cape, 2000), by permission of Lucas Alexander Whitley; **Robert Lowell:** *Day by Day* (Faber & Faber, 1977); **Roddy Lumsden:** *Mischief Night: New & Selected Poems* (Bloodaxe Books, 2004); **Thomas Lux:** poems from *New and Selected Poems 1974-1995* (Houghton Mifflin, 1997), reprinted from *Half Promised Land* (1986) and *Split Horizon* (1994).

James McAuley: *Collected Poems* (Angus & Robertson, Australia, 1980), by permission of HarperCollins Publishers, Australia; **Norman MacCaig:** *Collected Poems* (Chatto & Windus, 1990), by permission of Random House Group Ltd; **Gwendolyn MacEwen:** *The T.E. Lawrence Poems* (Mosaic Press/Valley Editions, Canada, 1982), *Afterworlds* (McClelland & Stewart, Inc., Canada, 1987), by permission of the publishers and the Estate of Gwendolyn McEwen; **Roger McGough:** *Defying Gravity* (Viking, 1992), by permission of Peters, Fraser & Dunlop; **Mairi MacInnes:** *Elsewhere & Back: New & Selected Poems* (Bloodaxe Books, 1993); **Jamie McKendrick:** *The Marble Fly* (1997), reprinted in *Sky Nails* (Faber & Faber, 2000); **Archibald MacLeish:** *Collected Poems 1917-1982* (Houghton Mifflin, USA, 1985); **Louis MacNeice:** *Collected Poems*, ed. E.R. Dodds (Faber, 1979), by permission of David Higham Associates Ltd; **Kona Macphee:** 'IVF' and 'My People', to the author; **Derck Mahon:** *Collected Poems* (Gallery Press, 1999); **Osip Mandelstam:** *The Voronezh Notebooks*, tr. Richard & Elizabeth McKane (Bloodaxe Books, 1996); **Glyn Maxwell:** *The Boys at Twilight: Poems 1990-1995* (Bloodaxe Books, 2000); **James Merrill:** *Collected Poems*, ed. J.D. McClatchy & Stephen Yenser, by permission of the Literary Estate of James Merrill at Washington University and Alfred A. Knopf, division of Random House, Inc; **W.S. Merwin:** *Flower & Hand: Poems 1977-1983* (Copper Canyon Press, USA, 1997); **Anne Michaels:** *Poems* (Bloomsbury, 2000); **Czeslaw Milosz:** *New Collected Poems*

1931-2001 (Ecco Press, USA; Penguin Books, 2001); **Adrian Mitchell:** *Blue Coffee: Poems 1985-1996* (Bloodaxe Books, 1996), *Heart on the Left: Poems 1953-1984* (Bloodaxe Books, 1997), by permission of Peters, Fraser & Dunlop, with an educational health warning: Adrian Mitchell asks that none of his poems be used in connection with any examination whatsoever; **Elma Mitchell:** *People Etcetera: Poems New & Selected* (Peterloo Poets, 1987), copyright © Harry Chambers; **John Montague:** *Collected Poems* (Gallery Press, 1995); **Edwin Morgan:** *Collected Poems* (Carcanet Press, 1990); **Esther Morgan:** *Beyond Calling Distance* (Bloodaxe Books, 2001); **Andrew Motion:** *Love in a Life* (Faber & Faber, 1991); **Paul Muldoon:** from *Why Brownlee Left* (1980) and *Quoof* (1983), reprinted from *New Selected Poems 1968-1994* (Faber & Faber, 1996); **Richard Murphy:** *Collected Poems* (Gallery Press, 2000); **Les Murray:** *Collected Poems* (Carcanet Press, 1998).

Howard Nemerov: *Collected Poems* (University of Chicago Press, 1981), by permission of Margaret Nemerov; **Pablo Neruda:** translation by Brian Cole of 'Dead Woman' (featured in the film *Truly, Madly, Deeply*) from *The Captain's Verses* (Anvil Press Poetry, 1994); translation by Alastair Reid of 'Fable of the mermaids and the drunks' from *Love: poems from the film Il Postino* (Harvill, 1995), reprinted from *Selected Poems*, ed. Nathaniel Tarn (1975), reprinted by permission of Random House Group Ltd; **Grace Nichols:** *I is a long memoried woman* (Karnak House, 1983, 2002); **Norman Nicholson:** *Collected Poems* (Faber & Faber, 1994); **Eiléan Ní Chuilleanáin:** *The Second Voyage: Selected Poems* (Gallery Press, 1986); **Nuala Ní Dhomhnaill:** *Pharoah's Daughter* (Gallery Press, 1990); **Eibhlín Nic Eochaidh:** 'How to kill a living thing', by permission of the author; **Alden Nowlan:** *Between Tears and Laughter: Selected Poems* (Bloodaxe Books, 2004), by permission of the House of Anansi, Toronto, and the Estate of Alden Nowlan.

Julie O'Callaghan: *What's What* (Bloodaxe Books, 1991); **Bernard O'Donoghue:** *Here Nor There* (Chatto & Windus, 1999), by permission of the Random House Group Ltd; **Dennis O'Driscoll:** *Hidden Extras* (Anvil Press Poetry, 1987), *Long Story Short* (Anvil Press Poetry, 1993), *Quality Time* (Anvil Press Poetry, 1997); **Frank O'Hara:** *Selected Poems* (Carcanet Press, 1991); **Mary Oliver:** *Dream Work* (Grove/Atlantic, 1986), by permission of Grove/Atlantic and the author; **Sharon Olds:** *The Sign of Saturn: Poems 1980-87* (Secker & Warburg, 1991), *The Wellspring* (Jonathan Cape, 1996), by permission of the Random House Group Ltd and Alfred A. Knopf, division of Random House, Inc; **Michael Ondaatje:** *The Cinnamon Peeler: Selected Poems* (Picador, 1989), by permission of the Ellen Levine Literary Agency, Inc; **Caitríona O'Reilly:** *The Nowhere Birds* (Bloodaxe Books, 2001); **Seán Ó Riordáin:** 'Switch', translation by Patrick Crotty of 'Malairt' from *Eireaball Spideoige* (1952), by permission of the translator; **Micheal O'Siadhail:** *The Middle Voice* (1992), from *Poems 1975-1995* (Bloodaxe Books, 1999); **Alice Oswald:** *The Thing in the Gap-Stone Stile* (Oxford University Press, 1996); **Wilfred Owen:** *The Complete Poems and Fragments*, ed. Jon Stallworthy (Chatto & Windus, the Hogarth Press and Oxford University Press, 1983), out of copyright.

Philip Pacey: *Charged Landscapes* (Enitharmon Press, 1978); **P.K. Page:** *The Hidden Room: Collected Poems*, two volumes (The Porcupine's Quill, Canada, 1997); **Marge Piercy:** *Available Light* (Knopf, New York, 1988), by permission of the author; **Katherine Pierpoint:** *Truffle Beds* (Faber & Faber, 1995); **János Pilinszky:** *Crater*, tr. Peter Jay (Anvil Press Poetry, 1978); **Sylvia Plath:** *Collected Poems*, ed. Ted Hughes (Faber & Faber, 1981); **Vasko Popa:** *Collected Poems*, tr. Anne Pennington, expanded by Francis R. Jones (Anvil Press Poetry, 1993); **Katrina Porteous:** 'Seven Silences', from 'An Ill Wind', commissioned by BBC Radio 3 for the 2001 Poetry Proms, by permission of the author; **Ezra Pound:** *Collected Shorter Poems* (Faber & Faber, 1926).

Hare: New & Selected Poems (Bloodaxe Books, 2003); **Wallace Stevens:** *Collected Poems* (Faber & Faber, 1955); **Anne Stevenson:** *Poems 1955-2005* (Bloodaxe Books, 2005); **Mark Strand:** *Selected Poems* (Carcanet Press, 1995); **Matthew Sweeney:** *Blue Shoes* (Secker & Warburg, 1989), by permission of the author c/o Rogers, Coleridge & White; *The Bridal Suite* (Jonathan Cape, 1997), by permission of the Random House Group Ltd; **George Szirtes:** *An English Apocalypse* (Bloodaxe Books, 2001); **Wislawa Szymborska:** 'The One Twenty Pub' from *Quality Time* by Dennis O'Driscoll (Anvil Press Poetry, 1997); 'The End and the Beginning' from *View with a Grain of Sand: Selected Poems* by Wislawa Szymborska, tr. Stanislaw Baranczak & Clare Cavanagh (Harcourt Brace & Company, 1993).

Dylan Thomas: *Collected Poems* (J.M. Dent, 1988), by permission of David Higham Associates; **Edward Thomas:** *Collected Poems*, ed. R. George Thomas (Oxford University Press, 1978), out of copyright; **R.S. Thomas:** *Selected Poems 1946-1968* (Bloodaxe Books, 1986), by permission of Bloodaxe Books Ltd, *Experimenting with an Amen* (Macmillan, 1986) and *Collected Poems 1945-1990* (J.M. Dent, 1993), by permission of the Orion Publishing Group Ltd and Gwydion Thomas; **Rosemary Tonks:** *Iliad of Broken Sentences* (The Bodley Head, 1967), copyright © Rosemary Tonks 1967; **Tomas Transtömer:** *New Collected Poems*, tr. Robin Fulton (Bloodaxe Books, 1997); **Chase Twichell:** *The Snow Watcher* (Ontario Review Press, USA, 1998; Bloodaxe Books, 1999).

César Vallejo: *Selected Poems*, tr. Ed Dorn & Gordon Brotherston (Penguin Books, 1976), by permission of Gordon Brotherston; **Ellen Bryant Voigt:** *The Forces of Plenty* (W.W. Norton & Company, 1983); **Fred Voss:** *Carnegie Hall with Tin Walls* (Bloodaxe Books, 1998).

Derek Walcott: *Sea Grapes* (Jonathan Cape, 1976), by permission of the Random House Group Ltd; **Harri Webb:** *The Green Desert* (Gwasg Gomer, Llandyssul, 1969); **Bruce Weigl:** *Song of Napalm* (Atlantic Monthly Press, USA, 1988), by permission of the author; **Susan Wicks:** *Night Toad* (Bloodaxe Books, 2003), by permission of the author; **Richard Wilbur:** *New and Collected Poems* (Harcourt Brace Jovanovich, USA, 1988; Faber & Faber, 1989); **C.K. Williams:** *Flesh and Blood* (Farrar, Straus & Giroux, Inc., USA, 1987; Bloodaxe Books, 1988), *New & Selected Poems* (Farrar, Straus & Giroux, Inc., USA; Bloodaxe Books, 1995); **Jeanne Willis:** *Toffee Pockets* (Bodley Head, 1992), by permission of the Random House Group Ltd; **Sheila Wingfield:** *Collected Poems 1938-1983* (Enitharmon Press, 1983); **Charles Wright:** *Country Music: Selected Early Poems* (Wesleyan University Press, Middletown, Connecticut, 1983); **James Wright:** *Above the River: Complete Poems* (Farrar, Straus & Giroux, Inc., USA, 1990; Bloodaxe Books, 1992), by permission of Wesleyan University Press; **Judith Wright:** *Collected Poems* (Carcanet Press, 1992); **Kit Wright:** *Hoping It Might Be So: Poems 1974-2000* (Leviathan, 2000), by permission of Michael Hulse; **Elinor Wylie:** *Collected Poems* (1932), out of copyright.

W.B. Yeats: *The Poems*, ed. Richard J. Finneran (Macmillan, 1991), by permission of A.P. Watt Ltd on behalf of Michael B. Yeats.

Adam Zagajewski: *Tremor: Selected Poems* (Collins Harvill, 1987), by permission of Farrar, Straus & Giroux, Inc.

Every effort has been made to trace copyright holders of the poems published in this book. The editor and publisher apologise if any material has been included without permission or without the appropriate acknowledgement, and would be glad to be told of anyone who has not been consulted.

INDEX OF WRITERS

INDEX OF TITLES & FIRST LINES